Side Parting

K T BOWES

SIDE PARTING

The Curly Fan Club

Copyright © 2021 by K T BOWES

ISBN 978-1-99-115460-6

All rights reserved.

No portion of this book may be reproduced in any form without written permission from the publisher or author.

Acknowledgement

My youngest daughter introduced me to the methods ascribed to in this novel. After 48 years of Hair Hatred, I did a Final Wash and never looked back. My routine has evolved in the subsequent years to something quick and manageable, and I no longer dread catching a glimpse of my head in the mirror. I know there won't be frizz.

Thank you, Sophia, for helping me to love my curls.

CHAPTER ONE
Curl Free

"Who are you?"

Kit froze in the doorway to the lounge, tension snaking up her spine to settle beneath the tee shirt covering her head. Two layers of plastic wrap and a shower cap nestled within the cotton folds of the stained fabric, a sizable helping of green henna baking her hair into a glowing amber. Kit gulped and her gaze swept the room for suitable weapons to defend herself. An unusual tidiness greeted her, and even Langdon's discarded newspapers sat on the breadboard in a regimented pile. Kit settled shaking hands over her hips and tried the ferocious approach. She blocked out her attire of an old dressing gown and ignored the tickle against her scalp of the henna heating and making a break down the back of her neck. "This is my house," she snarled. "Who the hell are you?"

"Oh." The woman lifted her chin and viewed Kit through narrowed eyes. Blonde hair covered her head and cascaded over her shoulders in waves. The Barbie doll effect didn't fool Kit's expert gaze. She saw beyond it to the repressed curls screaming for release. False eyelashes bounced once, and then ceased. The woman stared at her. Her full top lip rose in distaste as she assessed Kit's ragged appearance. "You're the landlady."

Kit gaped. "The landlady?" The title snatched her burgeoning anger and replaced it with hurt. She owned the house, but thought of Langdon, Raki and Jerry as her friends. Her family even. She cleared her throat and fixed a fake smile on her lips. Perhaps her constant absence over the past six months had damaged their relationship. "The boys are my friends," she asserted. She extended her left hand with her palm uppermost. "Who are you?" she repeated. "And why are you in my house?"

"I'm Melinda." The woman blinked again, and the eyelashes danced. "I'm cleaning." Her hand rose from beside her and a feather duster appeared, clutched in fingers edged with shiny, red nails. She moved from behind the sofa and Kit saw platform heels too high to walk in, let alone clean a house.

"I don't have a cleaner." Kit frowned. Her bare feet padded across the floorboards to the kitchen. She turned her back on Melinda and used the time to collect her thoughts. The items she'd got out earlier had disappeared from the counter. "Where's the lemon juice gone?"

"In there." Melinda pointed the fluffy end of the duster towards the biggest cupboard.

Kit's shoulders slumped, and she poked inside the pantry to retrieve the yellow bottle. Her protest seemed insignificant as she snatched it up and dumped it on the counter. Anger thudded in her breast as she clattered around the kitchen, finding the glass jug she used to mix her henna concoctions and pulling a new packet from her dressing gown pocket. Her mind ran through a list of possibilities. Why would the boys engage a cleaner and not tell her? Did they expect her to contribute cash to the cause? Fears for her empty bank account made her brain rattle. Petrol to Auckland every weekend, plus the cost of the motel had swallowed her wages from working at the dairy during the week. Her mother had lent her the money for the hairdressing course, but she still needed to repay her.

"You left it on the counter." Melinda's tone held accusation. She didn't bother to hide her irritation at Kit's negligence.

"I hadn't finished with it." Kit searched the cutlery drawer, her fingers prodding each of the compartments in a futile exercise. "It lives in the fridge, anyway. What happened to the scissors?"

"There." Again, Melinda used the duster to point as though it represented an extension of her arm. It rose and fell in Kit's peripheral vision. "Why are you making more if you've already got it on your head?" A sneer of disgust raised her top lip.

Kit slammed the top drawer and dug in the one beneath it. She clasped the rubberised handles and snipped across the lip of the henna packet. A cloud of green dust puffed free as she dumped the powder into the glass jug. "This is for next month, and three after that."

"I've already cleaned the kitchen." Heels clicked against wooden floorboards as Melinda approached. "Don't use the dishcloth to wipe it up either. I've washed it."

Kit flicked off the lid of the lemon juice and it squirted across the counter in silent support of her autonomy. Her fingers shook as she snatched a fork from the top drawer and dug it into the mixture. Tingles worked their way up her spine as Melinda's steps took her to the edge of the tiles and then halted. "I didn't ask you to clean my house," she growled. The prongs clattered against the glass as she stirred the citrus into the henna. "I don't understand why you're here."

"What are you doing?" Curiosity drove Melinda into the kitchen, though she stood far enough away from Kit's ire to leave time for a tactical retreat.

"Making henna for my hair." Kit mixed the green paste into a dough and pressed it against the bottom of the glass. Then she dumped the fork into the shiny sink with a clatter and reached into the nearest cupboard for the plastic wrap. She groaned as a tell-tale label appeared when she pulled a length free, advising her to add it to the shopping list. Melinda watched in silence as Kit ripped off a section and placed it over the jug. Then she fitted it down over the dough and stood back to admire her handiwork. Each packet of henna provided enough mixture to create four applications, which she would freeze in individual portions after it marinated overnight.

Kit sighed with relief. She'd made a list of her objectives for her first free weekend in six gruelling months.

1. Henna hair.
2. Make another batch and freeze.
3. Relax.

Two out of three seemed like short change. She'd fostered such high hopes for the weekend. Her muscles tensed, and she forced herself to turn and face Melinda. The edge of the counter dug into her spine. "We don't need a cleaner," she said. The brightness in her tone sounded even faker than she'd intended. "Invoice me for what you agreed to work today, and I'll pay you. I'm back now, so we can manage, thank you."

"Your fingers are green." Melinda pointed the duster at Kit as though she hadn't heard the dismissal. "Do you want me to wash your dressing gown?"

Kit stared down at the stained fabric. She fluttered her fingers over the fluffy lapels and hauled the trusty garment tighter around her body. "It is clean." Her voice bristled with defensiveness. "It always looks like this."

"It's disgusting." Melinda's pointy nose wrinkled into even lines. It created the appearance of rumpled velvet in the centre of her face.

Kit's jaw tensed. She wanted judgement in her safe space like she needed a hole in her head. "I only wear it while I'm waiting for the henna to dye my hair!" she bit. "It's my old one. I'll wash it as soon as my four hours finish." Her brain ran a mental check of how long she had left to wait. The first blessed hour had involved gutting her bedroom and ensuite bathroom after six months of cursory tidying between work and study. She'd laid on her bed and read for the next hour until the henna started dribbling down her neck.

Melinda groaned and leaned her head back to stare at the ceiling. "I bet that green stuff is all over the bathroom, isn't it?"

"No!" Kit ground her teeth and took a step towards her. "I clean up my own mess, thank you. Always have, always will. Now, I've said you can stop, so please leave."

Melinda used her index and middle fingers to move her fringe out of her right eye. She performed the action with delicacy, evidence of someone who'd taken time to straighten their hair and then added choreographed curls at the end of the process. "You can't fire me." Her voice held a sing-song quality. "I don't work for you." Her platform shoes clomped across the lounge and into the hallway, up the stairs and onto the landing.

A grunt of irritation reached Kit's ears alongside the whir of the vacuum cable winding itself back into the cylinder. Kit's jaw dropped at the clattering of a plug grinding against the innards of a wall socket and the buzz of her own vacuum cleaner sucking at the upstairs carpet.

Chapter Two
The Curl of Success

"Pardon?" Kit stuck her finger in her left ear and plastered her phone to the right side of her face. The vacuum cleaner burped outside her bedroom as it gobbled up the frayed tendrils of carpet where it ended at her door. Her wall shook as Melinda bumped the poor appliance against the skirting board.

"The Women with Curls Expo, remember?" Debbie's voice grated in Kit's ear as the vacuum gave a splutter and went on strike.

"The what?" She dabbed a wad of toilet paper at the green tendril of henna sneaking towards her right eye. Rising from the bed, she walked to the bathroom and stared at herself in the mirror. Smeared henna covered her forehead and dribbled down the side of her face like a ghoul from a horror movie. Kit shuddered. "Can I call you back later? I need to wash this henna off early. It's too runny." She pulled her phone away from her ear and dabbed at the goo covering the screen.

Debbie's voice boomed from the speaker and echoed around the bathroom. "You promised!" Her tone held an accusatory note.

"When?" Henna dripped from Kit's chin, tapping the front of her dressing gown and plunging to the floor. Jerry had spent two weekends renovating Kit's ensuite with leftovers from his uncle's last building contract. Her eyes widened as the drip headed towards the clean grout between the tiles. She dropped to her knees and wiped up the splat, limiting the damage. "Bloody hell!" she cursed. In desperation, she stood in the shower and closed the door behind her. He'd also installed a shower dome which encased Kit in a plastic bubble and blocked out the restarting of the vacuum cleaner. She leaned against the wall and stopped fretting about her dripping head. "What did I promise?" She exhaled and waited for Debbie to make up something horrendous.

"You agreed to man our stall at the Expo." Petulance gave Debbie's tone an edge. "The international group hired Claudelands Events Centre, and you said you'd do free hair consultations."

Kit blinked in surprise. She glimpsed her reflection in the mirror to her right, her face oozing henna through the cubicle's distortion. It summed up how she felt about life. "I don't remember that." She didn't, but then she'd stumbled through the last six committee meetings like a zombie just needing to get to September without collapsing in a heap. "But I'm sure we can work out something between us." Kit yawned. "Give me the details at the meeting this evening." She didn't give Debbie room for comment, killing the call and wiping the screen on the cuff of her dressing gown sleeve.

Showering took a good half an hour, but cleaning up proved easier than Melinda suggested. Experience meant Kit had a dustbin bag ready, and she stuffed into it her dressing gown, underwear, and the tee-shirt-head-cover known as a Plop. Those items had a date with the washing machine. Another bag took the plastic wrap and shower cap layers bound for the household rubbish bin. She used a homemade scrub of hemp oil and brown sugar to wash her hair, massaging her scalp with groans of ecstasy. Then conditioner, flaxseed gel and a helping of purple-willy-shaped-lube completed the process after a few moments of finger curling.

Kit washed and then used the shower head to rinse off the last of the green henna flecks before gathering her collection of eco cleaning sprays into a corner to dry. She emerged into her bathroom with a cloud of steam swirling around her damp body, stopping the escape of more condensation by closing the shower door. Scooping her red hair into a clean tee shirt Plop, Kit heaved a sigh of satisfaction. Jerry's skill surrounded her, and she paused to admire the neat finish of the tiles butting against the skirting boards and shower tray. A jack-of-all-trades, he'd settled on the most unlikely occupation of all. Priest.

Kit used a wipe to clean her phone and then mopped up the place where the henna had dripped onto the tiles. "Good job, Kit," she told herself. In a moment of gratitude, she flicked Jerry a quick text to thank him for all his hard work. Her finger paused over the icon, which would send the message. Mentioning Melinda's presence might serve as a backhander after the compliment. Her lips twisted in thought. But then she sent her message into the ether and decided to forget the insolent cleaner's existence for the moment.

Clean clothes, hair without faded orange regrowth, and a tidy bedroom and bathroom put Kit in the best of moods. She used her hairdryer and diffuser to dry the ends of her curls and then sat on her bed. Four file folders stacked in the corner evidenced the last six months of study and an exam. A salon wouldn't employ her on the strength of it, but the Queen of Curl had awarded her with a certificate which merited her capable of cutting curly hair in the approved international method. Kit smiled at the navy velvet case sitting on top of the pile. It contained a coveted set of matte black precision scissors worth over four hundred Australian dollars. Her mother had attended the awards ceremony and watched her daughter presented with the prize for the student with the most flare. Miriam had dabbed her eyes with a tissue and Kit bit her lip at the memory of her mother's extreme pride. "You're on your way now, darling," Miriam had whispered as she hugged Kit afterwards. "The sky's the limit."

Her shoulders slumped. Every weekday in her near future involved rising at four in the morning. Then would follow five full days at Mr Rashid's shop on Gordonton Road. The days merged into the same gruelling pattern, interspersed with alternate weekends. Her feet ached from the hours standing and walking around the store, filling shelves with groceries, serving customers and dealing with miscreant paperboys. She'd left the awards' night on Friday filled with promise and ended up right back where she started. "When do I fit in hairdressing?" she murmured.

The vacuum cleaner purred downstairs as Melinda continued working. Kit wondered if the boys had employed the cleaner as a one-off gift to mark the end of her half a year of driving herself insane. She shrugged, willing to accept their generosity just this once. She hadn't been home enough to monitor the rostered jobs, so perhaps it signified a new start and the household would return to its former state of routine now she'd finished studying.

Kit added mascara and lipstick and stared at herself in the mirror. "A new start," she sighed to herself. Then she picked up the soft case containing her new scissors. She tilted it and lifted the fold so that the scissors slipped forward to display their rounded handles. Without touching them, she closed the flap and pushed the case into her handbag. Tonight's audience wouldn't understand the full marvel of such an expensive pair of snips, but Kit did. They signified the start of a winning streak. The beginning of the rest of her life. If she could find the time.

Chapter Three
Blocked Curls

"So, this woman is just walking around my house in the most ridiculous shoes. Apparently, she's the new cleaner."

"Wow." Piper pushed her bottom against the sofa and sipped her coffee. "Is she expensive? I could use a cleaner for a few months. I don't know how I ever held down a job at the same time as running a home. It's all a big lie. Women can't have both, can they?"

Kit inhaled through her nose, the hiss making her eyes water. "The boys don't know why she's doing it." Her gaze shifted to the rest of the WWC committee still chatting in the open-plan kitchen. She leaned closer to Piper. "They think she's doing it for free."

"A free cleaner?" Piper's eyes rounded, and she blinked. "Where did they find one of those?"

Kit gave a huff of disgust and sipped her coffee. Pam had added enough granules to blow her head off and keep her awake until midnight. "Her mother attends their church and is enamoured with the boys. She's pimping her daughter on a free cleaning gig in the hope one of them will fall in love with her."

"Oh, no!" Piper's ringlets swished against her neck as she shook her head. "That's terrible. It's exploitation."

"It's prostitution!" Kit snarled. "I looked it up in the dictionary. It's the unworthy or corrupt use of one's talents for personal or financial gain. Prostitution."

Piper kept her head down and fixed her gaze on the flecks of coffee circling the rim of her mug in a gentle dance. "So, a bit like what you're doing with this Expo then?"

Kit gasped. She turned to Piper with her lips parted, indignation stampeding across her expression. Then she closed her mouth with a snap. "Yes. Don't tell anyone."

Piper smiled in her peripheral vision. "I guess if you use it to get some customers, we could class it as marketing. You could claim your travel expenses back from the tax man."

Kit's lips curved into a wicked smile. "That's right," she mused. "You did the accounts at the car dealership. Please will you help me set up a hairdressing side hustle in exchange for free haircuts?"

"I thought you'd never ask." Piper kept her head down and sipped her drink. Both women tensed as the conversation in the kitchen ceased.

"Right, girls!" Debbie waddled across the room and dumped herself into a recliner opposite Kit. It groaned and tipped back on its rocker. "Let's start the September meeting of the Women with Curls, Hamilton Chapter." She bounded forward with enough vigour to catapult her out of the chair, but gripped the arms with white-knuckled fingers to stay seated. "Piper is taking the minutes."

"I am?" Piper slopped coffee over her thigh and onto the sofa cushion. "I didn't know."

Debbie closed her eyes as though concrete blocks dangled from her lashes. Kit squirmed at the sight of her eyeballs moving around beneath the purple eyeshadow. "Didn't you get the email?" Debbie's eyes popped open, and Piper squeaked in alarm.

"No." Her head shook like a wet dog's. "No."

"I'll do them." Pam slumped onto the sofa next to Kit and settled a lined notepad across her knees. She offered Kit a genuine smile. "Is it nice having your weekends free again?" she asked, her tone soft. She pushed a blonde curl away from her left eye and the pen in her hand drew a blue line across her cheek.

Kit shot a wary glance at Debbie and pursed her lips. Pam outranked Debbie as WWC chairperson, but Debbie trumped her on the scary scale. "Yes, thanks," she whispered in an effort not to appear rude. She watched Pam's husband through the lounge window. He carried black dustbin bags along the side of the house towards the gate. Greying curls covered his shoulders like a cloak. He'd removed the customary band holding his ponytail. The glow from the streetlights refracted off the bald spot over his crown to give him an eerie halo.

Pam followed her gaze and lowered her voice to an almost inaudible whisper. "He just got a promotion." She jerked her head towards her husband as he retraced his steps, carrying a recycling crate in his arms. "He's worked so hard for it. Long hours and lots of meetings."

"Have we finished over there in the cheap seats?" Debbie snarled.

Pam gave an indignant grunt and stroked the cushion between her and Kit. Her attempt to exude sympathy for her insulted sofa resulted in another blue line across the cream fabric. "Just get on with it," she urged. She used the same tone with which she wrangled five-year-olds into obedience during her day job. She leaned closer to Kit. "Her husband applied but didn't get the job."

"I want to plan the Expo," Debbie began, her tone acerbic as she glared at Pam. "But first, I'd like to show you the wonderful new conditioner from the Professionals Range." She leaned sideways, and the chair tipped onto one rocker with a groan of complaint. After a set of primal grunts and what sounded like a greasy fart, Debbie retrieved a cloth bag filled with bottles and containers. She set the bulging bag in her lap and beamed around at the gathered Curlies. Her face transformed with the inner glow of a televangelist blessing donations. Kit tensed, waiting for the hard sell and not disappointed when it arrived with a price tag and persuasion. "I'm offering discounts to the committee," she stated. Her plump fingers extracted a white bottle and hoisted it high enough for everyone to see.

Piper spoke through the side of her mouth. "That means she's got a garage full and can't get rid of it."

Kit turned her snort to a cough and covered her mouth. Debbie's beady eyes locked on her face. "What about Mr Rashid? I could give him five percent off another order if he buys over twenty this time."

Kit shook her head from side to side and hoped she infused her denial with the right amount of determination. "No thanks. He blamed me for the exploding lube. I don't want to get involved again."

Debbie's lips curled back in a snarl. "It kinda was your fault," she concluded.

Pam cleared her throat. She waved the pen in dismissal. "But what a happy accident," she enthused in her best school teacher's voice. "If you hadn't sold all that lube from your garage, you never would have gone into the supply market and been able to quit your job."

Debbie frowned. Pam had stymied her guilt trip and as it formed her only plan for selling the many bottles of product, it left her speechless for long enough for Sharon to wade in with a rebuke.

"Stop hawking your dodgy products here," she growled. She narrowed her eyes at Debbie. "You can't use our group to make a fast buck. It's against the rules." In the scary-stakes, Sharon represented the unknown quantity. She outweighed Debbie by a few kilogrammes and got herself voted onto the committee as vice chairperson in the previous election. The little she said emerged from her lips with enough of a bite to kill all unwanted conversation. Her skill at policing conflict was the only reason Pam agreed to continue as the leader after a mini crisis of confidence a few months earlier.

Maintaining her familiar good cop routine, Pam used the diversion to move the meeting to its planned agenda. "The Expo is in two weeks and we need to organise our stall. I've created a roster from those who volunteered at the last WWC meeting and added in the committee members to fill the gaps. We'll need spot prizes to encourage people to give names and email addresses. What about a survey to see what the women need from our group? The aim is to increase membership and therefore revenue. So, ladies, what do we think?"

"I could sell my products." Debbie's eyes glinted.

A fire sparked behind her irises as Sharon shook her head. "No. We want to provide teaching and encouragement, not just dump more crap on them."

Debbie raised a gnarled finger and jabbed it towards Kit. "But she's doing free haircuts all day. That's advertising. I can if she's allowed."

Kit exhaled in a rush. "No, I'm not!" Her voice rose. "I said I'd do a shift, not a complete day!"

Debbie shrugged and dropped her bag onto the carpet at her feet. "I suppose you're not really qualified enough to do an entire day, anyway," she muttered under her breath.

"I am qualified!" Kit's cheeks flushed with a rosy hue as she regretted taking the bait. She flipped open her handbag and extracted the protective case containing her prized scissors. "The Queen of Curl presented me with a certificate that says I am." She jabbed an index finger into her chest, before peeling open the case to reveal the dull matte blades. A sense of unworthiness shrouded her despite the accolade. "I won the matte black precision scissors for the student with the most flare!" Kit brandished the case. She resisted touching the expensive matte blades. A shiver of anticipation ran along her spine. The first snip promised the most amazing moment of her entire life. She fastened the case to stop anyone else from getting any ideas about handling them.

Piper's fingers slid across the sofa between them to land on Kit's thigh. She gave a gentle squeeze of warning, but it arrived too late.

"Prove it!" Debbie snapped. She eased forward, her hands dangling between her thighs like a woman about to give birth. "If you're so bloody marvellous, you won't mind doing the entire day!"

Chapter Four

A Curly Adversary

"I'm not bloody marvellous!" Kit's fingers shook as she tweaked a red curl in the mirror of the downstairs cloak room.

Piper had sneaked in behind her and locked the door. Her friend closed the lid of the toilet and sat down, leaning her elbows on her knees and resting her chin on her fists. "I tried to warn you," she said. "She played you like a fiddle."

"I know!" Kit's face crumpled into a mask of despair. Her shoulders slumped as she turned and leaned her back against the tiny sink. "I can't do it. I'll have to pretend I'm sick on the day." Her new found resolve dribbled down the plug hole.

"You can't do that. Wait until the girls find out you're giving free Curly advice and demonstrations." Kit glanced back in time to see Piper roll her eyes. "I wouldn't want to be you."

Kit's knees trembled, and she reached her hand back to grip the edge of the sink. "And why am I only now finding out about a grand finale?"

Piper's eyelashes fluttered closed, and a beatific smile settled over her lips. "It's gonna be amazing," she sighed. "All the big towns in New Zealand will compete for the Curl Queen's coveted trophy." Her eyes popped open. "Win it for us."

"No, no, no!" Kit pressed her fingers over her eyes. "This isn't fair. I'm exhausted. What happened to my dreams of free weekends and lazy days at home?"

Piper's face scrunched into a mask of confusion. "But you work for Mr Rashid. And don't you have to man the shop on alternate weekends now you've finished your course?"

Kit groaned and stared at the ceiling. "Just let me pretend for a little longer, please?"

Piper shrugged. "It won't change the fact you just volunteered to spend the whole day with Debbie." She grinned at Kit's growled curse. "What if she wants you to use her for the demonstration?" She rose and unlocked the door.

"No. No way!" Kit lurched for the back of Piper's shirt. Her grasping fingers seized a chunk of her collar, causing Piper to cough as it constricted her throat. "Get back here! I'm demonstrating on you and that's it."

Piper wrinkled her nose. She turned in the small space to wriggle free of Kit's choke hold. "That won't work. You have to give four demonstrations across the entire day and then the grand finale. You need four other people."

A familiar tightening sent spasms into the muscles of Kit's chest. Shallow breathing caused her lips to tingle and a primal scream to form behind her ribcage. "I quit," she croaked. "I bloody hate these women. That's it. I'm done."

"Just breathe." Piper placed her hands on Kit's shoulders, her forehead furrowing into fine lines. "Everything is fine. You've weathered much worse." Her fingers tensed in a comforting massage. "You can demonstrate on my hair for the grand finale. We'll find four more Curlies for the other slots."

"I want nice Curlies only," Kit whispered. A yawn cut her sentence in half. "Not Debbie."

"Okay." Piper gave her a conspiratorial wink. "We can do a name-in-the-hat draw at the next meeting. I'll rig the results."

"Thank you, thank you." Kit wrapped her arms around her friend's neck and breathed in the scent of baby powder and pureed apple. Together they walked back into the lounge and prepared to resume the torturous part of the meeting, where Sharon ran through the dismal state of the accounts and argued with Debbie about her spending. Kit had snoozed through the last two gatherings, despite Piper's nudges.

"Come on then." Piper strode across the expanse of fluffy carpet with a light step, but Kit froze in the lounge doorway.

"You!" She lifted a shaking finger and pointed it at the blonde woman who'd taken her place on the sofa. Fear and rage mingled in her chest to create the kind of vitriol which would drive Langdon's hands to cover his ears. "You got me arrested!" Exhaustion and disappointment added to the other emotions as Kit balled her fists by her sides. Piper halted half way across the room and her eyes bulged like golf balls. She glanced towards Kit's nemesis with a wince.

"What's happening? Why is she here?" Kit's gaze tracked to Sharon, then Debbie, before resting on Pam. "Why wouldn't you warn me she was coming?"

Debbie gave a dramatic huff. "You can't decide who we're allowed to invite!" Her breasts wobbled beneath her blouse as she turned to face Kit. "It's a committee. Not the Kit Maguire appreciation society."

"Let's all calm down." Sharon patted the air with her right hand, though she shot a raised eyebrow in Kit's direction.

"Meaning me? You want me to calm down." Exhaustion and disappointment bit at the back of Kit's psyche. Questions revolved around her brain as her safe place grew a floor made from barbed wire.

"We need Cindy's help with the Expo." Debbie's jaw acquired a hard angle through her cheek, and she folded her arms. "I invited her, and she's staying. You need to get over it."

"I need to get over it?" Kit's voice rose to a screech. She stared at Cindy, seeing a smirk break out across the woman's painted lips. Temper flared in Kit's breast. "I'm not staying if she's here!" she shouted. She spun to face Piper, expecting her solidarity. Her eyes widened as Piper stared down at a loose button on her blouse. She lifted her index finger and flicked it, her cheeks reddening as she avoided Kit's gaze.

"Wow." Kit stared around the room. Debbie glared at her, but the other women fought to avoid eye contact. "Okay." She settled her shaking fingers over her hips. "Fine then. I quit."

"I'm sure we can sort this out." Ever the peace maker, Pam rose with a hand outstretched towards her. She used her best placatory voice to dampen the fire raging in Kit's eyes. Her tone reduced her dispute to that of a five-year-old throwing a tantrum. It lit the fuse of her rage and her fists balled by her sides.

"They arrested me, and she said nothing!" Her voice shook. She jabbed her shaking finger in Cindy's direction before facing her.

The new Curly of a few months ago had morphed into a butterfly. Coiled blonde ringlets cascaded over her shoulders. Veins bulged against Kit's neck as she shook her head in disgust. "You let the cops think I'd killed Mr Roy." She closed her eyes as a wave of sadness crept up her spine and settled at the back of her neck. Her venom surprised her. She hadn't realised she held Cindy responsible for one cataclysmic day which had changed her life forever. A safe bubble had shrouded her existence until that day. Then she'd lost her job, her freedom, and almost her home. Because of Cindy's silence.

Her shoulders slumped, and she squeezed the bridge of her nose between her thumb and forefinger. The unfairness percolating through her life hit her in the stomach.

Pam took a nervous step towards her. "We invited Cindy here," she affirmed, doubling the body blow. "She studied hairdressing at college."

"She's a computer programmer!" Kit's voice held an uncharacteristic screech.

Cindy rose, her neat stilettos forming a triangle at the bottom of tapered calves and sickeningly neat ankles. "You ladies inspired me so much that I did the refresher course in Melbourne run by the Queen of Curl herself." She fixed a determined gaze on Kit. "I qualified as a hairdresser when I left school. My father wanted me to run his company, so I went back to study IT at university to help him." She gave a nonchalant shrug. "He sold the business two months ago, so I can return to what I love." Her torso dipped as though taking a bow of its own accord. Kit's gaze slid to the other members of the WWC committee. Sharon appeared to melt under the lorry load of sugar, and Pam's eyelids fluttered. Kit couldn't look at Debbie. Cindy patted her chest with fingers edged by long, powder blue nails. "I'm happy to take the lead with the Expo if you think I'm suitable." Her jaw ground her teeth together in an almost imperceptible movement.

Kit nodded. An opportunity for deliverance presented itself. "I quit," she affirmed, her voice stronger. She strode across the room with determined steps. Her socks swished against the plush navy carpet. The bend in her spine appeared wooden as she snatched her handbag off the sofa and stalked towards the hallway. She didn't stop to fasten her plimsolls, jamming her feet into them and escaping through the front door. The laces flapped around her feet as she walked down the driveway to her yellow car. Unused to the sudden darkness, she squinted as her fingers fumbled in her bag for her keys. She hauled on her fluffy keyring with such vigour it detached from the metal link and flew backwards with her sharp yank. It disappeared into the bushes surrounding Pam's manicured garden. Too angry to engage in a search for it by the light of her phone torch, Kit abandoned it in favour of escaping before someone followed her to talk her out of resigning.

"I thought I recognised the car." The voice issued from the shadows, and Kit looked up with a scream. Jackson Delaney's eyes widened, and he reached for her, clapping a hand over her mouth. "Bloody hell!" he hissed. "Sorry."

Kit's heart rate shot to geriatric levels, and she dropped her handbag. Its contents clattered and tinkled as they hit the pavement. Laboured breathing stopped her thinking straight, and she lurched forward, wrapping her arms around the police officer's neck with relief. His Kevlar vest dug into her soft places, and the unexpectedness of the embrace pitched him backwards against her car with a grunt.

"Er, hi," he whispered against the side of her face. "I'm on a late shift and thought I'd drive around the suburbs."

Kit sighed against his shoulder and closed her eyes. "My warrant of fitness is out of date," she confessed.

"I know." Jackson's arms tightened around her. "And so is your car registration."

Chapter Five
Curly Cop

Kit sat in Jackson's police car overlooking Hamilton city. He'd helped her retrieve her belongings from the footpath and the gutter before suggesting a drive. His radio crackled on the dashboard and he listened to a message in his earpiece. "Show me helping a member of the public with car issues for the next half an hour," he said, his tone formal. When he turned to face Kit, his hazel eyes twinkled with humour. "So, Maguire, I haven't seen you around in a while."

Kit bent forward in the passenger seat to lace her plimsolls. Her efforts to do it with the police car in motion had resulted in a bump to her forehead. "The last six months are a blur. I worked at the shop during the week and drove up to Auckland every weekend." She sat up and turned sideways, bending her right knee on the seat. "You could have visited the shop if you'd wanted to see me." She didn't realise until she'd released it that the sentence held a veiled rebuke.

"What's in Auckland?" Jackson leaned his crown against the head rest and relaxed. He ignored her accusation.

"A hairdressing course." Kit dipped her head forward, and perfect ringlets cascaded against her cheeks and tumbled over her shirt. "It's specific for curly hair. The nearest one is in Australia, but they trialled one in Auckland for the first time." Her lips wrinkled into a sneer. "Unless your name is Cindy and you're a qualified hairdresser. Then you can do a quick five minutes and take over the world."

Jackson jerked his chin upwards, and his gaze followed a ringlet as it bounced forward over her shoulder. "The city seemed quiet without you. The crime rate is down, anyway." His lips curved into a smile. "It sounds like you're getting your life together. So, why did you leave that house with trouble written all over your face?"

Kit groaned. "I just quit the Women with Curls group." She dug the heels of her hands into her eyes. "I'll have to find another chapter now. It's the only way to operate as a legitimate Curly hairdresser. They're meant to oversee my business and ensure I'm sticking to the rules and expectations of the Queen of Curl." She bumped her head against the rest. "I'm such an idiot."

"There are more than one of these groups?" Jackson's voice rose at the end of the sentence. He gave an exaggerated slow blink. "It must just be yours that causes problems."

"The other nearest one is Cambridge." Kit sighed and picked at a loose thread on her jeans. "That's an extra half an hour on my driving time each way."

A raised eyebrow greeted her observation. "Not unless you fix that WOF and registration issue." Jackson narrowed his eyes to slits. "I have these pretty pink stickers I can decorate that yellow-mobile with and you don't want that, Maguire."

"No, I don't." She exhaled and pushed both feet onto the mat, sitting with her hands clasped between her thighs. "I'll visit the transport office on Monday as soon as my shift finishes to renew my rego. Kenny finally got a job at a local garage, so I'll ask him to deal with the warrant. It's only just out of date."

"You get twenty-eight days for the warrant." Jackson wrinkled his nose. "Why didn't you do the registration online?"

Kit sighed. "No credit card. No laptop either. Raki took it back because only bad things happen when I order products online."

Jackson nodded. "Ah yeah. The lube." He ran his hands through his hair and the silence spread between them. It tingled in the air, fading to a gentle hush as Kit settled back in her seat and watched the city. The ridge Jackson had driven to offered a panoramic view of Hamilton. Lights twinkled below as families moved around their homes and the power station glowed like a Christmas tree.

"Do you come here often?" Kit clapped a hand over her mouth as soon as the cliche became airborne.

Jackson smirked and bit his lip to stop himself from laughing. She appreciated the sincerity of his effort to avoid humiliating her. He sighed and watched the twinkling city lights below them. "Yeah." His reply held an element of reflection. "It's good to press the pause button and take stock sometimes."

Kit strove to lighten the mood, reaching for the easiest question in her social repertoire. "What's the weirdest thing you've ever had to do as a cop?" She smiled and turned sideways in her seat, her interest in his answer genuine.

Jackson inhaled and thought for a moment. "That's easy. I once turned up to arrest this girl, and she had my business card stuffed into her bra."

Kit released a hiss of dismay. The darkness hid the flush of embarrassment which attacked her cheeks and the tips of her ears. "Inappropriate," she grumbled. "And anyway, wrongful arrests don't count." A car shot past the layby, its brake lights blooming with guilt as the driver spotted the police car too late. Kit reran Jackson's sentence again in her head, and her features relaxed. "Thanks for calling me a girl, though. Thirty doesn't feel very girlish."

"Oh yeah, happy birthday for July."

She pursed her lips to stop her smile escaping at the fact he knew her birth date. Reality whipped away the minor victory when she remembered his police database also contained her height, weight, fingerprints and an unflattering mug shot from the previous summer. She changed the subject. "What are you working on at the moment?"

"Something quite interesting." Jackson covered a yawn with his hand as though to contradict the sentiment. "There's a significant rise in the number of cases of alcohol poisoning."

Kit shrugged. "People have overindulged since Noah landed. That's nothing new."

"It is when the same stuff keeps turning up repeatedly. Same formula, same local area. The chief thinks someone is running an illegal still and getting their calculations wrong. It's like paint stripper."

"Yuk." Kit wrinkled her nose. "I haven't seen the local news for months. Why would people want to drink paint stripper?"

Jackson rested his hands on the steering wheel. Kit understood their time together would soon end even before he fired up the engine. "Cost." He looked over his shoulder before turning the vehicle into a tight U-turn. "Accessibility. Why pay for shop bought spirits when you can get off your face for a fraction of the price? They're not looking for a nice whiskey to tickle their palate. The teenagers are pre-loading before they go out and those too young to buy it legally can get it without answering awkward questions."

Kit made interested noises and considered the alcohol in Mr Rashid's shop. "Should I ask at work if Mr Rashid has noticed any difference in sales? It might help to pinpoint a location if the regulars are going elsewhere."

Jackson lifted a finger and jabbed it in her direction. "See, this is why I've missed you, Maguire," he said. His voice sounded light enough for Kit to believe he spoke the truth. Until she glanced sideways and saw the smile he tried so hard to hide.

Chapter Six

Clipper Hell

"What the hell are you doing?" Kit's cry pierced the airwaves until they tingled in the resulting silence. She catapulted her handbag onto the sofa and fixed her hands over her hips. Jackson had dropped her back at her vehicle with a warning about the outstanding infringements, and she'd driven home with another lead weight added to the growing pile in the pit of her stomach.

"You're early." Jerry's smile didn't reach his eyes. Langdon sat on a stool in the middle of the kitchen, and Jerry waved a set of hair clippers over the top of his head. "Our usual barber retired last month. The verger commented we both looked a little too shaggy for the bishop's visit to the morning service." Jerry pursed his lips and frowned. The ex-lawyer held Kit's gaze and knew when to stop talking. He'd need to take up sprinting when Langdon attempted his next preening session because half the vicar's head revealed an awful lot of pink scalp.

"Wow." Kit's knees buckled, and she slumped onto the sofa next to her bag. "Just wow."

"You like it?" Langdon shook his head in a motion which usually gave his blond hair a ruffled flick. The right side swished as normal, but only his ear waggled on the left. "I wanted to ask you to cut it once you finished your training, but Jerry figured you'd get busy quite fast. So, he offered." Langdon's left hand rose, and Jerry's eyes bugged. He slapped the fingers a millisecond before Langdon contacted the bald spot above his ear.

"It's not ready yet!" he snapped.

Kit swallowed and enjoyed watching the unflappable Jerry flounder. An unusual sight, it offered much needed entertainment after a horrible day. Jerry mouthed something behind Langdon's head and jabbed his finger at the blade-end of the clippers. As though Kit couldn't already tell for herself that he'd forgotten to use the guard before starting, he picked it up and slotted it on and off again. Then he spread his hands in mute appeal. Kit rose. "Ah well," she said at the same time as releasing an exaggerated yawn. "I'll leave you to it."

Langdon gave a cheery wave as she grabbed her bag and headed for the stairs. Jerry choked, and Langdon continued his moment of benevolence. "I'll make you a hot chocolate as soon as we're done," he said with a smile.

"Not my circus, not my monkey," Kit whispered to herself as she reached the top of the landing.

Raki's bedroom door stood open, and Kit peeked in as she passed. She wished she hadn't, unable to unsee the sight of Raki's backside sticking into the air and his legs wound around his torso like a pretzel. "Night, Raki," she called with a yawn.

"Hey Kit." His voice sounded muffled. "Jerry said I could join him and Langdon next time they do hot yoga. I'm trying it without the hot."

"Nice." Kit released a sigh and closed her bedroom door behind her. She flicked on the bedside lamp, and a yellow glow blossomed from the energy bulb. Her earlier tidying rewarded her in the shape of clean sheets and the scent of floral furniture polish. Despite the early hour, Kit donned her pyjamas, cleaned her teeth and climbed into bed. She snuggled under the covers with a murder mystery her mother had presented to her as a birthday gift. Reminded of Marian, she lifted her phone and dialled her mother's number.

"Kit darling, I was just thinking about you." Her mother's gentle tone lulled her into a false sense of security.

"That's nice, Mum. Thank you for coming to the awards ceremony last night. I'm glad you got the opportunity to see how I spent your loan." She gave a fake laugh to hide how much Marian's generosity still hung like a weight around her neck. Especially since her hasty resignation from WWC had detonated her chances of launching a business and repaying it. She'd never needed a new Curly group more than she did right then.

"I'm so proud of you," Marian cooed. "My crocheting group wanted to know every last detail." She released a dramatic sigh, which created a whooshing sound in Kit's ear. "Your little face when the Queen of Curl called out your name, I thought I would just die."

Kit bit her bottom lip, but her proud smile still sneaked free. She drew her knees up to her chest and grinned into the phone. "Mum, do you think Dad would have been proud of me, too? He assumed I'd become a lawyer."

"Your father wanted you to be happy," Marian soothed. "He didn't care how you went about it as long as you stayed on the right side of the law."

"Thanks, Mum." Kit exhaled. "Do you think Kenny might do a favour for me?"

"Why don't you ask him?" A series of bumps and a serious clatter gave way to the sound of Kenny hawking something syrupy from the back of his throat. Kit winced and pulled the phone away from her ear. She jabbed the screen to activate the speaker and set the device on the bedspread.

"Kit?" Kenny's voice bellowed into the room. "Is that you?"

"Hi." Kit kept her tone civil. "How's your new job going?"

"Yeah, good." Her stepfather gave a guttural cough. "The boss says I fit right in with the crowd. We finish early on a Friday and drink beer."

"Great." Kit swallowed and considered the needs of her temperamental Volkswagen Beetle. "I'm pleased for you." The idea of handing over the Bug to a group of beer swilling mechanics didn't bode well. So, she made small talk with her stepfather before ending the call. He seemed pleased she'd rung, and she thrust aside the guilt for not congratulating him earlier. She admitted to herself that perhaps some of her issues with the infamous Kenny Rogers started with her own attitude.

Her phone buzzed with a text as she cradled her knees and listened to the argument break out downstairs as Langdon looked in the mirror. She held her breath and read it.

'I forgot to mention that one of my friends would like to explore becoming a Curly. Apparently, she's been straightening since 1987. I've given her your number. You've put Kenny in such a good mood. Talk soon.'

"1987," Kit breathed. She exhaled. "Trust my mother to bring the impossible challenge." She muted her phone and snuggled back into bed with her novel. A warmth spread out from the centre of her chest and gave her a sense of wholeness. She'd made Marian proud enough to recommend her services to a friend and accidentally enriched her relationship with her stepfather. For a little while at least, it caused her other issues to pale in significance and allowed her to drop to sleep with a smile on her lips.

Chapter Seven

Curly Cleric

The blissful fifteen-minute sleep gave Kit the happy sensation of drifting on a cloud of goodwill. Until the knocking shook her bedroom door on its hinges.

She woke with a start, clutching her chest as the paperback thudded to the floor.

"Kit?" Raki's voice wavered. "Are you awake?"

"No!" She groaned and turned off the bedside lamp. Squeezing her eyelids closed, she sought the euphoria of sleep for sleep's sake instead of the exhausted coma of the last few months.

"Kit?" Raki's voice lifted the end of her name into a squeak. "Something terrible has happened."

"If it's Jerry's hair cutting skills, I already saw!" She pulled the blankets higher and flattened her palms over her ears.

"No, it's happened to me. He didn't mean to do it." The handle turned, and the door creaked open. Light from the hallway bloomed across Kit's face to ruin the muted ambiance. All hope of sleep sneaked between Raki's legs and the door frame, slinking into the night and escaping.

"Bloody hell!" Kit shouted. She sat up and opened her eyes, wondering as her hand shot to her mouth if she'd stumbled into a strange nightmare. "What did you do?"

Raki sank onto the end of her bed with his head bowed. He stared at his bare feet and wrestled with several possible answers. In the end, he settled on the truth. "Jerry cut my hair."

Kit plumped her pillows to give her a moment to order her thoughts. Words like *scalped* and *butchered* had their place, but not in praise of an amateur hatchet job, which left bald spots showing through Raki's dark hair. His lips twisted as he looked up at her, his words muffled and stilted. "He did it this afternoon, but I hid it from you when you walked past my room." He swallowed. "I thought I might get used to it, but that was before Langdon started screaming. Apparently, there's a bald stripe at the back. Look." Raki whipped his head round and gave Kit a full view of the tram lines running along his head. It looked like the Overlander had come off the rails in the wilds of the King Country. Tufts stuck out either side of the bald spots like bush reserves. "I have a PhD meeting on Monday to defend my research. If it wasn't such an impossible task to get all the professors in one room, I'd cancel until my hair grows back again." His shoulders slumped and his usual genial expression morphed into down turned lips and sad eyes.

Kit groaned and scrubbed at her cheeks with her knuckles. "Can I fix it tomorrow?" she asked. "I think I'd make it worse if I tried to cut it now."

Raki brightened and nodded. Then he winced, and his lips flattened. "You can fix mine then," he agreed, "but Langdon is preaching to the bishop in the Matins service at seven o'clock tomorrow morning."

A howl drifted up the stairs and onto the landing, followed by the pounding of footsteps. Langdon burst into Kit's room with a tea towel over his head, forcing Raki's frightened face to recede into the background. She released an involuntary laugh but bit back the ready comment about shepherds and wise men. Jerry followed at a more sedate pace, the clippers still in his hand.

"Help me." Tears welled in Langdon's eyes as he clasped the diagonal edges of the tea towel under his chin.

Raki spluttered a laugh into the ensuing silence. "You look like the Virgin Mary, doesn't he, Kit?" His brown-eyed gaze slid to her, and she avoided it to prevent adding more humiliation to Langdon's pile. A fit of the giggles at his expense might send him over the edge. Kit sensed the tension weighing down the air and settling over the gathered crowd like a musty blanket.

"The bishop can't see this." Langdon released the ends of the fabric and whipped off his head covering. Kit tensed the muscles in her face and worked hard not to show the level of shock which ricocheted through her mind. Jerry cleared his throat and buzzed the clippers on and off a few times, distracting himself as Langdon showcased his handiwork. Langdon's lips moved without sound like a badly dubbed movie and Kit gave a decisive nod.

"Right," she said, swinging her feet to the cold floorboards. "Go back to the kitchen and I'll fetch my scissors."

"Thank you, thank you!" Langdon gushed. He clasped his hands together at his chest in prayer. Raki followed him from the bedroom, but Jerry hung around while Kit unwound herself from the bedsheets.

"It's called an undercut," Kit said. She wrapped herself in her dressing gown and stifled a yawn with the back of her hand.

"What is?" Jerry didn't look up at her, studying the clippers and running his thumb along the sharp combs.

"Langdon's hairstyle. It's where you shave one side or part of the head but leave the rest long. Apparently it's the most popular style this year."

Jerry nodded, and he lifted the clippers and gave them a shake. "I can turn my hand to most things, but not this it seems."

"Don't be daft." Kit bent to retrieve her hairdressing bag from the pile of folders. "I love my bathroom. You're amazing at everything you touch." Her fingers wrapped around his as she lifted the clippers. "Where did you get these?"

"A parishioner donated them to the second-hand shop attached to the church. I picked them up for a fiver."

Kit shook her head and dropped her hand. "They're rusty, Jerry. Put them in the bin." At his expression of devastation, she relented, rising on her tiptoes to kiss his cheek. "I'll fix it," she promised. "Don't worry."

By the time she arrived in the kitchen, Langdon already occupied the stool in the centre of the room. His closed eyes and blank expression exuded a practised peace, but his writhing fingers and planted feet betrayed his inner turmoil. Tufts of blond hair surrounded him in a lopsided arc like the evidence from a crime scene. Raki clattered around in the kitchen, clinking tumblers and pouring a healthy dose of the emergency alcohol. His bare feet padded against the tiles as he pushed a glass of amber liquid into Langdon's hand and clasped the other one himself. "I'll get you one after, Kit," he promised. "You'll need a steady hand."

"It's not as bad as you think it is," she soothed. Her tools clanked inside the cloth bag as she laid them on the counter. "Jerry didn't realise the clippers were blunt. I'll fix it."

Langdon's lips moved in prayer. He paused long enough to sip his drink before resuming his murmuring. The fact he didn't miss a beat impressed Kit. She'd borrowed the cooking sherry from Marian five years ago to adulterate a Christmas cake and forgotten to give it back. She hadn't made the cake either. Raki dug his index finger into his glass and chased an unidentified floater around the rim.

Kit extracted a comb from her bag and tried to make sense of Jerry's multi layered effort. Poor Langdon resembled an ageing punk rocker with bushy, jagged edges on one side of his head and a sizable bald spot on the other. She rediscovered his parting after some digging before hauling her trusty scissors from the folds of the bag. The urge to deliver a disclaimer rumbled through her brain. As soon as her fingers slipped through the ring handles and sensed the resistance of the pivot, doubt hit her like a freight train. She'd spent six months cutting curly hair, shaping it curl by curl like human topiary and learning which chemicals to avoid. Models had shuffled in wearing bramble bushes on their heads and walked out like super models.

Kit gave a definitive snip, and the bumper dulled the impact on her fingers. Cindy would know where to start. A year of hairdressing college followed by a refresher from the Queen of Curl had equipped her to deal with disasters like this. As Kit's confidence ebbed, Raki gave a sudden exclamation. "Why don't you use your new scissors?" His chocolate irises brightened, and he dumped his tumbler on the counter. "I can fetch them."

"I'll go." Jerry's voice held an uncharacteristic dullness. Kit hadn't noticed him lurking in the hallway beyond the lounge door, the clippers still clutched in his hand. "Where are they?"

Grateful for a moment's reprieve, Kit closed the blades and released a shuddering breath. "My handbag is on the shelf by my bedroom door. Just put your hand into the main pocket and you'll find a navy blue, velvet wrapper. They're inside but don't open the case." A serene smile played across her lips. This was her moment.

Jerry's footsteps provided his unspoken answer.

"Can you just start, anyway?" Langdon begged. He sank the tumbler of sherry and held it out to Raki. "More please."

"I'll start cutting if you stop drinking." Kit tapped his shoulder. "I can fix your hair, but I can't stop you breathing alcohol fumes over the bishop in a few hours' time."

Her brow knitted into a series of concerned lines. "And you have to promise not to fire Jerry."

Langdon gave a low growl in his throat. His jaw moved beneath the outline of the same chiselled face which broke hearts every Sunday. "I'll think about it," he conceded.

Kit took a step back and lifted her scissors away from his head. "No deal." Her voice remained calm as she called his bluff. "Forgive Jerry or I won't help you."

"Okay!" Langdon snapped. He wafted his hand in the same motion he used when commanding the octogenarian organ player to pump out her reedy notes. "Please begin cutting."

Chapter Eight
Curly Commitment

Jerry returned without the new scissors, bringing Kit's handbag instead. "I can't find them." He whispered the words, as though needing to diminish his presence in the room.

Kit set her old scissors on the counter and dug through her bag. "But they must be here," she mused. "Maybe they fell out and went under the shelves or my bed. Did you look there?" She frowned at Jerry's nod of confirmation.

"Just do it!" Hysteria laced Langdon's tone and Kit's shoulders slumped. The thrum of defeat beat alongside her pulse as she fought the urge to grab her old scissors and administer a skinhead akin to the abomination on Raki's scalp just to get it over with. Bare skin reflected the light on Raki's bald patches as he stood underneath the lampshade. He ran a hand over it and frowned, his mind elsewhere as he escaped into a world of chemical formulae and complicated potions.

Kit picked up her trusty scissors and her fingers slotted into position like holding the hand of an old friend. She took a fortifying breath. "What is the worst-case scenario?" she asked, her voice wavering.

"This!" Langdon jabbed at his head and screwed his neck around to glare at Jerry. "I look like a 1980s electro pop band member."

"A what?" Kit blinked at his reference.

"It doesn't matter!" Langdon's voice rose and his fingers twitched towards the sherry bottle. "Just fix it!"

"Okay." Kit ran her fingers through his remaining prized blond locks. She took a deep inhale. "To rephrase my question, do you want me to chop it all off so you can let it grow back, or should I attempt to style it?" Her fingers trembled at the thought of the second option, and she added in a rush, "I'm thinking I can give you something funky which would make the shaved part appear like it's meant to be there."

"Funky?" Langdon spun on the stool to face her. "I'm a vicar! There's nothing funky about me."

"That's true." Raki's eyes remained glazed, but his voice held clarity which showed he'd been listening the whole time. "Nothing trendy about Langdon."

"Not trendy?" Langdon froze, and his fingers fluttered up to touch the shaved side of his head. "Not funky is one thing, but not trendy is different. I thought I looked very trendy."

Raki pulled his phone from his back pocket and his fingers moved over the screen. Jerry sat on the sofa with a deep sigh. "I'm Googling it," Raki informed them. "Just wait a sec."

Kit waved her scissors in the air. "Don't mind me. It's not like I was asleep or anything."

Langdon raised his hand between them like a conductor halting a crescendo, and Kit ground her teeth. She slid her scissors behind her back to stop her from snipping off his fingers.

Raki cleared his throat. "Funky means having a strong dance rhythm." He wrinkled his nose. "Or a very musty smell." More finger scrolling. "Oh, look, it's a slang word. It means offbeat, unconventional or eccentric. Trendy means fashionable and up to date. They're kind of the same thing." He stuck his phone in his back pocket and folded his arms. "You're not funky or trendy, mate. I hate to break it to you."

Langdon bristled, and the air crackled with his offence. "I can be funky if I want to!" He raised his voice and jabbed his index finger in Kit's direction. "Funk me up, sister," he commanded.

Kit prayed to Langdon and Jerry's God for divine intervention before making the first cut. The natural mane which Langdon suppressed beneath hair spray and gel responded to Kit's scissors by springing into glossy curls. The vicar's ultra-sensible style paled beside the neat undercut on one side and the gentle waves cascading over his right ear. She neatened the back with her scissors, snipping away at the ratty ends and adding a neat curve along the line of Langdon's neck. Graduating the undercut into the rest of his hair proved easier than she imagined, despite it not being a cut demanded by any self-respecting Curly. She stood back to admire her work.

"I've made the undercut very short," she advised. "The bald spots will disappear in a couple of days and then I can trim the rest to match."

Langdon shook his head. "I can't have bald spots," he pleaded, closing his eyes and clasping his hands to his chest. "The bishop already hates me. She'll fire me in a heartbeat and give my parish to Alfie Dimwit."

Kit recoiled. The facade of the capable vicar faded amid his anxiety. Name calling seemed beyond his attained level of holiness and jarred with her perception of him. Jerry cleared his throat to the side of her and viewed her from beneath a raised eyebrow. "That's his actual name," he said, his tone wooden and without emotion. "And the bishop wants us to get married."

"To Alfie Dimwit?" Kit gave a visible shudder.

Langdon's shoulders drooped. "Not to him in particular. We can be gay or straight and she doesn't care which. But we need to be married to another person."

"Oh." Kit's scissors paused in mid-air. "But we're happy single, aren't we?" She looked at Raki and Jerry for confirmation. "We're a family. What is the world coming to when single people are outcasts?" A murmur of agreement added weight to her sentiment. She narrowed her eyes in thought. "Is it her perception of commitment, do you think? She's assuming if you're not with a special someone then your commitment to God and the church is also in doubt?"

Jerry nodded. "I think so. Also, marriage clips our wings and makes us less eligible. The other churches have dreadful problems filling rosters, but we have no trouble, do we Langdon? I suppose we could abuse our position to exploit our congregation."

Kit's mind strayed to the free cleaner they'd garnered and she bit her tongue. "Do you trust me?" she asked Langdon.

A trembling hand drifted to his head, and he ran his fingers through the glossy right side of his hair. "Yes," he replied, though he didn't sound sure.

Kit drew a thin battery razor from the folds of her hairdressing bag. She detached the guard and set the blades whirring. Langdon jerked sideways and glared at her. "Trust me," she soothed. "We'll teach her to doubt your commitment."

Chapter Nine
Jealous Curls

Kit stretched out on her bed and wiggled her toes. A watery sun poked through a gap in the curtains, and she sighed with gratitude. "Two lie-ins in one week," she mused. "Bliss." Her digital clock revealed the lateness of the hour, and she pushed herself to a sitting position. She'd slept until lunchtime after her late night antics with Langdon's hair.

"Kit?" A light knock sounded on her bedroom door. "Are you decent?"

"Yeah." She plumped her pillows and leaned back against them, resisting the urge for another stretch. The door opened and Langdon's face peeked through the gap.

"Sorry to wake you," he said. His muscles bulged through his black shirt, the dog collar crisp against its ebony folds. He proceeded into the room carrying a tray and strode across to the bed.

"Wow." Kit blinked, realising she must have woken to his initial knock on the door. She gaped at the tray he laid across her knees. Fresh coffee steamed in a take-out cup from her favourite cafe and a low carb treat nestled in a paper bag next to it. A tiny glass vase contained a single yellow carnation. Langdon bit his lower lip and his blue irises flashed with a hidden delight.

"Everyone loved my hair." His skin appeared to crawl within his black shirt as though excitement made it dance. His muscles rippled, moving the fabric taut and then releasing it. He stood on one foot and then on the other. "The bishop couldn't stop staring at your artwork." He turned his head sideways to reveal Kit's final attempt to fix up Jerry's hatchet job. A cross masked the bald spots, blending them into a seamless dedication to Langdon's first love. God.

Her shoulders relaxed, and she realised she'd held her breath when her chest started aching. "Thank goodness!" she exclaimed. She lifted the coffee cup to her lips and took a sip of the warming brew. "Thank you for this. It's awesome."

"It's the least I could do," he gushed. A pink tinge crawled into his cheeks. "She called it funky." He licked his lips, and a beam broke free and lit up his face. "I'm funky."

Kit clutched the coffee and freed her index finger enough to jab it in his direction. "You're also an honorary Curly. No more straightening those poor babies and no more sulfates or silicones. You need to do it properly like you promised last night."

"Okay." Langdon turned and bounced from the room, exuberance in every step. The midnight hair-wash with liquid dish soap over the kitchen sink had seemed like a step too far. But the Curly Approved conditioner, flaxseed gel and dab of lube had produced a stunning mop of curls. Interested in the process, Raki had analysed the chemical composition, which made the dish soap perfect for stripping out the terrible ingredients contained in Langdon's usual shampoo.

"I might try this Curly thing when my hair grows back," he'd mused. Kit winced in the cold light of day. Born with dead straight black hair, Raki's genetics predetermined his inability to create a single curl without artificial intervention. She stretched out on the bed and nibbled on her slice of keto heaven and sipped her coffee.

"Hey." Jerry stood in the doorway in his black shirt and dog collar. "Can I come in?"

Kit nodded, half way through swallowing a mouthful of slice. She jabbed a finger towards the end of the bed and an almond bounced back into the paper bag. "How are you?" She covered her mouth with her hand while she chewed.

Jerry shrugged and sat down next to her. His weight dipped the mattress. "All's well that ends well," he mused, his reply ambiguous. "I just wanted to thank you for fixing up my mess last night. I haven't felt that afraid since I told my father I wanted to leave his law firm and join the clergy." He ran a hand across his face. Bristles scraped against his palm.

Kit frowned and pushed herself higher on the bed. She spun her legs and set the tray on her bedside table. Jerry's misery cast a pall over her tidy room, dulling the weak sunlight and drowning it beneath a black cloud of doom. "It's okay now." She sat next to him and slipped an arm around his hunched shoulders. He gripped his lips and squeezed them into a beak with his index finger and thumb, to stop himself from revealing something he'd rather stayed hidden. Kit felt it hanging over them like a sledgehammer. "What's wrong, Jerry?" She kept her tone soothing.

He released his lips and inhaled. "I don't think I'm cut out for this," he whispered. His chocolate irises glittered with emotion. "Langdon preached this morning like his ass was on fire. It was the best closing argument I've ever heard."

Kit furrowed her brows and leaned back to observe Jerry's expression. "Closing argument? Like in a court room?"

"Yeah." Jerry nodded. "People pushed and shoved to get to the communion rail and wanted prayer after the service. We ran out of wine and wafers. It looked like one of those Billy Graham rallies. I wondered if Armageddon had struck outside, and we hadn't realised."

"I don't understand." Kit administered a series of gentle pats to Jerry's shoulder. His body hummed as though a motor idled inside his chest.

He dipped forward and pressed his face into his hands. His muddy brown curls bounced. "I don't like people much at the moment," he admitted. "That doesn't include you and Raki and sometimes Langdon. I like my mother, but not when she's nagging. But all those people with their judgemental attitudes and opinions about how I should live my life just irritate me. It makes me want to do the exact opposite. I don't want a cross shaved onto my head just to prove I'm secure in my faith and happy with my life."

Kit withdrew her arm from Jerry's shoulders and matched his pose. She rested her elbows on her knees and dropped her chin into her palm. "I hear ya," she soothed. "My mother keeps trying to fix me up with sons of random friends. She told me last night I'd made her proud and that all my father ever wanted was for me to be legally happy."

"Legally happy?" Jerry frowned and gazed at her sideways. His top lip curled up to convey his confusion.

Kit waved her hand in front of her face. "Yes. Happy but within the law. He prosecuted lots of ecstatic criminals."

Jerry exhaled through his nose. "I know what he meant. I've defended a few of those. Life is very unfair sometimes."

Kit shrugged. "Well then. We need to work out how to be legally happy. And to do it for ourselves. My mother might feel proud of me, but it won't stop her fixing me up with every available male who crosses her path. She needs to see I'm happy as I am, which means my face needs to get the memo."

"Yeah." Jerry released a heavy sigh. "Perhaps if I cease looking like I need help, people will stop trying to give it to me."

Kit turned to him and lifted her right hand. "Deal," she said. Jerry completed the high five before slapping his knees. He seemed less troubled. "But first things first." Kit raised her finger in the air and jabbed it towards his head. "Let's sort out this bird's nest. It leaves you open to the whole needing-a-good-woman cliche. Besides, we can't let Langdon upstage you, can we?"

Chapter Ten
Curly Consequences

Jerry tripped to his room in the sleep-out to change out of his clerical shirt. The back door slammed, and Kit picked up her hairdressing bag, knowing before she looked that her scissors weren't inside it. She made the bed and searched under it before tipping the contents of her handbag onto the bedspread. The velvet case containing her matte black precision scissors wasn't there. In desperation, she phoned Piper. Her fingers paused over the contact number, but she forced herself to give her friend the benefit of the doubt. Perhaps she'd wanted to speak up for Kit but hadn't found the courage.

"Hey." Piper's voice held an element of strain. A child wailed in the background. "I came after you last night, but you'd gone. Why did you leave your car outside Pam's house?"

Kit paused, the truth seeming more of a distraction from her actual issue than an answer. She didn't want Piper seizing on her ride with Jackson and turning it into something unmanageable. "I went for a walk," she lied. "Don't suppose you noticed my new scissors on the ground near my car, did you? I've lost them."

"No. Oh, that's terrible." Sympathy crossed the distance between them. "I might have missed them in the dark. You should drive around there now and see if they're still on the pavement or tucked against the curb."

"I can't." Kit's shoulders fell. "I don't want to see Pam right now."

Piper sighed, the sound whooshing in Kit's ear. "I wish you hadn't quit. Speak to Debbie. She can roster you on during the Expo to avoid Cindy and everything can go back to how it was before this."

"That woman has no integrity." Kit's jaw clenched at the mention of Cindy's name. Heat flared in her chest as though Piper had lit a hidden taper. "She knew the cops arrested me. She said nothing when she could have helped me. What kind of woman sets up another to take the fall like that?"

"It wasn't deliberate. She explained what happened. She's divorcing Paul because of the way he treated her." Piper's tone irritated Kit. She imagined the Curlies sitting in Pam's lounge after her dramatic exit and vindicating Cindy. She closed her eyes and performed a series of puffed yoga breaths. Piper waited, static drifting between them like an aura.

"Okay." Kit admitted defeat. "Thanks. I'll catch you another time."

Piper's audible gulp gave her a moment of regret. "Look," her friend began, "We're going for a walk with the pram soon. I'll wander around there and see if I can find your scissors."

"Thank you." A prickle of gratitude mixed with guilt as a shiver at the back of Kit's neck. "Please, can you check in the bushes near Pam's post box? I pulled my keys out and I might have lost them then. The fluffy part of my keyring is missing too."

"Okay. I'll phone you even if I don't find the scissors or the fluffy thing." Piper blew a kiss before disconnecting the call.

Kit stood in the middle of her bedroom as dread snaked around her heart. Like tendrils of doom, the idea formed in her mind and refused her feeble efforts to dispel it. Cindy took her place on the sofa while she was in the bathroom. Cindy sat next to her open handbag.

"I'm ready!" Jerry called up the stairs and Kit swallowed. She clutched her hairdressing bag to her chest and proceeded downstairs to the kitchen with leaden footsteps.

Jerry sat on a stool in the centre of the kitchen. He'd relinquished his curate's clothing in favour of skimpy shorts covered in paint spatters and a bare torso. A balled-up tee shirt sat on the counter. Hard plates of defined muscle covered his chest and stomach like armour. Oblivious, Raki moved around behind him, struggling to squeeze between Jerry and the sink. He carried a saucepan of boiling water and noodles. Langdon sang an impassioned rendition of a familiar hymn and grated carrot onto a bread board near the sink.

"Let's do it in the lounge," Kit relented. "Nobody wants hair in their food."

"Good idea." Jerry rose and his bare feet jogged towards the back door. "I'll fetch a tarpaulin and then I'll vacuum up the remnants." The door slammed behind him.

"Kit." Raki drained his noodles into a sieve and spoke without turning. She waited with her fingers on the stool. Raki dumped his saucepan in the sink and turned to her with a frown. "If I drew some chemical formulae on paper, would you be able to cover the bald spots on my head with them?"

She gaped. "I'm not sure. The blade managed to create the cross on Langdon's head, but I'm not convinced it's thin enough for fonts."

"Okay." Raki turned back to his noodles, lifting the sieve to shake out the excess liquid.

Kit dragged the stool into the lounge as Jerry arrived back with a blue tarpaulin flapping from his fingers. "The horse spooked at the tarpaulin," he announced with a wince. "He ran towards the gully end of the paddock."

Langdon dropped the grater but kept the carrot in his hand like a weapon. He shot towards the back door, and Kit listened to the familiar sound of him chasing his gumboots across the porch. Jerry's lips twisted upwards in veiled amusement as he slumped onto the stool.

She lowered her voice. "What did you do? Bouffant never spooks. He's deaf." She glanced up as Raki leaned sideways to stare through the window.

"Damn, he's lost that carrot," he announced.

Jerry closed his eyes to smile, creating a mischievous expression. "He jumped a little." He shrugged. "I didn't want Langdon to hear our consultation."

"Consultation?" Kit opened her arms to draw attention to her attire. "I'm still in my pyjamas and you're sitting on a kitchen stool with a tarpaulin underneath you. This is not a professional consultation."

Jerry leaned closer and, after a glance at Raki's back, dropped his voice. "I want you to do exactly the same to my hair as you did to Langdon's," he whispered. He flapped a hand at his head. "Could you reverse it so that my left side stays longer?"

Kit swallowed. She paused with her scissors in the air. "I don't think that's a good idea. You'll look like mirror images of each other. He'll hate it."

A smile lit Jerry's face from ear to ear. "Oh dear," he replied.

Chapter Eleven
A Curly Friendship

"I'm not doing it." Kit hid her scissors behind her back. "You'll look like weird clerical twins. You've got the whole Snow White and Rose Red thing going on already. I refuse to make it worse."

Jerry huffed out a breath. "But you don't understand. He got so much attention this morning. I'm just asking for a little of my own."

"Right." Kit stared at the ceiling and tapped the tips of her scissors on her bottom lip. "You'll get the wrong sort of attention, Jerry. Just let Langdon have his five minutes of funky."

"Okay." Jerry's head drooped, and he closed his eyes. "Please make me look marvellous."

"You already look marvellous." Kit nudged his shoulder with her elbow. "You're a Greek demigod wearing a cassock. I'm going to give you a Curly Cut and we'll see what happens. If you hate it, I can trim it back to the length you had it when you first arrived."

Jerry nodded and stared at the floorboards. "I trust you," he murmured.

Kit set about snipping curl by curl. Jerry's ebony coils created a mat beneath her bare feet. She relaxed into her method, the system creating a trusted rhythm which her mind and fingers responded to as safe and familiar. She stepped back an hour later to survey her finished work.

Hair prickled the soles of her bare feet and Kit's flushed cheeks exuded pleasure. "I enjoyed that," she admitted. She used an old blusher brush to chase the loose hair which had tumbled over Jerry's neck and shoulders before sending him to wash his hair. "Take the dish washing liquid with you," she insisted. "Wash your hair and then meet me in my room. I'll style it for you."

Jerry grumbled his thanks, sloping back to his sleep-out and leaving Kit to clean up the mess. Raki appeared with her ringing phone as she shook the tarpaulin onto the back lawn. He took over the job of shaking the rippling plastic sheet, laughing at Bouffant's snort of disgust as the horse shook his head at the sight of the waving object. Langdon had abandoned his lunch and rode the horse instead, pushing him into a loose canter around the paddock. He'd progressed enough to ride without a saddle, using the long rope from a halter to direct Bouffant's steps.

"Hey Piper." Kit blew out a breath and stared down at her dirty feet as she answered the call. "I just cut Jerry's hair. I have hobbit feet now."

"What?" Her friend's confusion crossed the distance between them. Kit winced.

"Sorry. I did it without shoes and the hair stuck to my pyjamas and covered my toes and the top of my feet. They look like hobbit feet." She winced and stood on one leg. "Did you know hairdressers are advised to wear covered shoes? Hair can penetrate your skin like a splinter and become infected." The need to labour the point negated the humour, and she admitted defeat. Piper's snippy tone indicated a lack of interest in Kit's head full of random facts. And her welfare. Hope replaced her deflated mood. "Did you find my scissors?"

"No." That single word sent a dart of pain through Kit's chest. "We searched the bushes by Pam's post box and the gutter along the street." Piper paused. "I found your fluffy keyring, but it's wet. Do you still want it?"

Kit swallowed and made the tough call. "No, thanks."

Piper grunted. "We saw Pam."

"Oh." Kit might have experienced a rush of curiosity about their conversation had her mind not began trolling through her movements the previous night. "Jackson!" she exclaimed. "I met Jackson outside Pam's place. Maybe the scissors fell out in his police car."

"He arrested you again?" Piper's incredulity stopped Kit in her tracks. She'd paced a circle around the lawn and tripped over the discarded tarpaulin. Raki stood at the fence, stroking Bouffant's muzzle. Langdon dismounted with a thud and patted Bouffant's neck.

"No, he didn't arrest me! We drove to Magellan Heights and chatted."

Raki turned to observe Kit as she raised her voice, his hand stilling over Bouffant's cheek.

"Pam is angry with you." Piper sighed, "And so am I. Your massive overreaction has turned the Expo into a nightmare."

"My massive overreaction?" Kit tensed. She'd thought as much to herself as she'd snipped the dead ends from Jerry's magnificent curls, but hearing her best friend voice the words hurt. Kit folded herself onto a wooden bench outside Jerry's sleep-out and watched water from his shower tumble into the drain beneath the window. The scent of floral dish washing liquid paid testament to his obedience. She opened her mouth, ready to admit her error, when Piper interrupted.

"If Cindy hadn't stepped in, we'd be screwed."

Kit gulped. "Cindy stepped in, did she?" Of course she did. Kit clamped her teeth shut to avoid releasing the barrage of vitriol which bubbled in her chest when Cindy's name crossed her lips. The woman had almost vomited at the sight of flaxseed gel cooking during her first meeting, yet she'd become the Queen of Curl's protege after one week in Australia.

Piper's final sortie detonated a bomb in Kit's core. "She filed for divorce from Paul and is now living with his cousin. She's got heaps more confidence. If you could set aside your petty grudge, you might make a decent team. We spent until after midnight phoning the other Curlies for help with the roster. All of them asked if you would be there. Apologise to Cindy and let's get back to winning the competition at the end of the Expo."

Kit stammered over her words. "She's living with Paul's cousin?" Piper wouldn't say his name out loud in her husband's hearing. She'd almost lost her marriage after a foolish kiss with Alec Roy.

"Yes." Her snippy tone implored Kit not to make her say it. "Cindy said she's willing to accept your apology. Debbie and Pam are very cross, but Sharon and the others just want peace. Auckland Curlies always bring in hairdressers who've done Curly Cuts for decades, and that's why they win. But with you and Cindy, we could take out the ultimate challenge."

"You want me to apologise to Cindy?" Kit's flat tone emerged as a whisper. Jerry bounced onto his deck wearing jeans and a tee shirt, damp curls leaking drips across his shoulders.

"What's next?" He jabbed a finger at his head and winced at the sight of the phone in Kit's trembling hand. "Oh, sorry." He sat down next to her and leaned forward so the drips pattered onto the boards between his feet.

"Thanks for looking for my scissors but I need to go." Kit cut across Piper's attempt to arrange a coffee date so she could apologise to Cindy. Her fingers shook as she shoved her phone into the top pocket of her pyjama shirt. A spreading sickness occupied her stomach, and she leaned forward and dumped her head between her knees.

"Kit?" Jerry's hand stroked her spine. "I'm so sorry. How could I be so thoughtless? I've pushed my issues onto you instead of letting you settle back into normal life. How can I help? Tell me what I can do?" He dipped forward to peer at her face just as a tear plunged from the end of her nose to create a darker patch on the wooden slats. She dashed away those following it with a jabbing motion filled with anger.

"Ugh," she groaned. "I hate crying. Why did I let her get to me?" She rose and ran a hand across her tender stomach. All the happiness of cutting Jerry's hair had disappeared down the plughole with the water from his shower.

Kit heaved in a shuddering breath. "Do you remember that woman who let me take the fall for Mr Roy's death last summer?" She didn't wait for Jerry's nod of affirmation. "She's the reason Jackson arrested me, and she said nothing and let the police search the house and take our stuff." Kit plonked herself back onto the bench with a thud. Spinning sideways in her agitation, she touched her knee to Jerry's thigh. "That same woman turned up at the Curly committee meeting last night. I think she stole my new scissors." Kit used the cuff of her pyjama shirt to dab at her damp cheeks. "I don't know what to do."

Chapter Twelve
A Curly Solution

"When is this Expo thing?" Jerry sat at the end of Kit's bed as she used praying hands to tease conditioner through his curls. He kept his head bowed while interrogating her with clerical finesse.

"Two weeks. It runs all day Saturday with a cutting and styling competition in the evening. It's the event of the year. We've never had a stall there before because we had nothing to offer."

"What's different this year?" Jerry's eyes remained closed.

Kit's sigh communicated her misery. "Me apparently. The committee thought they could utilise my new skills. I must have agreed to things during those late-night meetings when all I wanted was to get home and crawl into bed."

"Ah. That happened to me recently. I nodded off during one of Langdon's lengthy parish council meetings and it took three days to mow Mrs Cunliffe's lawns." He gave a visible shudder, and his wet curls bounced beneath Kit's fingers.

She frowned. "You fell asleep at the meeting and woke up at Mrs Cunliffe's place? My snooze wasn't quite that bad."

"No. My head bobbed at the wrong moment and I woke to the sound of applause. I'd somehow volunteered to stand in for her husband while he had an operation on his haemorrhoids." He sighed. "Once out of hospital he pointed out the ride on lawn mower in the garage. His wife made me use the hand mower and ogled me for three straight days."

"Oh, Jerry." Kit gave his shoulder a conciliatory squeeze. "Did you take off your shirt?"

"I wanted to, but I daren't. You can't imagine how much sweat one generates pushing a mower around three acres of paddock." Bouffant neighed from beyond the fence as though disputing Jerry's difficulties. He could do it faster, but without creating neat stripes.

"Will you apologise?" Jerry's question hung in the air between them. Kit's fingers tensed around the tube of purple-willy-shaped-lube in her hand. Then she reactivated and squeezed a giant blob into her palm.

"I should because I overreacted." She shrugged and spread the lube over her fingers before scrunching it through Jerry's curls. "But their attitude over the whole incident has irritated me more than I ever imagined it could. They knew how I'd feel and still did it. It's looking with hindsight as though I was set up, which would explain why Cindy arrived late while Piper kept me talking in the bathroom. Debbie had already got me to agree to everything and perhaps assumed I wouldn't back out."

"So, now you feel betrayed."

"I do." Kit nodded. "But I've also detonated a fantastic opportunity to launch my business and lost my new scissors." She pursed her lips to stop herself from accusing Cindy out loud again. Lying and hijacking a meeting were on a different level than stealing.

"What will you do?" Jerry blinked up at her, a black curl trailing across his eyebrow. "Could we get more scissors?" His insertion of himself into her problems caused a flush of affection to rush from her chest into her cheeks. She smiled and counted her blessings instead of her losses.

"Thank you, but no." She pressed a kiss to his damp forehead. "They were too expensive for someone like me. I won them using my old scissors, so that's how I should continue." She stood back to admire Jerry's head. "I need to bootstrap this business and then a set of new scissors can be my first proper reward once I'm successful." Her voice trailed away, creating the impression she didn't believe her own words.

Jerry rose and walked to the bathroom to admire his reflection. He tweaked a few curls and smiled at himself. "I love this." He tilted his head to gain an alternate view, smoothing his fingers over the shorter layers at the back and sides. "You're talented, Kit." He leaned his backside against the sink unit and folded his arms. "So, what's the plan?"

Kit shrugged and collected her hairdressing tools back into her bag. "I don't have one yet." She stared down at her pyjama pants and sighed. "Without the official backing of a WWC group, it's all academic. I can't trade."

Jerry pulled his phone from his pocket and scrolled through his contacts. Kit frowned as he lifted the device to his ear and spoke. "Hi, this is Jerry. Hey, is your wife still involved with that group of ladies with curly hair?" Kit's fingers froze over the zipper of the bag. "Ah yes. Huntly." Jerry waggled his eyebrows at her. "Do you know if they're taking part in this Expo in a couple of weeks?" He crossed his legs at the ankles and the sink unit groaned. "I'm just asking because a close friend just qualified to cut curly hair and is looking for a team." Jerry nodded and blinked a few times before the conversation degenerated into golf handicaps and the degree of what could be constituted as a bad slice off the tee.

Kit busied herself with choosing the day's clothing and laying it out on the bed, ready for after her shower. The previous morning's freedom and elation seemed a lifetime ago. Her interest returned to Jerry's conversation as she heard him read out her mobile phone number. "Ah yes, that's a weird business." He nodded a few times and after saying goodbye, ended the call.

"Did you just give my phone number to a strange man?" She stepped into the bathroom and flicked the switch for the heated towel rail. "And why is it a weird business?"

"I did." Jerry grinned. "And he's giving it to his wife who runs the Huntly chapter of Women with Curls. And the weird business is something different. Someone's stealing from the church. We can't seem to get to the bottom of it and he's offered to investigate. His family has worshipped at the church for generations, and he sits on the parish council with Langdon. If he can't get to the root, nobody can."

Kit gasped. "That's terrible. Is it money and holy ornaments?"

Jerry shook his head. "No. That would make sense. They're stealing our trash."

"Your trash?" Kit's brow furrowed. "That's very weird."

Jerry shrugged. "Anyway, the Curly group meets at a house fifteen minutes north of here. The same couple hosts our baptism classes." He lifted his hand to touch his hair but dropped it at Kit's frown of rebuke. "Their committee meeting is tonight."

"Oh. Thanks. They won't want me on the committee straight away. I'll find out when they hold their group meetings." She slapped Jerry's fingers. "No touching until it's dry! Find an old tee shirt and we'll use it as a Plop." She fluffed her towel on the rail and twisted her lips. "How did you know his wife was a WWC member?"

Jerry shrugged. "Snatches of conversation which popped into my mind at the right moment." His face creased into a grin. "Plus, the cut over his eyebrow last year from slipping on her hair products in the shower and the fact she has ringlets down to her waist." He paused as footsteps pounded up the stairs.

Kit pressed her hand against Jerry's chest. "Quick, tell me about the weird business."

Jerry's obvious discomfort increased the intrigue. He hissed through the side of his mouth and kept his gaze fixed on the door. "The empty bottles from the communion wine go into the church recycling bin. But I noticed they weren't there a few weeks ago. They keep disappearing. Someone is stealing them."

Kit jerked her head back and frowned. "The refuse collector probably took them."

Jerry's eyes widened, and his hazel irises glinted. "They disappear before the bins get put on the street. Someone is taking the bottles from inside the church."

A knock on the bedroom door heralded Langdon. He didn't wait for an invitation.

"Kit, please, can you help me? Is it time to Scrunch out my Crunch yet?"

Chapter Thirteen
The Curly Grenade

Kit dragged herself to the second WWC meeting of the weekend, aware she needed to get up at four the next morning to resume her early shifts at Mr Rashid's convenience store. Raki lent her his decrepit Toyota to stop her Bug attracting any more police interest. She found the rural address behind the sprawling humanity of Huntly West and parked in the only free space on the grass verge. Nerves assailed her shaking hand as she lifted it to knock on the front door of a timber clad house. The woman who'd phoned her earlier told her just to walk in, but it didn't seem appropriate.

A shriek greeted her sharp rap and Kit shot back a few paces, almost pitching off the narrow porch.

"She's here!" The door whipped open, an arm shot out, and grasping fingers snatched hold of the front of her jacket. A sturdy yank propelled her over the threshold and into a bright lounge lit by a million twinkling fairy lights.

"I can't believe you came!" Chunky arms embraced her, almost lifting her off her feet. Kit smelled familiar Curly Approved conditioner as ringlets slapped her face. The hair's owner disappeared and another set of arms wrapped around her. Then another and another.

She came up for air as the last person stepped back and regarded her with a delighted smile. Sparkling chocolate irises danced in a round olive face. "Welcome girl!" the woman gushed. "We're honoured to have you at our committee meeting. The Queen of Curl vouched for you."

"She what?" Kit's chin jerked forward. Her eyes blinked against the strobing lights. Five women encircled her in an arc of loveliness, oozing welcome and acceptance in their open, smiling faces. The atmosphere jarred with Kit's usual experience with the Hamilton chapter of the WWC. It left her floundering.

"Come and sit down for a moment." The woman who'd opened the door seized Kit's wrist and led her to a squashy sofa, pressing a palm to her shoulder to encourage her to sit. "You look like you could use a coffee."

Kit's nerves projected as awkwardness as she dumped her handbag on the carpet next to her. It bought her a second to settle herself before meeting the combined gaze of the room's other occupants. She heaved in a fortifying breath before seizing the moment. "I'm Kit," she said, her voice wavering.

The women chorused their names from a line in front of her.

"Ronnie."

"Lacey."

"Bronwyn."

"Jen."

Ronnie pointed to the woman pouring boiling water into a mug. "That's Vanessa. This is her house."

Kit forced a smile onto her lips and nodded. "Great. So, what do you ladies do for work?" She pressed shaking fingers to her chest, acknowledging she wanted their approval. "I work at a dairy, but I'd like to continue cutting hair."

"I'm a school librarian." Ronnie smiled and patted her mousy curls.

Jen narrowed her eyes. "I work at the council but I was in the army for eight years."

"Vanessa is a pharmacist and I'm between jobs." Lacey grinned. "I also have a toddler."

Bronwyn moved her wide shoulders in a shrug of irritation. "Raising a toddler is a job." She exhaled. "I work in a supermarket and have teenagers. That's a full-time job in itself."

Kit nodded in agreement and her mind strayed to affectionate thoughts of Piper. She stamped on them and leaned forward to study the women. "So, Vanessa is the group's chairwoman?"

"Oh, no." Lacey frowned. "We don't have one person as the head of our group. It's a democracy. We all take turns at the leadership role."

Kit gaped. Her mouth opened and closed like a fish. "How do you get anything done?" She struggled to keep astonishment from her tone.

Bronwyn laughed. Her wide shoulders shuddered up and down and short blonde curls bounced on her head. "Everyone asks that." She shrugged. "We just do. It's about commitment, not about who gets to be in charge."

"Right." Kit swallowed and her eyes widened. "This must be a new group. I haven't heard of the Huntly chapter before this afternoon."

Vanessa dragged a small table next to Kit's arm and placed a mug of coffee on a coaster. "I hope you like milk," she said, wrinkling her nose. "Sorry, I forgot to ask."

Kit's jerky nod acknowledged the drink. "It's fine, thank you."

Jen leaned forward in her seat. Dressed in a navy power suit, she oozed competence through the jab of her finger towards Vanessa. "The Queen of Curl and Vanessa are friends. They go way back to childhood." She spoke the words with a healthy element of awe, but raised a speculative eyebrow and lowered her head to hide a mischievous smile. Chestnut curls bounced against the lapel of her shaped jacket.

"Whatever." Vanessa sat next to her and nudged her with a sharp elbow. Jen frowned and crossed her long legs at the ankle. Vanessa regarded Kit with a sigh. "If you stick around, you'll discover a few secrets along the way. But we need to trust you before that happens." She delivered the warning with enough grace to cover the barbs, but Kit heard them anyway.

Lacey plopped down next to her on the sofa and gave her a sideways smile. Kit blinked in surprise at recognising the same hairstyle she'd given Langdon after Jerry's accident. Blonde curls tumbled over a neat uppercut, but the stylist had blended the layers with more finesse. Lacey lifted her hand and touched the bristly hair above her left ear. "Do you like it?" she asked.

"I love it," Kit replied with honesty. "A friend has a similar cut."

Lacey shrugged. "Something a little different." She jerked her head towards Ronnie. "Ron cut it for me this afternoon. Her vicar is a closet Curly and apparently he rocked up to their Matins service with something similar. She wanted to give it a try."

Kit swallowed a mouthful of hot coffee and attempted not to choke. So, Ronnie went to Langdon and Jerry's church. Vanessa had phoned her that afternoon and she assumed the man Jerry spoke to was her husband. It dawned on Kit too late that she might have left herself vulnerable to Jerry's manoeuvring. He'd invited her to events at his church and appeared to take her polite refusals in his stride. She placed her mug of coffee back on the table and wiped her sweating palms on her knees, sensing an ambush. "When are your group meetings?" she asked. Her voice croaked and squeaked at the same time.

Vanessa settled back against the cushions and smiled. "The last Monday of every month," she replied. "But we hold it here across dinner time. Some of the women are alone with children, so we have a pot luck dinner and the kids go to sleep in our spare bedroom."

Kit gaped. "They what?"

Vanessa exhibited endless patience. "We feed them and then they go to sleep. Most of the children are used to us bundling them into the car half asleep. We've done it this way for years."

"Wow." Kit swallowed and imagined Debbie allowing small people into her sanctuary. Sharon always said if the women wanted it badly enough, they'd work out their childcare arrangements and get there. It appeared Vanessa's group worked around the women and it created a different scenario altogether. She swallowed. "Years? So, your group isn't new?"

Bronwyn released a snort. "No. Our group is where it all started."

Kit shook her head to clear the fog. "I'm confused. Why have I never seen any of you at the Expo?"

"It all got a bit too frenzied." Vanessa's smile drooped to convey sadness. "The movement began to help women struggling with curly hair. It's become a cult along the way and too many get excluded from the groups for spurious reasons."

Kit stared at a framed photograph over the mantelpiece and her head bowed in a reluctant nod. Conflict burgeoned in her chest as she wondered if her efforts to fit in with the strong women in the Hamilton chapter had caused her to gain an exclusive view of the WWC. She ran a mental check of names and faces, blurred figures who'd stepped in and out of her life. She frowned and met Vanessa's steady gaze. "So, why this year?" she demanded. "Jerry said you're part of the expo."

"Oh, we most definitely are." Bronwyn waggled chestnut eyebrows at Ronnie and giggled. "As of today."

Kit licked her top lip, tasting tension in the air as the atmosphere tingled. A fire crackled in the grate and she tugged her collar away from her neck. Jen sat forward and pointed the sharp toes of her stilettos to meet in a neat triangle. She lowered her voice to a hiss. "We're gonna blow this thing wide open," she whispered. "And you're the grenade we've been waiting for."

Kit bounced to her feet in a fluid motion. Her handbag trailed next to her left foot and swung into Lacey's face as she lifted it by the strap. "I've gotta go," she breathed. The jabbing motions of her feet took her across the fluffy carpet towards the front door. Jerry had sent her to a terrorist cell by accident. She needed to warn him.

Kit kept her head bent and her gaze fixed on the door. The hairs rose on the back of her neck as feet pattered across the carpet behind her. She screamed as a hand touched her shoulder.

"Don't leave." Lacey cocked her head and the longer layers drifted over the shorn portion of her hair. "Jen always talks like she's in the mafia."

"I can't be part of this." Kit held her hands out in front of her. The strap of her handbag dangled over her left forearm. "I want to cut hair not blow things up." She gulped. "I live with vicars. We don't even have fireworks because we can't trust Raki not to modify them." She pressed her fingers over her lips to avoid talking herself deeper into her mess.

A throat cleared behind her and she turned to find Vanessa struggling not to release a laugh. "Come back," she soothed. "Let's start again."

A movement in her peripheral vision showed Lacey had edged in front of the door. But she maintained a calm facade which appeared non-threatening enough for Kit to realise she wasn't in imminent danger. "Just hear us out," Lacey implored, her hands wringing at her waist.

Kit walked with a woodenness to her movements. She allowed the women to lead her back to the sofa, sinking into the softness of the cushions as though falling into a ball pit. Vanessa sat next to her and took her hand. "We want to give the curly hair movement back to the women who need it." A ringlet tumbled forward over her shoulder to caress her sleeve. "We want to remove the exclusivity. It's become something it wasn't meant to be and it's time to turn back the tide." Vanessa's fingers trembled against Kit's. Her hazel irises sparkled with an inner fire. "We have the full backing of the Queen of Curl. She's spent the last thirty years of her life empowering Curlies." Vanessa's chest shuddered with a sigh. "She's ready to give up on the New Zealand branch of the organisation and I've persuaded her to wait until after the Expo."

"Give up?" Kit turned towards her and her body dipped in shock. She shook her head from side to side. "But I met her as part of my course. She handed me my certificate and my award. Why didn't she say something then about changing the culture of the organisation? She seemed so bright and happy." Kit slumped back against the cushions. "I don't understand."

Vanessa gave a sad shrug involving just the tips of her shoulders. "The winner of the Expo gets to set the tone for the year. An Auckland chapter always wins and the publicity carries photos of smiling white girls with perfect faces and blonde curls." She tapped an escaping ringlet and sighed. "Where are the Maori faces, the redheads and the girls with weight issues? They don't join the groups because they're already excluded by implication. If we can win the cutting competition, we can show New Zealand that our movement is for everyone."

"Just tell her." Jen rose, adjusting her tight skirt over her hips. She walked towards the kitchen and the scrunch of her heels in the thick carpet switched to clattering as she crossed the tiles to the sink.

Vanessa looked towards each of the other women in turn before tightening her lips and facing Kit. She released Kit's hand so her fingers could writhe together in her own lap. "The Queen of Curl is my sister," she confessed.

Other words followed her statement. Kit heard none of them.

CHAPTER FOURTEEN

Back Combing

Kit walked into Mr Rashid's shop just before five the next morning. She closed the front door behind her and shot the bolt home. The overhead lights flickered as they burst into life, blinding her even though she kept her eyes closed after pressing the switch. She walked straight to the stock room and dumped her handbag on top of a long freezer. Yawning, she unlocked the back door and pulled it open.

"Argh!" She clutched her chest and bent double. "You almost gave me a heart attack!" she squeaked.

"Sorry." A burly man slammed the back door of his van and smirked. The vehicle's headlights shone their twin spotlights on the fragile buds of a perimeter hedge. The engine purred and its exhaust fumes created a pungent white cloud in the cold air. "Running a bit late this morning." He jerked his head towards the heavy piles of newspapers, which he'd stacked outside the door. "Want me to pull those inside for you?"

Kit blew out a breath and leaned against the door frame. Her heart pounded in her ears as she nodded. "Yes please. That's my second shock in less than twelve hours."

The man laughed, grey curls bouncing in a buoyant fringe. A bald crown shone behind it in the glare from the security light. His muscles bulged through his tee shirt as he dragged the piles of paper through the doorway and deposited them on the tiled floor. "There you go," he said. He flexed his fingers in the leather gloves which protected his hands from the spiteful string binding. "See you tomorrow." He turned to leave and grabbed the door handle, frowning before giving Kit a reluctant smile. "Well, I probably won't, not unless I'm running late again."

Kit leaned against the freezer and covered a yawn with her hand. "Easily done when you're on an early shift," she agreed. She acknowledged the delivery driver's wave as he clicked the door closed behind him. Silence shrouded her with a gentle ringing as the shop settled back into its sedentary state. Kit stared at the piles of papers with a sigh. They wouldn't put themselves into the paper boys' sacks. She touched the green headscarf protecting her damp curls and yawned again. Her phone vibrated in her bag and she reached for it, finding the screen lit up with a text.

'Sorry if I made you late. Thanks for the Curly help.'

He'd even spelt Curly with a capital as though he'd already absorbed the rules and culture of the Women with Curls. "Oh, Langdon," Kit breathed. "I've created a monster."

She'd discovered the vicar waiting for her in the kitchen as she crept downstairs to the fridge for her flaxseed gel. He'd risen and showered at four in the morning just so she could style his curls for him.

Kit reached up to the shelf for the sharp scissors. She snipped the strings which held the newspapers into a bundle. With so many people reading their news online, it seemed surprising that the boys still delivered over two hundred in the local area every morning. The older generation stuck to their habits, claiming they preferred the scent of newsprint and the thrill of folding it back into one piece at the end of their perusing. Once read, the papers morphed into a staple household item used for lining bird cages, stuffing wet shoes and wrapping precious items.

Kit replaced the scissors and grabbed the list of addresses from the shelf. With a sharp pang of regret over losing her own precious snips, she bent to transfer the towering piles into their wrappers and fitted them into the boys' sacks.

The conversation from the previous night weighed on her and she made many errors which needed correcting. She'd spent years building an image of the Queen of Curl, awarding her a godlike status as the saviour of Curlies everywhere. Stumbling across the Women with Curls through Piper had changed Kit's life. It allowed her to complete her metamorphosis from an overweight, ginger, frizzy haired adolescent into a redheaded butterfly with enviable abdominal muscles. Getting her hair under control had been the first step in a stunning transformation. She owed all that to the Queen of Curl. The brave woman had fought the good fight for all Curlies, going public with her revelations about the curl-harming chemicals in shampoo. When the big pharmaceutical companies had tried to shut her down, she'd formed Women with Curls and continued her mission to rescue all frizzy heads from their capitalist clutches.

Kit hung the last filled sack on its peg in the stock room. She reached for her phone and pulled up the photo Marian had taken just last week. The Queen of Curl smiled from beneath greying ringlets, her kind brown eyes shrouded by black lashes. Her left arm curved around an embarrassed Kit, whose pink blush mottled her cheeks in the photograph. She clutched her certificate of merit and the velvet bag containing her scissors in white-knuckled fingers. Behind her, a crowd of eager students waited for their moment of glory, fear in their eyes that the Queen of Curl might not want to join a photograph with them.

Nausea rose into Kit's throat as a horrid lump lodged in her chest. It wasn't that the Queen of Curl was raised in Huntly or that she despised the organisation she'd built from the ground up despite all the odds. It was that she seemed more human and less divine. She'd lost her shine.

Kit reached up and touched the scarf which served as the Plop, protecting her curls until Mr Rashid relieved her later. Her shoulders slumped, and she frowned at her awestruck expression in the photo. "She needs your help." Kit spoke out loud. "And she'll get it."

"Talking to yourself again." Mr Rashid's rasping voice made Kit jump, and her phone skittered across the top of the freezer. She clutched her heart for the third time in twelve hours and blew out a ragged breath. Mr Rashid's pyjama bottoms sagged at the backside as he strode across the stock room. Tiny motifs of the Taj Mahal dotted the fabric, though the bottoms didn't match his white shirt and striped tie. Kit gaped at him.

"Why are you up so early?" she demanded. She jabbed an index finger at his pyjama pants and bare feet. "And did you get bored half way through dressing?"

"No, no. I forgot my pants." Mr Rashid leaned across the corner desk and displayed way too much ass crack for Kit's stomach to bear at that time of the morning. She closed her eyes and counted to ten as a belt buckle clanged against the computer keyboard. She opened her eyes to discover Mr Rashid dangling yesterday's trousers in front of her face.

"I don't want to know," she growled. "Please, just keep it to yourself."

Mr Rashid's head bobbled from side to side as he shrugged. He'd already shaved, and his hair lay flattened across his head as though tamped down by an oil slick. "I'm taking Mrs Rashid to breakfast," he announced.

Kit tilted her wrist to examine her watch. "It's five thirty in the morning." She wrinkled her nose. "Are you taking her to a drive through?"

A satisfied grin spread across Mr Rashid's face. His black eyebrows lifted, and his lips flattened. "I'm driving her up to Auckland for breakfast and then taking her to Sylvia Park to indulge in her love of shiny things." His shoulders slumped enough to convey fake bravado.

Kit gulped. "But what about the shop? What about me? You can't leave me alone all day!"

Mr Rashid bolted for the door and waved a hand over his shoulder. "Sorry, I must have forgotten to mention it."

"Get back here!" Kit shouted as he picked up speed along the toiletry aisle. She gave up the chase after a few steps. "Fine, I'll just shut the shop."

Mr Rashid's face poked from the end of the aisle; his raised eyebrows hidden in his fringe. "Do not shut the shop!" An olive finger jabbed the air.

Kit groaned and covered her hands with her eyes. She'd expected payback for her refusal to work weekends for the last six months but hadn't imagined him exacting it so soon. Bare feet pattered across the tiles, and Mr Rashid ventured back into the aisle. "Raj is coming at eleven," he conceded. "Then you can use the downstairs bathroom."

Kit gritted her teeth and her words ground from between her lips. "Upstairs bathroom. And it's not fair to expect me to work for five hours straight without a break. It's illegal." Her tone acquired a whine and Mr Rashid shrugged.

"You did your silly hair snipping thing every weekend for the last six months. That's twelve weekends you didn't come to work, and I still kept your job open for you." He lifted his chin in defiance, a sure sign he had no intention of budging. Then his eyes narrowed. "Today when Raj comes, I want you to drive to that woman's house and get more product. Customers like it and I love the profit margin. I left a list for you on the front counter."

He turned away and Kit jogged down the aisle after him. "Wait! What woman? Why can't Raj go?"

"I'm asking you!" Mr Rashid's eyes rounded like fat almonds. He wagged his index finger at her while his other hand hauled his pyjama pants higher. "And no talky talky with your friend when you collect the supplies. Raj can only mind the shop for half an hour. Deepak is coming at two o'clock ready for you to go home." He jerked his head towards the counter and his hair moved as a single piece. "Float is already in the cash register." His bare feet padded towards the internal door set next to the counter, and he pressed the numbers for the key code.

Kit ran after him. "What friend?" Her shoulders slumped at his ignorance. "What if I need the toilet?"

Mr Rashid hauled the door open and stepped through the gap. He paused for long enough to wag his finger at her. "Did you worry about my bathroom breaks when you were snip-snipping in Auckland?"

By the time the door to the apartment clicked shut, Kit had seized the note laid over the cash register and released the first of many agonised groans. "No, no, no!" she hissed. Mr Rashid's rambling scrawl had recorded a list of items he wanted from his supplier. Below it, he'd written the address of Debbie's garage enterprise.

Chapter Fifteen
Curly Thwart

"Your dad asked if you'd mind watching the shop for a couple of minutes so I can sort out my hair. Then you need to pick up these items from this address." Kit struggled to maintain a blank expression and avoid suspicion. Her heart pounded as Raj's olive fingers snatched at the paper and his eyes raked his father's slanted handwriting. Kit held her breath. She folded her arms to stop her fingers from trembling and giving herself away.

"Nice try." Raj pushed the list between her wrists and chest. A smirk flowered on his handsome face as the paper fluttered to the floor. "I phoned Dad on my way here. Mum's spending it up large at the mall. He said you need to go because she's your friend."

"But you have a van!" Kit protested. She unfolded her arms and spread her hands in protest. "I can't fit heaps of boxes into my little Bug and besides, you'll find it easier to do the lifting."

Raj tugged a set of keys from his back pocket and dangled them in front of her face. "Use the van," he instructed. "But I need to arrive back at my shop in twenty-five minutes." He looked at his watch to accentuate the urgency. "The Cola supplier is delivering a new drinks fridge. Deepak can't relieve you at two o'clock. I'll come back again so you can go home." He raised a black eyebrow. "But only if you go now and don't make me late."

Kit's shoulders slumped, and she snatched the keys. "I need the toilet," she complained. "This isn't legal. I'm allowed bathroom breaks."

Raj made a spinning motion with his hands and raised a black eyebrow. "Why are you still talking?" He turned away and ducked beneath the counter to serve a customer waiting to buy a loaf of bread.

Kit pursed her lips as she bent to retrieve the fallen list. She'd actually had two bathroom breaks by shutting the shop and putting a note on the door. Whipping off her Plop during the first one, she'd got away with the three-minute dash upstairs and found no one waiting when she returned. But the second attempt resulted in an angry customer who hadn't wanted to wait four minutes for her to use the toilet and wash her hands. His urgent need for a carton of milk trumped her health needs by a country mile, according to him. If he complained, Mr Rashid would check the security cameras and deny all bathroom breaks for a week as punishment.

Kit jogged out to Raj's van while wondering if Mr Rashid had spent the morning watching her on the camera app installed on his phone. She imagined him eating his breakfast while complaining to his wife about the way she'd stocked the vegetable tins in between serving customers.

She wasted valuable time changing the position of the driver's seat. Raj's long legs meant Kit couldn't touch the pedals. She altered the mirrors and then examined the controls before setting off for the suburb of Flagstaff. Six minutes from the Gordonton Road to Debbie's house seemed like pure luck, the mid-morning traffic sparse on the main roads. Kit parked on the street for long enough to wipe her sweaty hands on Raj's seat before reversing up to Debbie's garage door. She negotiated the turn and fought to keep the vehicle straight as she avoided dinging Debbie's red station wagon.

She glanced at her watch as panic seized her. Raj wanted her at the shop and the van unloaded by eleven thirty, which gave her less than twenty minutes to deal with Debbie, get Mr Rashid's list fulfilled, and drive back again. She pulled the crumpled paper from the passenger seat, killed the engine and pushed open the heavy van door. The cloying scent of jasmine and lilies wrapped around her head as she jumped to the concrete driveway with a dull thud. Kit swallowed and pushed her shoulders back in an attempt to bolster confidence. "This is business," she told herself. "I'm just the delivery driver."

No one responded to the tentative knock on Debbie's front door. A wooden sign instructed visitors to 'Please remove your shoes.' Two sets of flip-flops snuggled on the mat as though the owners had obeyed, ejecting out of them and disappearing together. Kit glanced at her watch and quailed. "Debbie?" She knocked harder, the sound from her knuckles reverberating through the house. She surveyed

Debbie's car with confusion as no one answered her knocking. If Debbie's rounded backside wasn't in the driver's seat, then it would be inside the house. She walked nowhere and snorted with derision at anyone brave enough to use public transport.

Kit walked to the front of the house and knocked on the garage door. The lack of echo paid testament to the many boxes of stock stacked behind it. "Debbie?" Kit's voice held a plea. "Mr Rashid sent me." She glanced down at the list in her hand. "He wants a lot of stuff. I'm just the messenger."

She halted at the sound of cardboard dragging against gritty concrete. Her temper flared, and she ground her teeth. Another glance at her watch showed the time as marching past the quarter mark. "Fine!" she snarled. "This is ridiculous. I'm coming in now!"

Kit skirted the left of the one-storey house and reached over the back gate. Her fingers scrabbled to release the bolt, and the hinges creaked as she pushed it open. Debbie had hosted enough committee meetings and group gatherings for Kit to pick her way along the familiar crazy paved path to the rear of the house. It wound through flower gardens and a vegetable plot before arriving at the back door. Fragile tomato seedlings waved against the canes they didn't yet need.

"Debbie!" Kit hammered on the frame and pressed her nose to the glass. A half cup of coffee sat on the counter next to a plate of toast. Butter oozed from beneath a thick layer of purple jam, creating a stained puddle. Kit stamped her foot and balled her fists. Bloody Debbie!

Her phone vibrated with a text and she hauled it from her back pocket.

'I need you back here!' Raj stated. *'My delivery has arrived early.'* An emoji with an angry face followed in a second text. Raj must have considered Kit's tendency to disobey men who told her what to do, because the third text contained a pair of yellow praying hands.

"I'm trying!" she grumbled. She stuffed her phone into the back pocket of her jeans and wrapped her fingers around the metallic door handle. "Here goes nothing," she hissed.

The door squeaked and Kit held her breath. An open window elsewhere in the house created a vacuum and made it harder to push the door. Warm air rushed past her as she increased the pressure. "Debbie!" she called. "It's Kit." She winced after saying her name, suspecting Debbie ignored her on purpose. "I'm not here to talk about Women with Curls. Mr Rashid sent me." She closed the door behind her, struggling to stop it from slamming. Creeping through the kitchen, she passed another mug of coffee. It sat on the island, which divided the dining room from the kitchen. Kit glanced at her watch again. "Debbie!" Her tone held a wail of frustration. If she upset Raj now, he'd make life difficult when she needed him to return at the end of her shift. She'd get stuck behind the counter until Mr and Mrs Rashid deigned to return from their shopping spree.

The TV played to an empty lounge and Kit's shoulders slumped. She stepped into the hall and saw the internal garage door standing ajar. Her breath exhaled in a whoosh. The list flapped in the breeze and then stopped, causing Kit to look along the hallway. She frowned, imagining she'd just heard the click of the front door shutting. Tension rode across her shoulders in waves as time ticked by at a frantic rate. She strode towards the garage door and hauled it wide enough for it to thud against an object behind it. "Stop hiding from me!" she snapped. "We're grown-ups and you obviously need Mr Rashid's custom!"

Boxes crowded the space, creating a tiny area for walking across the centre of the garage. The door handle had dented the side of the nearest box. Debbie sat on a child's three-legged stool at the end of the walkway with her back to the door. She leaned forward with her hands buried deep in a box. Her shoulders rounded in a lumpy arc. She wore a voluminous mustard tee shirt, which clashed with a green scarf dangling across her left shoulder.

Kit halted just inside the garage, struggling to see in the dim light. Spinning around, she sought the light switch and gave it a jab with her index finger. A rumble began overhead, and she squeaked as the garage door rolled up by slow degrees. "Sorry, sorry!" she gasped, turning to locate the light switch having hit the garage door opener instead. The grey daylight from outside lit up the scene and she paused, no longer needing the overhead bulb and unable to locate it.

Boxes covered the opening between the interior and the driveway. Marked with the branding of an expensive whiskey, someone had sealed them closed with brown parcel tape. Stacked to above Kit's head, they prevented access beyond them. She groaned, realising she'd need to take Mr Rashid's products through the house and out the front door to the van. Glancing at her watch again, she saw that even more time had passed. She lifted the list and flapped it. "Please, can we do this quickly?" she implored Debbie. "I'm running short on time."

Debbie continued to ignore her, and Kit gritted her teeth. "I'm sorry for quitting the committee," she ventured.

"Please can we just get this done and then I'll come back and talk about it another time?" She had no intention of talking about her decision, but urgency fed the lie.

Desperation and curiosity drove her to Debbie's side. Kit navigated the boxes, turning sideways at points to squeeze past them. She arrived next to her and peered into the cardboard box to identify the thing which engrossed Debbie so much. She noted the neat lines of Curly Approved conditioner bottles standing like little cream soldiers. One leaned at a jaunty angle below Debbie's left hand, its lid off and white goop dripping from its open mouth. "What are you doing?" Kit asked. She glanced around the garage at the eclectic mix of gardening tools and boxes. A spade leaned against the wall next to a precarious pile of empty seed trays. "How can you work in this mess?"

Curiosity furrowed her brow, and she peered over Debbie's shoulder.

Her hip bumped the other woman's tilted head and for a moment, Kit imagined herself falling backwards and her arms flailed. Her fingers grabbed at the side of the cardboard box and the bottles of conditioner danced and rattled. A bottle beneath Debbie's hand fell over and landed on the bottom of the box. Conditioner pumped onto the cardboard with enthusiastic glugging. Four full bottles joined it like falling dominoes.

Then Debbie tipped sideways and sprawled across the concrete floor. A length of green fabric fluttered to the ground next to her.

Kit's lips parted in a primal scream and she shuffled backwards, slamming into boxes which complained with the sound of clanking glass. Her left foot struck something plastic, and it bounced away with a happy skittering sound. "No, no, no!" Kit wailed. She held her hands out in front of her to block the sight of her prized matte black precision scissors sticking out of Debbie's flaccid purple neck.

Chapter Sixteen
Trapped Curl

Kit scrambled backwards and her plimsolls stuck to the floor. A crackling sound issued from her soles as she moved sideways to avoid the ochre coloured puddle. She lifted her hands and her gaze darted over them to check for contamination, not knowing what she expected to see but finding nothing different about her fingers.

But she'd touched Debbie.

She'd touched Debbie's dead body.

A lump rose into her throat. She'd handled pretty much everything on her way into the house. "Oh no! Not again!" Kit covered her eyes, but when she pulled her fingers away, Debbie still lay on the floor. She resembled a sleeper, relaxed in slumber with her eyes closed. But her lips parted in a familiar smirk, their swollenness creating an eerie pout. Kit's scissors protruded from her neck and a trail of blood soaked into her mustard shirt.

Kit backed towards the door's location in the narrow space available, jerking forward at the clank of bottles from a box she bumped into on her way. Panic blinded her and the smell of alcohol mixed with floral scented conditioner created a nauseating haze. Kit struggled to fight her way through boxes she'd passed before with such ease. Her body no longer fitted through the gaps and she forgot to turn sideways to navigate the narrow spaces. Trapped between a sealed box labelled 'Whiskey' and another which was sealed but not labelled, Kit froze. Her heart thudded blood through her eardrums and her laboured breathing denied her brain the oxygen it demanded. A maze of brown walls halted her progress as she found herself in a cardboard cul-de-sac. A vivid black line scored a diagonal slash on each of the boxes facing her, as though she'd strayed into a bizarre cataloguing prison.

"Jackson!" She whimpered his name before focusing her energy on conjuring him up in person. Her fingers scrabbled in her back pocket for her phone, failing to grip it as she yanked it free. It clattered to the concrete floor, and she banged her forehead on a box which contained rattling bottles as she bent to retrieve it. A corner of the phone's plastic case had fractured and crumbled, its rough texture offering a dose of reality as she held the screen in front of her face. A red funnel bounced away as she moved her foot, recreating the skittering sound as it rolled against the concrete floor. Kit stood and forced herself to calm, pushing controlled yoga breaths in through her nose and out through her mouth. The red of the funnel reminded her of Debbie's blood, and nausea rose into her throat.

The phone lit up as she tilted it and her fingers shook. She unlocked the screen with her code and found Jackson's number in her contacts. It seemed to dial forever as she held her breath and waited.

"What do you want, Maguire? I'm working." His reply sounded even and unruffled, a hint of humour behind the abruptness as though pleased to hear from her.

"Jackson," Kit whispered. Her gaze tracked towards the open garage door blocked by heavy boxes. Grey sky winked through narrow gaps and over the top of the furthest stack. She nudged the box in front of her with her knee and the contents rattled, but it didn't move. "Help me!" She lifted her voice to a wail. "I can't get out and she's dead!"

"What?" His voice switched to a business-like tone, and an engine roared in the background. "Where are you?"

"Debbie's house." Kit's breathing hitched in her throat. "Mr Rashid sent me for supplies, and she didn't answer the door and I came in and found her in the garage and she fell off her stool and she's dead." The lengthy sentence depleted her energy levels, and she inhaled to replace the breath. "I feel sick."

The powerful engine purred, reminiscent of Kit's drive with Jackson two nights ago. "Are you coming for me?" she pleaded, hating the need in her voice. She cleared her throat and feminism and autonomy stamped all over it. "I mean, I don't need you to. I can find my own way out but she's still dead." Kit swallowed. "I feel very sick."

"Do not puke on the crime scene!" Jackson barked. "Touch nothing! Are you in the same street as the other night? I'm on my way."

Kit shook her head and realised he couldn't see her. "No. No. It's two streets away. I'm on Endeavour Avenue. Number forty-eight." She glanced back towards Debbie, and her gaze drank in the scene. The box of adulterated conditioners remained in place, but the stool had tipped onto its side and Debbie's chunky thighs remained in view. The backs of her striped leggings bore darker patches beneath the shirt, which had ridden up to reveal the pink skin across her spine.

Kit hiccupped. "Definitely gonna be sick," she announced. Acid rose into her throat, and she clamped a hand over her mouth. A lone siren split the airwaves outside, competing against the rustling of open box lids tugged by the breeze. The wail increased in volume, creating an odd stereo through the phone against Kit's ear. She registered a slight delay in the sound, which lessened with each passing second.

"I'm almost there," Jackson barked.

Kit pulled the phone from her ear as the siren occupied the remaining space in her brain. Blue lights strobed against a narrow arc of the garage ceiling and a car door slammed. The siren stopped, leaving a ringing in her ears. But the strobing continued, bouncing off Debbie's prone legs as though willing her to get up and dance.

"Kit!" Jackson called her name, and she sensed his presence beyond the wall of cardboard. The hammering of a fist rattled the glass in the front door. "Kit!" The stereo effect occurred again as he shouted into the phone. Kit raised it to her ear.

"I'm stuck in the garage," she whimpered. "The entrance is blocked by boxes, but the back door is unlocked."

Jackson didn't reply, but he kept the call running and his steady breathing accompanied the pounding of his work boots against the crazy paved path. Kit held her breath as the air changed and he released a hiss at the internal garage door. "Where are you?" he demanded. "I'm ending the call so I can find you in person." The line went dead, and desperation filled the space in Kit's ear. Jackson's voice replaced it, calling over the boxes to her. "Just talk to me," he encouraged. "Say anything."

"I didn't kill her." The words rolled off Kit's tongue. "I found her like it." Her voice rose to a wail, and she dropped her forehead against the sealed box in front of her. The implications of her presence filtered through the mind fog. "Just leave me here," she begged. "They'll think I killed her. I can't go through all that again."

Kit jumped as a dark shape appeared in her vision. She pushed out her hand in self-defence and contacted the hard edge of a Kevlar vest. "It's okay," Jackson's firm voice soothed. "It's all gonna be okay. You're safe now." He gripped her wrists and pulled her towards him, edging her free of her cardboard prison.

Chapter Seventeen
Kiss Curl

"I'm not a feeble woman." Kit cleared her throat and brushed at her clothes with her fingers.

"I didn't say you were." Jackson tilted his head to observe her. "Stop doing that."

Kit sniffed. "I wasn't afraid of the body and I didn't get lost in a cardboard maze." The denial helped to stiffen her spine. She wiped her nose with the back of her wrist and noticed the hands on her watch. "Oh, no! Raj! I need to get back to the shop!"

Jackson winced. He maintained a firm grip on her elbows before shouting over a new cacophony of sirens which robbed Kit of the ability to think straight. "Just wait!" he mouthed, adding, "Please." He checked on Debbie and returned to Kit, shaking his head. She blocked out the view of Debbie's sprawled legs in her peripheral vision and ran through a mental checklist of Curly Approved products to keep herself calm. It didn't work.

Kit groaned and rubbed a hand over her forehead. A crunchy curl bumped against the back of her index finger, and she wrinkled her nose. She still needed to Scrunch Out the Crunch. Twisting her lips, she wondered if Jackson would let her do it before she became a public spectacle. She opened her mouth to speak, but his head shaking began with authority. "No. Don't ask me for special favours. Please, Kit." His plea encompassed her predicament. She was in big trouble. Again.

"But I didn't do it. I didn't kill her," she whispered, her tone urgent. She took a breath and stared into his fathomless chocolate irises. "Do you believe me?" Forcing him to choose seemed like a good idea at the time, but she hadn't factored in his determination to choose justice over friendship.

"It doesn't matter." He shrugged and stood on tiptoe to shout over the boxes to the incoming officers. "The back door is open. We're in the garage." He settled onto his heels and conflict darkened his irises to anthracite. "They'll take your clothing and treat you like a suspect. Get ready and please don't compromise me?"

"Compromise you?" Her voice rose to a squeak, and Jackson tensed. He swallowed at a thud from the kitchen followed by the heavy tread of multiple police officers.

His eyes widened. "You phoned me instead of the emergency services. How do you think that looks?"

"Oh." Kit closed her eyes and her body slumped. A tremble in her knees grew to involve her torso and arms. Her neck shook as though trying to eject her head. "Sorry," she whispered. "I'm so sorry." She couldn't look at him.

"Damn you, Maguire!" Jackson whispered. He tilted her chin upwards with his fingers, and she jumped as his warm lips touched hers. The kiss lasted less than a second, an explosion of heady senses with the backdrop of imminent arrest. Kit inhaled as Jackson broke the kiss and rose to shout over the boxes. "There's a witness. She's here. The body is on the other side of the garage. I've checked her, and she's deceased. Go back outside and wait for Lane."

"Okay, Sarge." The footsteps stomped away and resounded as an echo beyond the open garage door.

Kit raised her gaze to study Jackson's chin. His rigidity conveyed his discomfort, and his jaw moved beneath the skin as he gritted his teeth. Small scars lined his neck, the residue from a childhood accident which had killed his brother. A white mark across his temple had once contained broken glass from a windscreen, and the sight of it reminded her of his link to her father. He'd pushed hard for the hit-and-run driver to serve a decent punishment and failed. It gave them a shared understanding of her powerful father and added a welcome tangibility to his memory.

Jackson's right palm remained beneath her elbow. He jerked and his fingers closed as Kit rose on tiptoes. She pressed her lips over his and his pupils exploded into fathomless black pits. His Kevlar vest dug into her breasts and Jackson gave a sharp inhale. The stubble on his chin grazed her cheek as he tilted his face sideways and ran his tongue between the seam of her lips. Kit's tongue trembled as it met his, the action both seeking and tentative. The vest dug into the soft skin of her forearms as she wrapped them around Jackson's waist. His skin smelled of faded aftershave and maleness, a remembered concoction which set off firecrackers in her brain.

"Delaney!" A shout from just metres away sent them skittering apart. Jackson swore and struggled to stop the box at shoulder height from tipping over sideways. Kit blinked at the sight of Debbie's legs, and guilt bubbled into her chest. Lane's voice called again from the driveway beyond the box wall. "Are you there? What do you suggest?"

Jackson pressed his index finger over Kit's lips to silence her and gave a slight shake of his head in warning. "If you're facing the garage, the deceased is to your left. She's lying on her side with what looks like a pair of scissors sticking from her neck. There are boxes everywhere. The witness found the body, panicked, and walked into a cul-de-sac. I've got her with me, and she's happy to do whatever you need. Can you get the crime scene guys in and then we'll work out how best to get the witness out without disturbing anything?" He dropped his chin and raised an eyebrow for Kit's benefit. She pushed away thoughts of Raj's ire and nodded in agreement.

It seemed like hours before men and women in white suits and covered shoes flooded the garage. They photographed and sampled, labelled and processed before allowing Kit to leave her cardboard prison. Jackson remained with her but put distance between them, conscious of the rising damage to his integrity. He turned sideways as though to avoid looking at her, frantically building an emotional wall between them. Kit didn't blame him. She knew she'd need to tell him that the scissors sticking out of Debbie's neck belonged to her, but the optimum moment came and went.

Lane appeared at the end of the row of boxes. He wore white bootees over his shoes and blue disposable gloves covered his twitching fingers. White streaks had filtered through the grey since Kit last saw him, and he appeared thinner and even more ragged. He groaned and threw his head back when he recognised her. "What's she doing here?" he snapped at Jackson. "Please tell me she's not the witness?"

Jackson's blank expression offered nothing in return. He gave a nod of affirmation. "She doesn't know how it happened, so I kept her here to avoid contaminating the scene further with her DNA."

"Good thinking." Lane pulled a plastic bag from his jacket pocket and flicked it open. Then he held out his hand to Kit. "Phone," he demanded. "You know the drill, don't you, Miss Maguire?"

Chapter Eighteen
Frazzled

"I didn't kill her." Kit swallowed and repeated herself for good measure. Her voice echoed in the formal interview room. "I did not kill Debbie."

"Okay." Lane brushed her off with a wave of his hand. "Don't forget you're still under caution." He concentrated his efforts on the technology, fiddling with a connector before sitting up with a sigh. Kit held her breath, wishing her father could still stroll through the locked door and rescue her. She pursed her lips and in the next second, experienced an overwhelming gratitude that he wouldn't witness her in yet another legal scrape.

She cleared her throat, and Lane held up his hand to stop her speaking. He peered at the flashing red light on his recording equipment, and the perfunctory action rankled Kit. She ground her teeth together until her jaw ached, but the mischievousness still wriggled past her common sense. "I'm surprised at you, Officer," she said with a sigh of deep sadness. "And anyway, I don't carry that much cash."

"What?" Lane's gaze switched to her face and his colour heightened as two red circles on his pale cheeks. Confusion broke over his features like a tidal wave.

"Write it down." Kit jerked her head towards the pad contained in the top pocket of his tweed jacket. He'd scribbled in it at the scene until his miniature pen became a blur. "I'm under caution, so you need to write everything I say."

Lane jerked back in his seat. It rocked on its rear legs. "I'm not writing that!" he snapped. "That's ridiculous."

Kit folded her arms in front of her chest and crossed her legs. "Write it down," she snarled. "I'm telling my lawyer you didn't record everything. You cautioned me under Section 8 of the Police (Questioning of Suspects) Act, but you can't pick what information to write in your little notebook and leave out what doesn't agree with your theories." Her eyes narrowed. "Have you called my lawyer yet?"

Lane's lips twitched. "Yes." He ground out the single word like he'd pushed it through a cheese grater. "Please state your name for the recording."

Kit darted a glance at the red flashing light. "It's not working, Detective Lane. I think we should wait for Jerry to arrive."

Lane rose and kicked his chair underneath the table. Kit lifted her gaze to the ceiling to avoid letting his discomfort make her lose control of the laughter, desperate to break free. The sound recording might have left him high and dry, but she knew the video feed still rolled through the cameras fitted in two corners of the room's high ceiling.

Lane slammed the door on his way out, and Kit released a heavy sigh. She leaned her elbows on the scratched table top and rested her head on her wrists. She yearned to walk around the table and straighten Lane's chair, anxiety setting off a wave of compulsiveness.

The door clanged, and she jerked upright, her eyes widening at the sight of the uniform. Jackson stepped into the room carrying a mug, which emitted steam. He pushed the door closed behind him with his foot. "Stop winding him up," he cautioned. His irises sparkled with the infection of her mischief. He placed the mug in front of her and fished three biscuits from his trouser pocket. "A latte with a dusting of cinnamon," he announced. The biscuits shed crumbs onto the scratched surface as he dumped them on the table. "Gingernuts. No pun intended." He shot a glance at her auburn curls, and his eyes crinkled in the corners.

"Thanks." Kit raised her chin and peered at the scum floating on top of the coffee. Strange flecks danced around the rim in a frenzy. "I wish it was a latte with cinnamon," she mused. "Is this what you have to drink all day?"

Jackson smirked. "It'll put hairs on your chest."

Kit frowned and leaned back in the plastic seat. "Is Jerry coming?"

A line came and went as a furrow in Jackson's brow. "The charge sergeant left a message on his voicemail."

Kit nodded. "Maybe he's in a meeting. Or a funeral." She sighed. "I need to tell you something." The image of the precision matte black scissors sticking from Debbie's neck made her wince.

Jackson's posture changed as his muscles stiffened. "No. I don't want to know." He swallowed, and the tendons became hard ridges in his neck as he resisted the guilty urge to check the camera above her. His speech sounded strange as he spoke without moving his lips. "He'll ask you why you called me," he whispered.

Kit reached for the mug and drew it towards her. She leaned forward as though to blow on the hot liquid. "Don't worry." She rushed the words and then drew out her second sentence. "Thank you for the drink and the biscuits."

"Get out, Delaney." Lane's sentence preceded him into the room. A thin man with spectacles followed him like a puppy. As the newcomer turned, Kit saw a lank ponytail hanging down the centre of his spine. A name tag dangled from a lanyard around his neck, and he carried a screwdriver. Lane held the door open for Jackson and waited for him to leave before closing it behind him with a click, which echoed around the bare walls. He jerked his head at his companion. "Can you fix it?" he demanded, not giving the poor man a chance to check the flashing red light.

The skinny man gulped and darted a glance at Kit. He pointed at a blank wall to her right. "I need to access it from in there." His ponytail quivered like the tail of a frightened dog. Kit studied the flyaway ends lifting with static and sighed.

Lane released an exasperated groan. "Then, why didn't you say something?" he demanded. He pursed his lips and jerked his head towards the door. "Just knock and go in. Let me know when you're finished."

Kit stared at her fingers, wondering what kind of person would kill another Curly in such a particular manner. The tech shot from the interview room with a nervous glance at her over his shoulder. She shook her head and her mind moved over her memory of the scene. A tut escaped her lips at Debbie's last activity. She'd been one of the Queen of Curl's first converts back in the early 2000s, founding the Hamilton chapter of Women with Curls with Pam and ruling them with a rod of iron. Kit shook her head and tapped her nails on the table. "Why would Debbie open conditioner bottles?" As she mused over the murmured question, another one added itself. "And how did my scissors get to Debbie's house when I lost them at Pam's?" That fact alone meant one of the committee members knew something about Debbie's death. Kit exhaled, and her tapping intensified.

Lane paced the interview room, alternately checking his watch and staring at the red light flashing from the recording device.

Kit looked up and opened her mouth to ask again for Jerry. At that same moment, the flashing light switched from red to green, mirroring the evil spark in Lane's eyes. A grin split his face, and he ran to the chair opposite Kit's, as though taking part in a game of musical chairs. Thumping himself into it, he yanked his notepad from his jacket pocket and produced the miniature pen. "Right," he began, "let's get this show on the road."

Chapter Nineteen
Curly Criminal

"Why did you use Sergeant Delaney's phone number instead of calling for the emergency services?" Lane rested back in his seat, a smug smile stretching his lips into an uncharacteristic expression of pleasure.

"I want Jerry." Kit folded her arms. "I'm saying nothing until he gets here."

Lane shrugged. "It's a simple question, Katharine. Personal interest more than relevant to the case."

Kit rolled her eyes and considered the predicament she'd dumped Jackson into without a second thought. She sighed and broke a rule which would have made her dear father's face fall in disbelief. He'd taught her better than to speak to a detective without a lawyer sitting next to her. "I saved his number first in my contacts." She shrugged. "You've taken my phone. You can check. I put an extra 'A' in front of important numbers. My mother should be first, then Jerry and Langdon, but '*J*' comes before '*M*'. '*Ja*' is before '*Je*' or '*L*'." Kit blinked away the image of Debbie.

Lane waved away her explanation with a disappointed wafting action. His shoulders sagged.

"I panicked." Kit bobbed her head and stared at the table. "Officer Delaney gave his number to me earlier this year. He saw my manager being aggressive and intervened. He asked if I needed help and gave his card to me then. We've crossed paths a couple of times since, and he's always been kind and professional. After finding Debbie, I wanted a kind person to help me. He took care of calling an ambulance and other police officers, just like I hoped he would. I'd got myself trapped in all the boxes and I couldn't leave without passing Debbie. If I moved, I'd touch something, so I needed to stand still." Kit frowned. "I noticed a noise when I knocked on the door and assumed I'd heard Debbie dragging boxes around in the garage. She might not have registered me knocking, but Mr Rashid seemed to think she'd be waiting with his order all ready. He only gave me half an hour to collect it and get back to the shop." She winced. "Raj needed to leave. He's gonna be so mad at me." Kit released the lie amid a sigh. "I think I arrived just as Debbie died and the killer was in the house."

She directed her gaze at the table to avoid Lane's perceptive stare. The truth of what she'd said made the hairs rise on her arms and she shivered. A gulp betrayed the thoughts flooding her brain as the subconscious realisation took hold. She'd disturbed the killer.

Lane cleared his throat. "You think you interrupted the perpetrator?"

"Yeah." Kit nodded and clutched her arms around her stomach. "That's why I called Jackson and not a total stranger. He'd understand I was in danger and not assume it was a hoax." Kit rocked forward with a groan.

She'd been inside the house with Debbie's killer.

Delayed terror danced through her mind like confetti. "I feel sick," she admitted. "Please, can I visit the bathroom? And then can you fetch Jerry for me?"

"Okay." Lane rose with a frown. "I'll ask a female officer to escort you to the bathroom and phone your lawyer again." His tone sounded more sympathetic. "Just wait here for a moment and don't touch that coffee. It looks terrible. I'll make you another."

Lane left the room, and the door clicked behind him. Kit pushed her chair back and pressed her face against her knees. The thin white fabric of her jumpsuit released the strange whiff of plastic and institutional dust. The desk sergeant had taken her clothing for forensic examination.

Yoga breaths helped her regain her equilibrium, but the terrible realisation blossomed in the forefront of her mind. She'd heard Debbie's killer in the garage moving boxes before she walked around the side of the house. Mental images flooded through her brain as she revisited the scene and walked through it again. The closed front door had faced her as she turned right into the garage, which meant they hadn't left that way. "Unless they were fast," Kit mused under her breath. She shook her head. "No." Debbie's husband had fitted a device above the door to stop it from slamming after a grandchild trapped his finger. The door inched closed at a millimetre per second, and often after meetings, Kit had reached her car before it sealed shut. She swallowed, and her tongue felt too big for her mouth.

She sat up, and the room spun for long enough to make her stomach churn. A female officer stepped into the room, a look of enquiry in her raised eyebrow. "There was a drag as I opened the back door. I assumed someone left a window open, but I also thought I remember the front door clicking as I stood in the hallway."

The officer shrugged. "Tell Lane when you get back here. Come on," she said, her tone gentle. "I'll take you to the bathroom now. Lane asked me to explain your lawyer is on his way." A blonde bun bobbed at the back of her head every time she moved. Flawless makeup gave her a doll-like appearance.

Kit nodded and pushed herself to a standing position. She swayed on her feet. "Every time I shut my eyes, I see Debbie just lying there," she whispered. "And now I've realised the killer was in the house with me when I found her." She leaned her head back and stared at the ceiling. "They might have killed me!"

"But they didn't." The officer smiled, but the flapping of her hand indicated her rising impatience. "Come on. I need to get you there and back before someone else wants to go too."

"Okay." Kit stumbled across the tiled floor and followed the woman from the room. Shouting issued from beyond a set of double doors, and she paused, looking over her shoulder. The officer jerked her head in the opposite direction.

"Delta just arrested a guy with a knife."

"Delta?" Kit forced her feet to move.

"Dog squad." The woman set off ahead of her, sensible boots rapping staccato squelches against the tiled floor. Kit followed, the cloth bootees creating a skating rink beneath her.

"Will I get my stuff back?" she asked. "I'm not bothered about the clothes, but my mother gave me the bag for my birthday. Detective Lane also took my best plimsolls."

The officer shrugged. "Sorry. You'll need to ask Lane." She stopped and stood aside to let Kit pass through the door she held open. A stencilled image of a female wearing a skirt decorated the door. Someone had added a hand drawn radio and a truncheon to the silhouette. The officer jerked her head before following her into the bathroom.

"I don't understand. I'm not under arrest." Kit waved her hand towards the nearest cubicle and frowned. She didn't want an audience while she used the toilet.

The officer shrugged again. "You found the deceased, which makes you a suspect until Lane proves otherwise." She jerked her head towards the cubicle. "You can push the door a little but not close it."

Kit released the zipper on the jumpsuit with a sigh and wriggled free, grateful Lane hadn't confiscated her underwear. She flushed and repeated the exercise in reverse before emerging from the cubicle. The hand soap smelled of pure chemicals and she wrinkled her nose as the slimy liquid spurted from the dispenser into her palm. Even after rinsing her hands under the scalding water, her skin still smelled like insecticide. A glance in the mirror made her wince. Stringy ringlets dangled around her face where she hadn't yet Scrunched Out the Crunch.

The officer hurried her back to the interview room, not waiting for Kit as she slipped and slid on the tiles in her booties. The door opened as they arrived, and Jackson appeared from the room. His flushed cheeks and the brightness of his eyes indicated his discomfort, and he glanced at Kit and swallowed. "Lane asked me to reset the tech," he said to the officer.

"Hey gorgeous." The woman's manner changed. She reached up and ran her hand along Jackson's forearm. The action appeared proprietary and familiar.

"Hey." His lips twitched into a smile, which didn't reach his eyes. He ignored Kit as though she didn't exist.

"One more hour to go." The woman smiled, and her blue irises sparkled. "Same again tonight?"

"Yeah." Jackson swallowed and freed himself from her grasp. He made the light shake of his arm appear unobtrusive. Still, he ignored Kit, and she held her breath. She'd enjoyed their kiss, giving far too much of herself than she'd wanted. She'd broken rules she'd forged from the ashes of her last disastrous relationship and the realisation caused her stomach to clench. Her teeth ground in her jaw as she stamped on the embers of passion. She set her face into a blank mask and stared past Jackson to the double doors beyond him.

They flew open as though on cue, and three male officers wrestled a man through the aperture. He struggled between them, dropping to his knees and forcing them to carry him along the corridor. The approaching hazard caused the woman to push Kit into the interview room, closing the door behind them. The overpowering scent of neat alcohol filtered through the narrow gap between the door, and the officer rolled her eyes. "He's a regular," she said, cocking her head. "Nothing to worry about."

Kit's jumpsuit rustled as she sank back into the plastic orange chair. Emotions crackled like fireworks beneath her skin. Jackson Delaney was a cheat and a Woman With Curls had died at the blades of her missing scissors. And somewhere in the city of Hamilton, a killer perhaps wondered how much Kit Maguire knew.

Chapter Twenty
A Curly Crisis

Lane released Kit after taking her statement. Part of Jerry's delay had involved dashing to the second-hand shop attached to the church to grab clothes for her. She squirmed in the front seat of his car wearing a tee shirt which smelled of someone else's sweat, and a pair of shorts discarded by an eight-year-old.

"Sorry I took so long." Jerry shot her a sideways glance as he pulled away from the curb outside the police station. "Langdon made me turn my phone off before the funeral."

Kit snuffed out a soft laugh. "It's fine, Jerry. I didn't know who else to call. Perhaps I need to pay a retainer for a local lawyer." She sighed. "Lane seems keen to put me behind bars at some point in my future."

"Na." Jerry shook his head, and his curls gave a gentle bounce. "It's all circumstantial. Statistics show it's often the person who reports the death who is the killer." He reached a hand across to lay it over Kit's writhing fingers. "But I believe you didn't do it and so will Lane."

Kit sighed and linked her fingers through his. "Thank you, Jerry. I don't deserve your faith in me. Anyway, Jackson reported the death so maybe Lane will think he did it."

"With you watching? That's a stretch." Jerry took his hand back to indicate the turn onto the expressway. "Unless you're in it together. Even Lane can't prove that."

Kit turned sideways in the passenger seat and bent her knee beneath her. The seatbelt tightened across her neck, but the discomfort caused by the shorts lessened. She studied Jerry's profile as he navigated a set of roadworks and the broken glass from a two-car shunt. The drivers argued at the side of the mess, their vehicles occupying all the outside carriageway.

Jerry's black shirt hung open at the neck. He'd removed his dog collar and pushed it into his top pocket before entering the police station. Black bristles protruded through the skin on the lower half of his face like a shadow. Kit closed her eyes with a sigh. "I can't believe Debbie's dead." The words sounded jarring when she spoke them out loud. "She was always larger than life and someone just snuffed out all that energy."

"Yeah." Jerry's tone held a hint of approval. "It was very brave of you to tell Lane about your missing scissors. I realise it implicates you, but it's better to give the cops all the facts rather than try to hide something. It sends them on wild goose chases and destroys your credibility further down the track when they catch the lie. Which they will." He spoke the last three words with a sense of finality. His years as a defence barrister meant he'd witnessed the little untruths which spiralled out of control and implicated the wrong person.

"Thank you." Kit reached across and rested her hand on his shoulder. The contact brought her comfort and grounded her in her truth. She didn't kill Debbie. Jerry, at least, believed her.

"The forensics guys will fingerprint the scissors. Langdon and I can verify they weren't in your possession on Saturday night. Whoever killed your friend will have left prints. Unless they wore gloves and then they'll have smudged yours." Jerry smiled sideways at her; oblivious he'd just added more fuel to her fear.

Kit cleared her throat and removed her hand. "They won't find my prints on the scissors," she whispered. Jerry's knitted brow turned in her direction, and she cringed. The vehicle behind theirs honked to warn him he'd crossed the dividing line, and he jerked the Mustang back into his lane.

"Why is that?" His tone indicated he didn't want the answer.

Kit sighed. "I've never touched them." It seemed ridiculous to admit they'd been too precious to handle. She'd lifted the flap of the navy velvet case and stared at them, but she'd saved her big revelation for the committee meeting. It became another thing added to the list of triumphs Cindy's presence had denied her.

"Oh." Jerry clicked his tongue. "That's both good and bad."

Kit nodded. "I realise that. If the killer wore gloves, it will look like I killed Debbie and wiped the scissors clean. Lane will believe she died as the result of a premeditated attack."

Jerry frowned. "You listed the bad part first. If the killer didn't wear gloves, then their prints will exonerate you. Yours won't exist to incriminate you."

Kit nodded. "You make it sound so simple," she mused. "But the fact is that my scissors killed Debbie. I never even got to use them and now I've lost them forever."

"I'm so sorry." Jerry's words contained empathy and understanding. "We need to face the likelihood you'll never see them again. They'll stay in an evidence locker for an exceedingly long time."

"I don't want them." She shuddered. "They've lost their specialness now. I'll stick to my old ones."

Jerry ran a hand through his curls and smiled, but he kept his thoughts to himself.

Kit straightened her legs and the shorts bit into her skin. "Lane seemed excited about the fact I shared air space with the killer." She shivered. "I'm less thrilled."

Jerry shot a glance in her direction. "As soon as we get home, I'll interview you myself. We'll use a voice recorder so you can play it back and listen to your own story. It's great for jogging your memory."

"But I saw nothing!" Kit protested. Hunger, tiredness and fear had turned her mood towards the dark side. "What more can I say that I haven't already told you and Lane? I don't know what I don't know."

Jerry clicked his fingers, and his handsome face relaxed into a beatific smile. "But it's possible that you also don't know what you do know. Just give me a chance, Kit. We'll work it out."

She relaxed against the seat, and the tension in her stomach lessened. She loved how Jerry had looped himself into her crisis by using a first-person pronoun. *We*. It soothed her battered nerves enough to forget Jackson's inappropriate behaviour and the fear of Raj and Mr Rashid's disappointment. She enjoyed a moment of relief that Lane had confiscated her phone for examination. Raj's angry calls had started while she was still in the car on the way to the police station. Then Mr Rashid had text bombed her when she didn't answer. Her shoulders slumped against the seat, and Jerry reached for her hand again. "Don't worry," he soothed, as his fingers closed around hers.

"What if Mr Rashid fires me?" Kit groaned. "The police confiscated Raj's van. He'll never forgive me either."

"Mr Rashid won't fire you. His wife won't let him. And the van issue is temporary." Jerry's thumb smoothed the back of her hand. "Forensics officers will go over it with a fine-toothed comb and find nothing. So, they'll have to release it back to its owner. They'll pull the data from your phone, swab it for blood, fingerprints and anything else they can think of and give it back to you."

"Broken!" Kit snorted. "Like last time!" She inhaled and held the breath, releasing it seconds later as a wail. "Oh no!" She turned sideways in her seat, a waft of the shirt owner's sweat wrinkling her nose. "I can't remember what I said about Cindy. They'll look at texts and calls and realise I argued with the committee. Debbie is a member, and she attended that meeting." Kit pressed a hand over her eyes. "I had a motive."

Jerry shook his head. "You're looking at the worst-case scenario. Lane can see texts and phone numbers, but he can't get transcripts over digital mobile. The murder weapon won't contain your fingerprints. Someone else handled them in order to stab Debbie."

Kit's lips twisted down into a grimace. "That is potentially as bad as the worst-case scenario," she said. "You might find yourself with two defendants."

"How?" Jerry slid his car onto their driveway next to Langdon's and activated the hand brake. He turned in his seat to face her. "Whose fingerprints might they find on the scissors?"

Kit's muscles tightened as her body shrank in her seat. "She was so proud of my achievements she kept taking them out of the case and admiring them." She closed her eyes and her jaw showed as a hard line through her cheek.

"Who?" Jerry demanded.

Kit gulped. "My mother." She raised her hand to brush a curl from her forehead and her fingers trembled.

Chapter Twenty-One
Curly Confusion

Kit sat on the sofa in the lounge, her knees drawn up to her chin. The hugging action of her arms did little to soothe her frayed nerves. Jerry paced the lounge, a toe peeking through a hole in his sock. The discarded dog collar coiled from the pocket of his jacket, as though even the angels feared the nightmare unleashed on Kit. He whirled to face her and held up his hand for silence, even though she hadn't spoken.

"You're sure your mother touched the scissors."

Kit gave a shallow nod. "Yes. Lots of times. Some of her prints might have wiped off when she pushed them into the cloth case, but I can't guarantee it."

Jerry exhaled and spun again. "I don't think we should say anything to Lane just yet."

"What? No!" Kit lowered her knees. "Because then they'll start looking for an unknown killer who'll turn out to be my mother! It's too risky. You said it's the little lies which cause the biggest mess."

Jerry closed his eyes and scrubbed at the air as though wiping a blackboard. "Not necessarily. Unless she's committed a crime, they won't have her fingerprints. Let's wait and see how this runs before we drag your poor mother into it." He snatched a notebook and pen from the arm of the sofa. Kit's eyes widened at the irony of his behaviour, the similarities to the detective spinning a knot in her stomach. He jabbed his index finger at Kit. "Lie on the sofa and close your eyes." He grabbed his phone from his trouser pocket and frowned as he searched for the voice recorder app.

"What?" Her head jerked forward. "What will you do to me?"

"Yes, what will you do to her, Jerry?" Langdon stood in the doorway to the lounge, a tube of purple-willy-shaped lube clutched in his fingers. Jerry's eyes widened, and he gaped at the sight of his vicar wielding a sex aid. Langdon bobbed the tube at Kit like a threat. "Please, can you show me how to use this?"

"In what capacity?" Jerry's voice held an uncharacteristic croak. His gaze shot from Kit to Langdon and back to her.

"For his hair," she groaned. She rubbed her eyes with her knuckles and fought through a wave of exhaustion.

Jerry bridled and threw his shoulders back, giving him a few centimetres height on Langdon. "We're having a client consultation here." For a moment, he sounded like the barrister who'd once wooed the juries of the nation. Kit pulled her hands away from her eyes and drank in the magnificence. Jerry pushed his thumbs into the pockets of his waistcoat and cocked his head, assessing Langdon with an unblinking stare. "We need a few moments of peace. Please close the door on your way out."

"Oh. Right." Langdon backed away, clattering with the door frame on his way through it. He gave a feckless wave with the purple-willy-shaped lube and closed the door behind him. When Jerry blinked at Kit, she obeyed without question, shooting back against the cushions and closing her eyes like a child caught evading bedtime.

Jerry's tone changed, gentling to a soothing lilt containing the illusion of endless patience. "Inhale and exhale. Create a gentle rhythm." He paused and Kit sensed him holding his breath. "Now, go back to this morning in your mind. Run through everything you did. What sent you to the victim's house?"

"The note," Kit murmured. She pictured it, the list of items and the number of boxes. "I thought Mr Rashid stopped buying from her because of the exploding lube. He left a note of what he wanted, and Raj lent me his van." She remembered the council's tow truck hitching the vehicle onto its winch as Lane observed the operation and groaned. "He's going to kill me."

Jerry continued, brushing over her immediate concerns with the same smooth tone. "You drove to the house and then what?"

Kit inhaled. The exhale seemed to wobble from her lungs like a drunkard. "I backed the van onto the driveway and knocked on the front door. She didn't answer, but I knew she was home."

"How?" The immediacy of Jerry's question bit into the mood and Kit jerked. A whine entered her voice.

"I saw her car. And she left her shoes on the doormat."

"Describe the shoes."

Kit squeezed her eyes closed and forced the image to paint itself on the inside of her eyelids. "Red. Flip-flops, you know, the thongs with the painful bit between your big toe and the next one." The image stuttered and winked out in her mind, leaving Kit with a picture of a child's bleeding foot. "I haven't worn them since the age of six," she said with a sigh.

"Go back to the shoes," Jerry commanded. "Just red? Fabric or rubber?"

"Rubber. And a pair of blue ones. Bigger size. They faced the house. You know, how people take them off and step through the door?"

"Two pairs?" Jerry's tone contained urgency. Kit lifted one eyelid to find his chocolate irises glittering as though back-lit by a flame. "Were the other pair for a male or female, if you had to guess?"

Kit exhaled and closed her eyes. She pictured the shoes on the mat. The blue ones looked less worn than the red, the rubber not bowed and dipped at the heel. "I don't know," she concluded. "Just bigger. Some men have little feet, and some women have clodhoppers. I can't say for sure." Her stomach growled and her mind flicked instead to the items contained on her shelf of the fridge. She groaned. "I didn't shop at the weekend. Jerry, I need to grab some food and get to the Women with Curls meeting." She glanced at her wrist and missed the watch which Lane had kept hold of for the time being. Her gaze found the wall clock, and she released a squeak and shot upright. "It's right now! I need to leave." Another realisation sent her head into her hands. "My car is still at the shop!"

Jerry drove her to the meeting, silence pervading the journey. He said little, tapping his fingers against the steering wheel as he paused at junctions. Kit got out at Vanessa's house, bending to thank him before she closed the door. Wood smoke drifted through the darkness as a grey haze, underscored by the subtle scent of melted plastic and her mother's washing powder. "Concentrate," she said, pointing through the windscreen. "Forget about it for now." A tractor emerged from a narrow lane adjacent to the house, ambling along the road with mud flicking from its giant tyres. Jerry gave himself a shake and nodded, but his eyes still appeared glazed.

"Call me when you're ready to leave," he replied, forcing a smile.

Kit slammed the door and waited as Jerry pushed the gear lever into place and pressed the gas. The magnificent, guttural roar of the engine apologised for the spots of oil decorating the road where it had idled.

"Here goes nothing," Kit breathed. She brushed at imaginary specks on the clean tee shirt and denim skirt she'd hauled onto her damp body after the fastest shower in history. Her curls dripped water down her neck, and she raised a hand to haul them away from a soaked patch on the back of her shirt.

"You came!" Vanessa weaved her way through the parked cars filling her driveway to meet Kit on the road. Kindness radiated from her twinkling hazel irises. Perfect coils brushed her cheek and continued behind her shoulder. "Bronwyn is just serving dinner. You want some?" She glanced along the street at Jerry's retreating tail lights and gave a nod of satisfaction.

Kit clutched her stomach as it produced an answering growl. Words spilled from her lips before she could contain them. "I'm starving. My flat mate forced me to use lube on his hair and I didn't have time to Plop." Her fingers gave an involuntary twitch. A length of auburn curl sneaked over her shoulder to leave a wet trail across her shirt. She swallowed, realising she'd just betrayed Vanessa's vicar. "I shouldn't have come. My hair is a mess. It's a terrible way to meet new Curlies."

Vanessa smiled, the action curving her eyes. "It's a perfect way to meet new Curlies. We all struggle, Kit. It's what makes us human." She tugged Kit's hand away from her head and kept hold of it, leading her along the snaking path to the front door. The vehicles parked bumper to bumper occupied the driveway and the grass lawn next to it.

Kit gulped. "You must have a sizeable group." Her voice cracked with nerves. Booster seats and a collapsed pram filled the interior of an eight-seater parked near the door and her steps faltered. "I'm not great with kids," she admitted.

Vanessa blinked and her Mother Earth image wavered a little. "You'll like these," she said, a hint of promise in her tone. She released Kit's hand to walk up the steps onto the porch.

Kit shook her head from side to side behind her, mouthing, "No, I won't." Vanessa opened the door and stood back to let her pass, a wry smile on her lips. As she kicked off the old pair of plimsolls requisitioned from the back of her wardrobe and stepped around her, Kit noticed the mirrored glass on the front door and held in a groan of dismay, realising Vanessa had witnessed her whispered rebellion. She took a deep breath and crossed the threshold to the sound of clanking cutlery and the giggle of children. Her fingers shook on the handle of her rucksack. Then a voice rose higher than all the rest.

"Oh my gosh!" it gasped. "Everyone shut up for a minute!" Silence spread like an infection, and Kit glanced toward Jen's jabbing finger. A newscaster squared his shoulders and faced the camera, a severe expression on his face.

"Hamilton police are investigating the death of a woman after they discovered a body in the garage of her house." An image of Debbie's front door scrolled behind his head on a video screen and his brows narrowed. "We'll bring you more on our main news at six o'clock."

Nausea rose into Kit's throat as all eyes turned from the TV to her. Bronwyn scurried towards her, bearing a steaming plate filled with mince and potatoes. "You came!" Kit glanced back at Vanessa with a frown. They'd trusted her with their secret without expecting her to fulfil her side of the bargain by returning. Excitement lit Bronwyn's round face, and she pushed the plate into Kit's hands. "Come and sit with us. You can tell us all about your day." She pressed her palms together in delight, and Kit's appetite fled outside to sit with her second-best plimsolls.

Chapter Twenty-Two

Curly Kids

"Don't you like it?" Vanessa frowned as Kit pushed a smooth blob of mashed potato to the side of the plate. She gulped, formulating lies in her brain and then discarding them.

Bronwyn gasped. "You're not a vegan, are you?" Her cerulean irises rounded to giant blue orbs in her face. "I didn't think to ask. We have a vegetarian option."

Kit pursed her lips and shook her head. It would have been so easy to accept the excuse, but she imagined carrying it on for the rest of her time in the group and failed at the first hurdle. She cocked her head and pictured them catching her eating bacon or fried chicken at the age of eighty. Or she could become a vegan for real, and then it wouldn't be a lie. "No," she replied with a sigh. "I like bacon too much." She glanced up at the concerned faces surrounding her at the dining table and her shoulders relaxed. "I got nervous about meeting everyone." A rueful smile pressed her lips flat as her left hand lifted to touch her soaked curls. "I'm having a bad hair day. Not a great advert for Women with Curls."

Choruses of consolation and encouragement rose in a cacophony to dismiss her fears. Bronwyn leaned across the table to tap Kit's hand. "Don't be daft," she soothed. "I kept mine short for years after I joined the WWC. We all struggle at some point. We'll forgive you the odd blunder if you'll return the favour when the time comes."

"Blunder?" Kit dug her fork into the mince and lifted it to her mouth. Gravy dripped onto the mashed potato, reminding her of the line of blood leaking into Debbie's shirt. She frowned as a thought pervaded her subconscious and wriggled free. She needed to speak to Jerry. Her fingers scrabbled around her body before she remembered Lane confiscating her phone. Ever observant, Vanessa cocked her head at the myriad of emotions stampeding across Kit's face.

Jen detailed the never-ending list of potential blunders for a Curly. "Brushing, straightening, oils, non-approved gels." Her brown eyes narrowed, and she jabbed her finger at Kit's head. "Do you always leave the house with your hair soaked? Don't you use a Plop?"

Kit lifted her fingers to her fringe and nodded. "I do, but I got delayed and needed to shower." She shot a look at Vanessa and winced. Her face broadcasted her earlier sentiment that she shouldn't have come. Vanessa jumped into the fray.

"Kit lives with the reverends Langdon and Jerry," she announced. A dozen sharp intakes of breath issued from the surrounding women. Forks ceased their clatter against the plates as a barrage of comments hit her like a wall. The Curly crowd took shape as a home group formed from the vicars' curly congregation.

"I love Reverend Jerry best." A woman with vibrant blue eyes and black curls fluttered her eyelashes. "He's gorgeous."

"Langdon's like an angel." An older Curly in her sixties chased a green bean around her plate. Grey curls morphed to white by the time they reached her fringe. "He makes me wish I was twenty years younger."

Kit pursed her lips against the objectification of her flat mates. She dipped her head to stare at her food, wondering how women could complain about sexism when they used the same measurement for handsome men. Her mind blocked out the women's inappropriate chatter as it returned to its earlier thread. *Blood*. There should have been more in the garage and around Debbie. Lane confiscated her clothes, but they'd find nothing. It should have covered the killer. Kit frowned as she turned the thoughts over in her mind. A stabbing to the neck would have generated a blood bath.

"Kit." Vanessa tapped her shoulder. "Are you finished?" She turned to speak to someone else and didn't wait for an answer.

"What?" Kit stammered the reply as the image of Debbie's garage winked out. She sat at Vanessa's dining table alone, and Bronwyn collected discarded crockery. A baby in a high chair had appeared next to her right arm, and it leaned across her to dip its spoon into her mince. She fought the urge to recoil at the brown streaks across the child's button nose. Long black eyelashes blinked as it beamed at her. Blue pants and a pink shirt added to her confusion when deviating from the pronoun *it*.

Kit held her breath and shoved the plate nearer to the small person. Giving a squeal of delight, it dug a red plastic spoon into the mashed potato. And flicked a blob clean across the room to splatter against the TV screen. Kit followed its trajectory and waited for an eruption of complaint. Two children watching a cartoon leaned sideways in unison to avoid looking through it, but they made no removal attempts.

"Oh, sorry. He shouldn't have that. We're vegetarians." A woman appeared behind the high chair stirring a bowl of biscuit coloured vomit. "I'm starting him on warm breast milk and rusk." Kit's gag reflex went into overdrive as the woman leaned forward and moved the plate aside again. She dropped her voice into the same pitch and intonation as Langdon used when speaking to his cantankerous horse. "Does Alfie-walfie want some din-dins?" The child grumbled and waved its red spoon. Another child wearing a blue dress hung off the woman's skirt, sucking her thumb and glaring at Kit. The woman patted the child's head and issued something akin to a threat. "Watch TV with the others, Lottie," she soothed. "Or sit on Kit's knee."

Kit tensed in horror and pushed her chair back with her calves. She rose and seized her plate, chasing Bronwyn across the room and into the kitchen. The older woman turned to her with a grin. "Don't you like children?" she asked. Her eyes twinkled with mirth. "Wait until you hit twenty-eight and the body clock starts ticking. Then you'll be popping them out like candy."

Kit ground her teeth together and set her plate on the counter. Pausing for a beat, she lifted a drying towel and attacked the teetering crockery tower balancing on the draining board. Bronwyn frowned at her plate before scraping its contents into the waste disposal. She pressed a button, and it gurgled away, devouring scraps of food and vegetable peelings. When the noise stopped, Kit looked up to discover her staring at her as though waiting for an answer. She sighed. "I'm thirty and my body clock is broken or defunct. I've no interest in reproducing a small replica human who will make me feel perpetually inadequate." She glanced back at the table as the mother attempted to push the vomit-coloured rusk between Alfie-walfie's lips. He squirmed in his high chair and spread it across his cheek. The small girl glared at Kit from across the room and cemented her life decision. Why produce something to highlight her own deficiencies when other people could do it for her?

The girl-child leaned sideways so she could eyeball Kit's movements as she manoeuvred around the kitchen behind Bronwyn. Her gimlet eyes blinked hatred from beneath a mop of uncontrolled blonde curls. Kit turned and dumped the dried plate onto the counter. "I don't have a maternal bone in my body," she admitted with a shrug. "People always said I'd change my mind, and I didn't."

Bronwyn stood with her hands in the sudsy water, her eyes glazed as she stared through the window at the rolling landscape. "How does that work with regard to relationships?" she mused. "Do you need to disclose something like that at the beginning?"

Kit heaved out a sigh and considered the cringeworthy personal question. "I guess so," she replied. "I'll let you know if it happens."

A clatter behind her denoted the plastic bowl hitting the tiles, and the baby exuded a squeal of rage. The harried mother popped up from behind the table, bowl in hand, and the rusk spread across her face and through her hair. Bronwyn shot Kit a sly grin from the side of her mouth, and her eyes crinkled at the corners. A further protest drew the women's attention as Vanessa switched the TV channel from cartoons to the news. Tension rode across Kit's shoulders like a buffalo stampede, and she held her breath. The national news had picked up the story of Debbie's death and as her fingers knotted the drying cloth into a twisted rope, Detective Lane walked down the steps of Hamilton Central police station to speak to the waiting reporters.

Chapter Twenty-Three
The Upperhanded Curl

"Flagstaff. That's the suburb at the top of Hamilton, isn't it?" Lacey looked at Vanessa for confirmation.

Jen replied instead. "Yeah. It's an older suburb than Rototuna, but I've never heard of a murder there."

"Someone's helping them with their enquiries." Ronnie rocked back on her heels and grinned at the rusk spattered mother with her matching child. "I wonder who found the body. The killer always turns out to be the person who found them." She chucked the baby under the chin, and he chased her finger with his mouth like a piranha. The kid was a raging carnivore. Why could nobody see it? Kit bit back her comment in defence of the unfortunate people of the world who happened across dead bodies. She allowed her gaze to slide sideways to where the blonde child still clung to her mother's skirt and glared at Kit. Her shoulders slumped in defeat. Vanessa used the remote to restore the psychedelic cartoon characters to the screen and the two children resumed their places right in front of it. They stood shoulder to shoulder like sentinels.

The mother winced and spoke to Kit. "We don't have a TV at home," she whispered. "They love coming here."

"I didn't hear your answer earlier." Vanessa turned towards Kit. Women milled around the lounge as they dropped into existing seats or carried dining chairs in front of them like ants. "Did you bring your scissors?"

Kit gave an audible gulp and shook her head. "Sorry. I left in a hurry."

"Oh." Vanessa's tone carried her disappointment. "We wanted to run through a demonstration and try some different cuts ready for the Expo."

Kit sank into a nearby dining chair, hearing a soft grunt behind her as the grey-haired woman frowned. Before Kit could stand again, she'd walked back to fetch another. "But Ronnie cuts hair. I assumed I'd be her reserve." She jammed her fingers beneath her thighs to prevent them from vibrating their terror along her arms and into her neck. She shot a look of hope towards Ronnie.

"I have the skill but not the flare," Ronnie replied. She jerked her head towards Kit. "But you do."

She closed her eyes and exuded a low groan. "I don't. I really don't."

"Well, the Queen of Curl says you do." Vanessa folded her arms. It didn't seem an appropriate moment to disclose that an arrest loomed in her near future. Unless she could find Debbie's actual killer, Kit would spend the Expo weekend in jail. Vanessa shook her head. At the same moment, she flapped a hand in Ronnie's direction. "She's right. She has skill, but you have the flare we need. It's flare that wins the

Expo. Something different to the usual helmet of curls. Something radical." She closed her eyes and lifted her face to the ceiling. Kit peered up at the white plaster, tempted to say a prayer of her own.

"I don't have my scissors." She said it with finality, adding a dollop of regret in just the right measure to put them off the scent. But the hopeful breath exhaled in a rush as Ronnie stepped in with a rescue plan.

"Vanessa has some. Hey, can Kit borrow your snips?"

"Where's my handbag?" Vanessa huffed and puffed, searching behind the sofa and frowning towards the kitchen counter. She winced. "Damn. I left it in the bedroom. I've already disturbed my husband twice. He's trying to watch a movie."

"Don't worry. I'll fetch mine." Ronnie patted her jeans pockets and retrieved a car key. "I'm parked on the street and I only live three minutes up the road. Back before you know it." She barrelled across the room, and the front door slammed behind her before Kit could protest.

"Wonderful." Vanessa clapped her hands. "That gives us time to get the children into bed and put the tarpaulin on the floor. Who wants to go first?"

Hands lifted into the air and Kit baulked at the sheer number. Ten women twinkled their fingers at her, their faces lit with hope. They expected her to stay all night cutting hair for free. She eyed the closed front door as plans of escape drifted through her mind. She couldn't call Jerry without her phone, but she could perhaps walk home. The scratchiness of her lids against her eyes indicated tiredness. She could trim ten heads in the time it would take her to walk back to Gordonton.

Jen jumped to her rescue. "She's only doing one person tonight. You have two minutes to decide who that is for now. If you're interested in modelling at the Expo, put your name on the list in the kitchen. Ronnie can pull names out of a hat at the end of the evening." She frowned and searched for Vanessa. "Do you have that woolly hat around somewhere?"

Kit stared at her knees and cringed. This Expo nightmare had sucked her in and spat out the bones. The usual day out with Piper had turned into an impossible mission. She gave a sharp intake of breath at the memory of her friend agreeing to be her model. That moment in Pam's downstairs bathroom seemed a lifetime ago, longer than a mere forty-eight booby trapped hours.

The women chatted among themselves, and Kit rose on wobbly legs. She walked to the kitchen and retrieved a mug from a cabinet next to the fridge. Hot water spurted from the tap and she ran it for a moment, holding her hand beneath the flow until it cooled.

"I don't like you."

She glanced down to see the grumpy girl-child glaring up at her. Water spilled over the edge of the mug and soaked her sleeve. She sighed and sipped the bubbles from its rim. The tightness in her throat eased. "That's nice." She paused to reply and sipped again. "Because I don't like you either."

The girl gave a sharp intake of breath and indignation marched across her sharp features. Her lips pursed into an ugly knot. "You can't say that."

"Just did." Kit shrugged and gulped water.

"But you're not allowed." The girl's voice rose. "My mum said."

Kit stared through the window at the darkening sky. It mirrored the foreboding in her soul. "Whatever," she breathed.

The girl shook her head. "You can't say that either! It's rude."

"So, bite me." Kit turned to face the mini guerrilla. The child shook her head and blonde curls bounced against her shoulders. She epitomised the image of a wolf in lamb's clothing.

"I don't eat meat, so I can't bite you." She jabbed a finger at her mother's retreating spine. The woman carried the grizzling baby from the room, a heavy bag dangling from her wrist. "Our family doesn't eat meat, but you fed it to Alfie."

Kit finished the rest of the water and dumped the mug in the sink. "Kid, I don't care." Her tone exuded a practiced disinterest. "What do your friends think about your stinky attitude? I guess they're used to your rudeness. But what about when you get new classmates?"

The child blinked. Enormous hazel irises disappeared and winked back into view. "Am I getting new ones?" she demanded.

Alarm bells fired in Kit's brain. She had the sensation of being stuck in a maze that had changed since she entered. A divine hand had walled up the exit and rearranged the signage. She swallowed and chose the principle of inevitability. "Well, yes," she replied. "Of course, you'll get new ones."

The girl's eyes widened until she showed more eyeball than iris. Her mouth opened into a wide O. "Is my mum having another baby?" Distaste dripped from her tone. "Not another one!"

Kit jerked backwards, and her brow furrowed in confusion. "How should I know that?" she demanded.

The girl turned and jabbed a bitten nail towards the children glued to the TV screen. "They're my classmates," she replied. "We're home schoolers."

"Oh." Kit snorted and shook her head. "Then I don't know. Sorry."

"I'm telling Mum you said she had a baby in her tummy." The child narrowed her eyes.

"Lottie!" The mother reappeared and shepherded the other two children into the hallway. She jerked her head towards her daughter. "Bedtime." Kit's eyes widened at the implications of a throwaway comment involving the roundness of a woman's belly. She gulped.

"Don't do that," she snarled. "She'll think I called her fat."

The girl shrugged. "What's in it for me?"

Kit pursed her lips, and her gaze roved across Lottie's curls. Dead ends created frayed edges at the bottoms, and a haze of frizz dusted her head like a haze. Kit cocked her head. "A free haircut." She raised an eyebrow and jerked her chin towards Lacey's new style. "Like hers."

Lottie narrowed her eyes, and a sly smile spread across her lips. She fixed her hands over her hips and pulled out the clincher. "I want a cross," she hissed. "Like Reverend Langdon's."

Kit swore beneath her breath and the child's eyes swivelled like something from a horror movie. But that was how Lottie got to stay up later than her sibling-classmates and Kit got to practice scalp calligraphy with Vanessa's husband's nose hair trimmer.

Chapter Twenty-Four
Ponytails of the Unexpected

Lottie's mother stepped from the hallway after putting her other children to bed. She froze at the edge of the lounge rug. Her forthright daughter wore a grin from ear to ear as Kit added the finishing touches to her hair. The woman gulped. "I said you could trim her curls." She choked on the words. "But you've scalped her!"

"No, she hasn't Alexis. Don't overreact." Vanessa's tone held a note of warning. "It's exactly what we were looking for. Edgy, sophisticated. Kit is definitely our secret weapon."

"Grenade." Jen lifted her wine glass and aimed a pointed wink at Bronwyn. The merlot left a pink stain on her teeth as she smiled. Kit stepped back from her handiwork, misgiving creeping across her shoulders. Lottie had said she wanted something different, a style like Lacey's with a cross like Reverend Langdon's. But her ten-year-old's imagination had intervened and demanded the holy angels, poor crucified Jesus and the disciples in attendance. All crowded into a space measuring five by five centimetres. Instead, Kit had used the nose hair trimmer to inscribe the word 'Faith' into the short layers above Lottie's left ear. Blonde curls tumbled over her right side, the split ends banished amid the promise of ringlets.

"Did you do a poor Jesus?" Lottie opened her eyes and her long lashes swished. The glare returned in the side eye which she administered to Kit, although it contained less aggression.

Kit stepped back with an exhausted sigh. "No. It's a surprise. You need to wash your hair with a sugar scrub. Ask your Mum to add hemp oil if you have it. Then condition and style. I think your hair might benefit from Finger Curling rather than the Praying Hands method."

"Okay." Lottie slid off the stool. She waited for Kit to remove the towel from around her shoulders before heading towards her mother. "Can we do it now? I wanna see how it looks?"

Vanessa stepped over the tarpaulin and dodged the escaped clumps of hair. She held out her hand to the girl. "Yes, we can do it here. I'll help Mummy if you're okay with that?"

"I'm good." A skip entered Lottie's walk as she headed towards her speechless mother. She slipped her hand into Vanessa's and permitted herself to be collected into the woman's amicable bubble. With another glare in Kit's direction, the mother turned and followed them to the bathroom.

Kit moved the stool off the tarpaulin and began shovelling the hair into the centre. A glass appeared in front of her face, and Ronnie swished the tinted liquid into an eager whirlpool. "You sit down," she urged. "Have a sip of this whiskey and soda. We'll clean up the hair."

"Thanks." Kit took the glass from her fingers. The first sip sent a heady rush to her knees. It had a vinegary taste and not the usual whiskey burn.

"Please, can you just do one quick Unicorn Cut on me?" A slender woman wearing her hair in a ponytail rose to her feet. Frown lines marred her forehead and down turned her lips. She touched her frizzing hair with tentative fingers. "I don't mind paying." She bent and seized a tan leather handbag. "I'm new to this. I'm doing my best, but I made the mistake of visiting my old hairdresser last week." Her shoulders slumped. "She insisted on using the salon shampoo and then cut my hair wet. She refused to listen to me. There's a weird step at the back and I didn't notice at first because she'd straightened it." Her eyes sparkled with tears, the humiliation still fresh in her mind. A wad of twenty-dollar notes crinkled in her fingers. "I was ready to just give up and my husband treated me to this Curly Approved conditioner." She tugged at the band holding her ponytail in check and the gathered Curlies leaned forward to see the result. Lacklustre waves cascaded over her shoulders, frizz rising like a heat haze to cover her head. Kit twisted her lips. A warmth in her chest told her she couldn't take the woman's money when she'd already been stung.

She tugged the stool back onto the tarpaulin and patted the seat. "Let me have a look," she said, her brow furrowed. The woman performed a death-defying leap across the blue plastic tarp and almost slipped in her haste. She settled on the stool, the cash still clutched in white-knuckled fingers.

"Go Danni," someone joked.

Kit ran her fingers through the hair, registering the straw like texture and the knots which snagged at her touch. She frowned. "Did you use dish washing liquid to remove any sulfates and silicones when you got home from the salon?" She didn't attempt to address the hairdresser's behaviour. Within WWC, they lumped in hairdressers with male doctors and car mechanics. None of them seemed capable of listening to their female clients.

"I did!" The woman's eyes rounded, and her head nodded with emphasis. She gulped. "What should I do?"

Kit inhaled and took a step backwards, but she rested her hand on Danni's shoulder to maintain the connection. "We're going to fix it," she soothed. "So, put your money back into your purse."

The women whispered to each other, their voices creating a general hum of approval. Jen rose and stepped across the tarpaulin to finger a strand of Danni's hair. Her brow creased in a frown. "What product do you use?" she demanded. "Are you sure it's approved?"

"Yes!" Danni bristled. "I promise."

Jen returned to her seat with a shrug.

"A few of us have struggled recently." Lacey patted her uppercut and winced. "I think it's the weather."

A grumble of solidarity surrounded them as Kit got to work. When a phone rang in Ronnie's back pocket, she dragged it free and peered at the screen. A frown spread across her forehead. "I need to take this," she murmured. "My husband knows I have WWC tonight. It must be important." She stepped through the front door and onto the deck.

Kit borrowed Danni's hair tie and finger combed her locks into a high ponytail at the top of her head. "You must always think about how you position the ponytail when attempting a Unicorn Cut," she advised. The women silenced and fixed their attention on her busy hands. "Do it too far forward and the layers end up short at the front and longer at the back."

"Like a mullet?" someone asked, and the women laughed.

"Yes." Kit raised an eyebrow. "Nearer the bottom will give you more of a bob style, but you'll end up with a V at the back. You need to consider the length of your hair and what you're trying to achieve before you tie up the ponytail." She ran her fingers through Danni's new ponytail, surprised to notice how the tension eased in the woman's thin shoulders. She stopped twisting the money and closed her eyes. Kit paused to address the women. "Curls are very forgiving. It's okay to experiment. If you're only using Curly Approved conditioners, your hair will grow back stronger, and any minor accidents will grow out in a few weeks." She tapped Danni's shoulder. "It'll be okay. I've seen a lot worse than this, I promise." Her mind flicked to an image of Gabby hiding out in her bathroom after a disastrous visit to a local hairdresser. She frowned and pushed the memory aside before she became maudlin. They all had her number on speed dial in case of emergencies, but not one of them had reached out to her after the disastrous meeting. Her old committee had chosen Cindy. She needed to learn to live with their decision.

Kit moved the ponytail twice before satisfied with its position. Then she picked up Ronnie's matte black precision scissors and started snipping. She jumped and almost closed the blades around her index finger as a figure barrelled back from the porch, bringing a cold draught with her through the open front door. "Gotta go!" Ronnie snapped. She lurched for her handbag and turned in a fluid movement.

"What's wrong?" Lacey rose. "Do you need anything?"

Ronnie shook her head, and tears filled her eyes. "I said Damien could go to a friend's place while I came to the meeting. I texted him when I drove home for my scissors and he said they were gaming. My husband just arrived to pick him up after he finished work and he's called an ambulance. He's on his way to the hospital with them now."

"What happened?" More of the women rose in concern.

Ronnie shrugged and jangled her car keys. "Don't know. He said they're out cold and Damien is fitting." Her voice broke. "I need to leave."

"Not like that. I'll drive you." Bronwyn met her at the front door with her handbag and chased her shoes around the porch. "We'll fetch your car tomorrow. Vanessa won't mind." She plucked Ronnie's keys from her hand and threw them back into the room. They landed on the doormat. "We'll leave the keys in case she's blocked anyone in, and they need to move her car. Bye girls." The door closed behind her.

Chapter Twenty-Five
Flattened Hair, Deflated Hearts

A hush followed Bronwyn's exit. An engine started in the distance and a vehicle sped away on the quiet street. Lacey retrieved Ronnie's keys and placed them on the kitchen counter after peering from behind the curtains. "I don't think she's blocked anyone else in," she concluded. "She arrived first."

Kit retrieved her scattered thoughts and lifted Danni's ponytail. "I'm cutting now," she warned, not wanting to lose a finger if the woman hadn't realised. The room buzzed with the group's speculative chatter, so she abandoned her attempt to instruct them on the finer points of Unicorn Cuts. Her fingers melded with Ronnie's scissors, snipping and blunting Danni's ends until the layers stood like regimental soldiers between her first two fingers. She repeated the action until she'd created a straight edge from every direction. Then she released the ponytail.

"Is it done?" Danni leaned sideways to snag a lock of hair. She hauled it up to her face to inspect it.

"I've finished cutting." Kit lifted the longer layers and then dropped them into place. She shoved the scissors blade first into the back pocket of her denim skirt. "I don't want to take off too much. The salon cut was a little uneven, but that's because she cut it while wet. I've sorted that out, but the actual issue is the condition." Kit exhaled and inspected another lank wave. "It sucks that hairdressers always insist on using their own products, but it's not on long enough to cause any damage." She shrugged and looked for confirmation from the gathered women. "My friend, Piper was a bridesmaid last year. The bride demanded they all get their hair straightened to match. She washed it with dish washing liquid the next day and restarted the process. She conditioned the heck out of it and apart from a little heat fatigue, I'd say it returned to normal in a few days." Thoughts of Piper and their ailing friendship sent a dart of pain through her chest. But she'd set the cat among the pigeons and the women chased it.

"Curlies should never straighten."

"I've told my sister I'm not straightening for her wedding."

"My sister-in-law got thrown out of the Albany chapter of WWC for shampooing to get rid of build-up. They blocked her on their Facebook page."

Kit winced, thinking of all her blunders and deliberate deviations over the years. The Hamilton chapter had excommunicated no one, not to her knowledge anyway.

She stared at the back of Danni's head and her brain sifted through solutions. "Are you sure the conditioner you bought is Curly Approved?"

Danni bristled, and her lips flattened into a line. "Yes! I stood in the toiletry aisle taking photos for the Facebook group. I dashed there on the way home from my hairdressing appointment on Saturday. Someone said it was fine." She leaned forward to include the women in her peripheral vision. "I can't remember who answered my post."

"Me." Jen raised her hand to a reluctant half-mast. "It's the same one that I use."

Kit shrugged. "Then I don't understand." She stepped off the tarpaulin and walked to the kitchen island, withdrawing Ronnie's scissors from her back pocket and placing them next to her keys. "I suggest you start again with dish washing liquid and a different conditioner. It makes no sense that your hair is so dry. It's desperate for moisture."

"I bet Vanessa has some olive oil." Lacey rose and hauled open the pantry cupboard. "Yes, she does. Why don't we do it here?" Lacey bent over and searched through a drawer. "She has plastic wrap. We can bind it around your head and then you can leave it on all night."

Danni wrinkled her nose and stood. "What about my pillowcase?"

"Wear your Plop over the plastic wrap," Kit suggested. "I imagine your hair is going to drink everything you put on it, so you won't see leakage."

"Okay." Danni smiled for the first time that evening. "You guys are amazing."

Kit's shoulders slumped as she stopped moving, and a leadenness filled her legs and feet. Exhaustion nipped at the fragile threads of energy remaining. "Does Vanessa have a land line?" she asked, leaning against the counter for support. "I need to get up at four in the morning. It's been a hell of a day."

Lacey led Kit into the hallway and pointed at a low bureau containing a cordless phone. It sat in its charger, and Kit fumbled it as she lifted it free. "You make your call." Lacey jerked her head back towards the lounge. "I'll just clear up the tarpaulin. Thanks for what you did for Danni. I know the girls appreciated it. It's exactly what the spirit of the WWC should be." She offered a rueful smile before walking back towards the hum of conversation and closing the door behind her.

Kit released a groan and stared at the ceiling. Giving free haircuts and consultations wouldn't pay her mortgage.

The clang of the shower door closing along the hallway galvanised her, and she dialled the digits for the land line at home. The exercise tested her memory of the number. She'd promised herself she'd write down the boys' numbers after Lane confiscated her phone last time, but she'd lost the piece of paper. Raki picked up after the fifth ring. "Yep." He sounded busy in his absent-minded way. Kit crossed her fingers behind her back and prayed he hadn't just left something chemical burning on the stove. His last experiment with salt had rendered her best saucepan fit only for life as a planter outside on the deck.

"Please, can you tell Jerry I'm ready to come home?" Scuffling and giggles behind the bathroom door suggested that Vanessa, Lottie, Lottie's mother and Danni had gone into the bathroom together. Tension raked down Kit's spine. She didn't have the energy to style two lots of wet hair before escaping. Her confidence leaked through the soles of her feet and she pushed away the realisation that she didn't want to see the result of her cutting. What if Lottie hated it and pitched a fit?

"You left!" Raki's horror drifted through the connection. "What happened? Did you have a fight?"

"What? No!" His meaning filtered through the cogs of her brain. "I didn't leave. Well, I did, but Jerry gave me a ride. I want him to come back for me."

"Ohhhh." Raki dragged out the word, but he remained on the line. A shout sounded in the background and Kit recognised Langdon's voice.

"Where's the blue smoke coming from?"

Raki swore. "Gotta go!" The line went dead.

Kit heaved out a sigh of defeat and replaced the handset. "Fine then," she whispered. "I'll just walk."

She'd hoped to slip past the women, gather the rucksack serving as her temporary handbag, and wave from the door. But her new celebrity status rendered that dream impossible. The women mobbed her with their questions as she emerged from the hallway, shouting over one another as though she possessed the pink fairy dust which would make all their hair problems disappear. Lacey rescued her, putting her body on the line as the women blocked the front door from Kit's line of sight. "That's enough for one night!" she announced, raising her hands in front of her face. "Kit works the early shift at Rashid's dairy on the Gordonton Road. We should let her go home. I'm sure she'll do another demonstration before the Expo." A frown creased her forehead. "Ronnie's meant to pull a name out of the hat for the Expo model. Never mind. Put your names in and I'll ask Vanessa to do it before you all leave." She glanced towards the hall door. "The girls will be out any second."

A stampede ensued as the women dived as one for the pen and pad. The pushing and shoving looked as familiar as that of the Hamilton chapter of WWC.

"My ride is here." Kit wrinkled her nose against the lie. She snatched up her rucksack and waved over her shoulder. "Bye girls. See you next time." She cast her gaze around the room, hoping not to catch anyone's eye. She found Jen staring at her, thin lips tightened with displeasure.

"Same time next Monday!" Jen approached her with a frown. "We usually meet once a month, but we'll add an extra one to practice for the Expo. The committee meets every other Sunday."

Lacey drew her shoulders up to her ears with excitement. "One more practice until the Expo!" A mini cheer rose around her, and Kit nodded. And fled.

Chapter Twenty-Six
Run, Curly, Run.

Kit set off along the country lane, aiming for the general direction of her house. She figured if she kept the lights of the power station behind her and to the right, she'd either end up in Gordonton or fall into the Waikato River. Determination set the pace at a steady clip until she'd covered the first few kilometres, and then exhaustion began its insipid whine. Vehicles passed on both sides of the road, forcing her onto verges made up of squelching mud. Each set of headlights brought the hope that Raki had passed on the message and sent Jerry, but their tail-lights accentuated the failure of all her recent plans.

Self-pity set itself up as her companion. "What made you think you could change your life?" it grumbled. The voice sounded strangely like her own. "Now, you owe your mother for the hairdressing course and you still don't have any clients." Kit's mind flicked back to Danni's offer of cash, and she chewed on her bottom lip. The notes had been right in front of her and she'd rejected them. Kit spent the next two kilometres trying to work out why. She came to the sad conclusion that she didn't rate her skill high enough to risk taking money for her craft. Possession of the scissors had affirmed her, and she'd lost them less than twenty-four hours later.

A car pulled up behind her and its headlights lengthened her shadow to alien proportions. She'd passed the last house ten minutes earlier, and a tick of fear caught in her throat. Dodging a single murderer seemed more than enough drama for one day. Two would be greedy.

She contemplated running, but the mud glued her feet to the verge. Temper flared and she spun on the spot, her torso moving faster than her legs. The headlights blinded her. Flickering spots dominated her vision. With flight no longer an option, she decided to fight. "Keep driving, buddy!" She lifted her fingers and formed the shape of a gun. "I have a weapon and you don't wanna mess with me!"

"Kit?"

She shielded her eyes, and the click of a car door drew her gaze to the left. "Langdon?" Her shoulders drooped, and she released a sigh of relief. "I don't really have a weapon." She lowered her hand and pushed the makeshift finger gun behind her back. The lights moved as he stepped in front of them and faced her.

"We've been looking for you everywhere." His voice held more concern than anger. "Get in the car. I need to phone Jerry. He's five minutes away from getting the cops to mount a search."

"I'm sorry." Kit squelched towards Langdon's silhouette. "I left a message with Raki. I guess he forgot."

Langdon clasped her wrists and led her to the car. He leaned her against the bumper and bent to look at her. "No, he didn't forget. Jerry left ages before that. He must have missed you on the road. What were you thinking?"

Kit sighed. "I'm thinking I get way too much wrong for a woman my age. Everyone wants too much from me and I'm so tired."

"Okay. Let's get you warm and perhaps things won't seem as bad." He opened the rear door. Jerking his head, he told her to get into the car. "Get in the back for now. I think I've got the passenger side stuck in the mud."

"I'm sorry," Kit groaned. She peered down at her feet. "My plimsolls are filthy. I'll mess up your carpet."

Langdon grinned and his teeth glowed white in the eerie light. "Don't worry about it. I've got a bale of hay in the boot for Bouffant. Can't you smell it? The scouts are raising money for their annual jamboree. I'm letting them use the church driveway for car valeting, so they'll give me a good rate."

Kit found a plastic bag under the driver's seat and removed her plimsolls and socks before accepting the ride. She belted up and held her breath as Langdon slipped and slid the station wagon off the verge and back onto the road. Then he phoned Jerry, the conversation audible through the car's speakers. "I've got her," Langdon said.

"Thank God for that!" Jerry replied. The sentiment sounded genuine. "Okay, thanks for letting me know." Engine noises revved, and someone honked their horn in the background.

"Should we head home?" Langdon asked, and Kit tensed. She leaned sideways to stare at the back of his head.

"Maybe not." Jerry's cautious tone offered no reassurance. "Let's meet at that fast food place just off the expressway. I could murder an ice cream sundae."

Langdon shuddered. "What about the keto diet?"

"I'm having a night off." The humour in his tone confirmed what Kit had always believed, that Langdon cared more about Jerry's health than Jerry.

"Whatever." Langdon's huffy reply indicated he knew it. "See you there in about ten minutes." He killed the call and took the turn towards Hamilton, edging up his speed to match the other few travellers on the road.

Kit sat in the back seat and clutched her rucksack to her chest. "Why can't I go home?" She released a sigh and stared at a strand of escaped hay clinging to the ceiling. "Raki burnt the house down, didn't he, and you want to tell me in a public place so I can't kill him?" A groan escaped her lips. "No. I bet Lane turned up at the house with a search warrant and took my henna powder again."

Langdon snuffed out a laugh and his blond curls wobbled on his head. "None of the above." He paused for a moment to check the intersection before joining the main road. "It's true. Raki created a blue haze earlier this evening. This time, it wasn't a science experiment. He forgot about his noodles. It may or may not be the case that staying out longer will give him time to get rid of the smoke. I suspect Jerry just wants a sundae. And he has some news."

"Oh. Great." Kit's stomach dropped with a sickening sensation. She no longer believed in good news, which meant anything Jerry had to say would be bad. For her.

She stared through the side window and contemplated her threatened freedom. The journey ended far too fast and she padded into the restaurant on bare feet. Jerry waited inside the entrance and he pulled Kit into a bear hug. "I'm sorry," she whispered, her words muffled by his jacket.

"It's okay." He kissed the top of her head and released her, but his fingers closed around her left hand and held it tight. "I'm just glad you're okay." He squeezed her freezing digits. "I remembered you no longer had your phone and set off for Vanessa's place. She said you'd left a few minutes before, so I drove up and down her road but didn't see you."

Kit groaned. "So, she knows I lied and ran out on them."

Langdon interrupted Jerry's confused frown with questions about the menu. He gathered their order after finding a table. "Are you sure that's what you want?" he demanded, cocking his head at Kit.

"Yes, please." She gulped. "I'll pay you back."

"Two sundaes?" Jerry leaned on his elbow in the booth and turned to face her. "For the girl who doesn't eat carbs."

Kit leaned her head back against the faux leather surface and closed her eyes. "I figured I'd enjoy my last supper. Langdon said you had news, which means Lane is coming for me. I doubt there are many late-night dessert deliveries in Waitakere Prison."

"Hi, Vicar." A man slumped into the booth next to them and spoke to Jerry over the partition. "Late night snack, is it?"

Jerry pursed his lips together and darted a look at Kit. She sensed his anxiety at the man's unfortunate timing. "Something like that," he replied. When she sneaked a sideways glance at Jerry, she found him frowning. He leaned closer to her and lowered his voice as he tugged his dog collar free and stuffed it into his pocket. "Lane isn't coming for you," he growled. "Not on my watch." His expression softened and he flattened his lips into a line of concern, steering the conversation into safer territory for a public venue. "Why did you run from the house?" He glanced sideways at the other customer and then at Kit.

She exhaled. "I already cut two people's hair and I knew they'd want me to style it too. It felt like someone pulled a plug and my energy drained away at the thought of them not liking what I'd done. I didn't want to see their disappointment."

Langdon stood at the counter and an assistant took his order. She held up two fingers to represent Kit's greed. The moment for changing her mind had passed. Her gaze shifted back to Jerry's face to discover he hadn't moved.

"How did you know you'd disappointed them?" A line bisected his brows. "How do you know you didn't miss their excitement and thanks?"

Kit shrugged. "I don't. The second person offered me money and I turned it down, even though I need it." Her chin wobbled. "What's the matter with me, Jerry? Do your vicar thing and tell me what's wrong."

Jerry's eyes crinkled at the corners as he smiled. He reached out a hand and brushed a stray red curl behind her ear. "Okay. But can I eat my sundae first?"

Kit nodded, and her shoulders relaxed. She let her gaze move across the other patrons in the restaurant. They occupied the booths in various states of dress and undress. A man in a business suit sat with a child wearing pyjamas. Kit raised an eyebrow as the child scarfed her chicken nuggets and moved on to the man's chips. Perhaps she could eat her two desserts and let tomorrow worry about itself for a while.

The click of Langdon's soles grew louder as he carried the tray containing their order. He made a bee line for their table in his usual commanding style, nodding to the parishioner occupying the adjacent seat. Kit offered him a smile of appreciation before a prickle in her spine told her someone watched her with a little too much interest. She tipped sideways to look past Langdon, keeping her movement slight enough to appear casual.

Jackson Delaney studied her from a booth near the counter, his expression blank like a mask. The female cop sat opposite him, her blonde waves cascading from a ponytail which touched her shoulders. She kept her back to Kit's table, digging into a box of fries in front of Jackson with slender fingers. Kit looked down at the tray Langdon set in front of her, eager to distract herself from the discomfort of Jackson's stare. Langdon slumped into the booth, blocking her view of the restaurant and of Jackson. Gratitude soaked up Kit's spine and into her brain.

"Hello, Reverend." The man in the booth next to them leaned over again to acknowledge Langdon. He gave a feckless wave before turning back to his newspaper.

"Oh, hello there, John." Langdon settled himself in the seat and leaned forward. He opened his mouth to say something else to the man, but after a glance at Jerry, chose not to bother. Then, he jerked his head towards the tray, at the same time as lifting a steaming hot chocolate to his lips. "I got you both sugar free hot chocolate and a keto cookie each," he said. "Your waistlines can thank me later."

CHAPTER TWENTY-SEVEN
Friends that Curl

Jerry released a dramatic sigh and ran a fingernail around the rim of his mug. "A decadence free hot chocolate and a carb-less cookie." He repeated Langdon's sentence with the hint of a grimace. "Thank you," he added with reluctance.

"Thanks." Kit reached for hers and gave Langdon a warm smile. "For the drink and for safeguarding my curves. I don't know why my mind goes straight to food when I'm distressed." She glanced sideways at the parishioner as he folded his newspaper and left, grateful that Jerry hadn't introduced them while she had a terrible case of frizz.

"I have a theory on why we reach for carbs." Langdon leaned forward in his seat opposite Kit. "Psychologists think there are two figures on our shoulders, an angel and a demon. I'm concluding there's only one. It tells you it's okay to eat rubbish and that you deserve it, but as soon as you swallow the last bite, it turns on you. It ridicules you and makes you feel dirty. That's why people are so affected by mental battles over food. It's not about ice cream or chips, it's about feeling betrayed by a best friend."

"Oh." Kit cocked her head, her interest immediate. "I think you're right." Her chin dropped as the realisation gripped her.

Jerry grunted and gave an exaggerated sigh. He sipped his chocolate and wiped his top lip with the back of his hand. "The sugar free one isn't as satisfying." Disappointment dripped from his words.

Langdon shrugged and sat back in his seat. He reached for his drink, but ignored the small stack of cookies. "You can't tell." His tone dared Jerry to list the differences.

Kit contemplated Langdon's theory about diet in the light of her years as an overweight woman. She realised she'd banished the kilograms, but not the voice of temptation and condemnation.

Langdon shifted sideways as he removed his jacket, and Jackson's steely gaze bore into her face from across the restaurant. Unnerved, Kit edged sideways until her thigh touched Jerry's. She craved his trustworthiness and solidity to ground her. Jackson had kissed her, despite having a girlfriend. And she'd compounded the emotional tie by acting on impulse and returning his affection. She forced herself to add him to the growing pile of cheats she'd encountered, along with Alec and many others.

"Are you cold?" Jerry responded to her shiver by removing his jacket and laying it across her shoulders. He wrapped a protective arm around her and rubbed his palm up and down her arm to infuse her with his warmth.

"Thank you." A yawn split Kit's gratitude in half. She sighed. "What a horrid day."

"Jerry's news should improve things a little." Langdon eyed the cookies as though facing wrappers infested with demons. He fingered the cross around his neck. His reaction to the amassed carbohydrates seemed enough to stop Kit from craving them. She focussed her attention on Jerry's moving lips as he lowered his voice to a whisper.

"So, she didn't die from the impact of the scissors." He finished his sentence and frowned as though sensing he'd left Kit too far behind to catch up to his conclusion.

"I don't understand." She rubbed her right eye with her knuckles. "The scissors didn't kill Debbie?"

"No." Jerry's frown persisted. He lifted a finger to his lips. "Look, you're too tired to take this in for now. Let's go home and we'll talk about it in the morning."

Langdon leaned back and strained to haul his phone from his tight trouser pocket. "I'll call Raki and see if he's got rid of the pong of burnt noodle." He rose and turned his back on them, jamming a finger in his ear and striding towards the sliding doors. Kit glanced at Jackson's table and heaved a sigh of relief to discover he'd left and another late-night munchies sufferer had taken his table. Her shoulders slumped, and Jerry tightened his grip. She allowed him to pull her tighter against his ribs.

"I have work in a few hours." Kit lifted her wrist and stared at her watch. She groaned in dismay. "I have four hours of sleep left before I need to get up again."

"No, you don't." Jerry's jaw tightened in her peripheral vision. "I paid Mr Rashid a visit after I dropped you at your group. You're taking paid leave for the next two days on compassionate grounds."

"He won't pay me." Fear edged Kit's tone like fragile lace.

"Yes, he will." Jerry sounded buoyant and his chest muscles tensed like rock. "Hurt and humiliation can prove costly for employers when they're taken to tribunals. He pays you to work in his shop, not run around the city collecting supplies. His demands were unreasonable and led to your current trauma."

"Trauma." Kit sampled the word on her tongue. Was that responsible for the hard knot in her chest? She exhaled and gave a slow nod. "Okay, thank you. I must admit the prospect of a sleep-in tomorrow morning makes me want to cry with relief."

"Good." Jerry squeezed her. "I'm glad."

Kit exhaled a ragged breath. "Can you explain again how Debbie died, please?"

Jerry nodded, and his fringe touched hers as he leaned sideways to whisper. "Strangulation. The killer, or someone else, added the scissors as an afterthought. According to my father's contact in the coroner's office, an initial check of your clothing shows no blood at all. A blade to the neck would have created a blood bath and he says the crime scene looked clean. So, when the scissors entered her neck, she didn't bleed to excess because her heart already stopped pumping."

"Ohhh." Kit drew out the word. She closed her eyes and pressed her fingers over her lips. "I wanted to speak to you about that. It occurred to me when I tried to eat the mince at dinner time. Poor Debbie. What a horrible way to die. All alone in her garage."

Jerry wrinkled his nose at the food-based tangent and shrugged. "Not completely alone. Lane will get the results from the tests on the scissors in the next day or so. We'll need to decide whether to tell him about your mother's prints before then."

Kit ran a hand across her eyes. "Okay. Please, can you drop me at the shop on the way home? I should grab my car."

"Not tonight. You're too tired to drive. You left the keys, so I drove it around to the back and Mr Rashid locked the gate. We'll fetch it tomorrow."

Kit gnawed on her lower lip. "Was he furious with me?"

"More concerned than angry. I think you underestimate how much he values you. The man has an odd sense of humour and I think he enjoys riling you." Jerry removed his arm as Langdon strolled back towards their table. He straightened the jacket around Kit's shoulders and drew the neck closed at the front.

"Raki says the stink is gone." Langdon shot Kit a tired smile and covered a yawn with his hand. "Let's drive in convoy."

A bitter wind snatched at the borrowed jacket and whipped around Kit's bare feet as they emerged from the restaurant. The scent of late snow drifted up from Ruapehu in the south. She shivered, and Jerry slipped an arm around her, smiling when she snuggled against his ribs. He waited as she dropped into the passenger seat of Langdon's station wagon, and then he closed the door.

"I think winter has a sting in its tail this year." Langdon rubbed his hands together after turning up the heat. Kit leaned her head back against the seat and breathed in the mossy scent of mud and wet grass emanating from the foot well behind him. She shuddered at the thought of what her second-best plimsolls might look like after squelching across verges. Jerry's sleek Mustang slid past and they followed, pausing at the exit for an empty space in the traffic. Kit stared through the side window, admiring the overhead stars flickering from the Milky Way. Hamilton's streetlights created a haze beneath the inky blackness of the night sky, as though it tried to hold the dark at bay. Her skin prickled, and she frowned at the sensation of being watched.

Just a slight movement of her head brought her gaze to Jackson's. He sat in a car outside the restaurant, staring straight at her. The vehicle vibrated from the motion of the engine, but the headlights remained unlit. Kit lifted her hand to wave to him and then dropped it into her lap. He didn't deserve her time or acknowledgement. As soon as Lane gave her back her phone, she'd delete his number forever.

Chapter Twenty-Eight
Curly Accusations

Kit sighed with satisfaction as her head hit the pillow. Hours of glorious sleep stretched before her, undisturbed by the phone alarm, which would frighten the entire police station in three hours unless Lane had deactivated it. She stretched out each of her muscles in turn, hoping to achieve a state of mindfulness which would send her brain to the same point of exhaustion as her body. Sleep claimed her between flexing the toes of her left foot and her right, plunging her into a cardboard garage filled with corpses.

Darkness still surrounded her when she woke with a start two hours later. Sitting bolt upright in bed, she gulped for air and pressed a hand against her chest. Her heart hammered fast enough to dim her vision into a series of bright spots and shadows.

Kit shoved the sheets aside and forced her wobbling legs to carry her to the bathroom. She snatched up the glass she kept by the sink and filled it, her fingers fumbling with the tap and letting the water overflow the rim. The glass banged against her teeth as she slurped the liquid, the coolness providing calm and solidity in her panic. A slight earthiness brought her back to reality with a bump. The UV filter connected to the rainwater tank needed maintenance. "More money," she breathed, resting her forehead against the mirror.

A knock on the bathroom door made her jump and she turned, still rubbing her head. "Yeah?" A switch clicked and light flooded her bedroom.

"Are you okay?" Jerry stepped into the small ensuite with a frown marring his features. His hair stuck up in peaks and troughs as though he'd slept on one side. A frayed tee shirt covered his torso, and ripped shorts completed his night-time ensemble. "I heard you crashing about."

Kit turned and leaned against the sink unit. She grabbed the hand towel and scrubbed excess water from her chin. "I dreamed about Debbie." Her voice wavered. Her fingers wound the towel into an elongated rope, which she twisted in front of her. "What time is it?" A yawn punctuated her question.

Jerry tilted his wrist and squinted at the hands of his wristwatch. "Three o'clock."

Kit groaned and pressed a hand over her heart. "That's so unfair! I had fantasies of snoozing in bed until midday."

Jerry ran a hand through his fringe and it snagged on the curls. He withdrew his fingers and stared at them. "Trauma affects sleep. I'm not surprised you dreamt of finding the victim." He tilted sideways and leaned against the door frame. He'd called Debbie a victim. Kit frowned and dropped her chin to her chest. It would have seemed impossible a week ago to imagine Debbie anything other than vitriolic or abrasive.

"Why are you awake?" Kit tilted her head and observed Jerry's growing discomfort as it spread a blush across cheeks already covered by bristly hair.

He shrugged and drew a line down the door frame with his index finger. "I couldn't sleep." Black eyelashes flickered as he considered his words. "I have some personal issues playing on my mind. It seemed easier to lie on the sofa in the lounge and watch television." Jerry inspected the paint work with more interest than it warranted and Kit took the hint. He couldn't or wouldn't talk to her about his issues. She imagined it pertained to the strange behaviour of the rubbish thief at the church.

"Want some company?" She inwardly acknowledged a reluctance to return to bed and invite Debbie's corpse back into her dreams.

Jerry nodded and offered her a smile. She followed him into the hallway, pausing to snag her bedspread from the floor where it had fallen. The stairs creaked as they descended and Jerry took the bulky fabric from her half way down when she almost tripped. He left her getting settled in the lounge and clattered around the kitchen, making hot drinks. Kit pushed the cushions up to one end and used her bedspread to cover the sofa. She clambered beneath it and squashed herself against the crease, turning onto her side to take up less room. When Jerry returned with two mugs of hot milk, she lifted a corner and invited him into her makeshift bed. "What are we watching?" She lifted her head to peer at the television and wrinkled her nose at the muted screen. "Anything but rugby."

Jerry used his shins to move the coffee table closer to the sofa before dumping the mugs onto its tiled surface. He scooted beneath the bedspread like a naughty child afraid of rebuke. His glance at the hallway door told Kit he feared Langdon's disapproval. She flattened her body to make space for his bulk, but it proved impossible for them to share the sofa without him putting his arm around her. Though he'd done it a hundred times, the action seemed to carry more emphasis than it should. Kit pursed her lips and spread her fingers beneath her cheek to create distance between her face and his chest. She sighed and focussed on the television as racing cars powered around a sunlit track somewhere else in the world. Jerry's muscles bunched beneath her fingers as he reached for his drink and sipped the hot milk.

"You okay?" He asked the question again, as though he hadn't believed her the first time. His voice rumbled through her fingers and vibrated into her ear.

"I think so." Kit nodded and her hair swished against his tee shirt. His chest rose and fell as he swallowed his drink. She closed her eyes and plugged into the sense of perpetual calm which Jerry exuded, envious of his ability to soothe the ragged souls of others. Her fingers traced the outline of his pectoral muscle to where it dipped in the centre of his chest. She tilted her head back and looked up at him, meeting his steady gaze with a blink. "Jerry," she whispered. "I think Cindy killed Debbie."

Chapter Twenty-Nine
Erroneous conclusion

"Tell me everything. From the start." Jerry balanced his cheek on his fist as Kit's ear pressed against his chest. He stared down at her, his expression unreadable.

Kit groaned. "Saying it out loud makes it more serious." Her voice became an irritating whine. "Just forget I mentioned it."

Jerry snorted. "Not gonna happen. Is this the same Cindy who let you take the fall for Mr Roy's death? The one who got you expelled from your group?"

"Yeah." Kit sat up and reached across him for her drink. She stuck out her tongue at the white skin wrinkling its opaque surface. Wasting time, she slid it across to the rim using her index finger. Jerry continued to stare at her, waiting to pick apart her ludicrous theory. Her shoulders slumped. "She didn't get me expelled. I just left and on reflection, my behaviour seems a little extreme." She bent her left leg in the small space and turned to face him. Jerry's hairy thigh prickled against her shin. "But I took my scissors to that meeting. When I came out of the bathroom, she'd claimed my seat. She had ample opportunity to steal my scissors from my open handbag and hide them until after I'd gone."

Jerry's eyes glazed as his quick mind worked through various scenarios. "But why kill Debbie? Didn't Debbie want her there either?"

He gave a grunt as Kit leaned across his stomach to lay her mug on the table. A sense of defeat shrouded her when she turned sideways and snuggled against his armpit. "I think Debbie invited her." She exhaled. "Debbie was the one person justifying her presence at the meeting. I suspect she asked her to come late to prepare the groundwork. She needed me to agree to cut hair at the Expo before upsetting me." The thought sat heavily in her head and Kit narrowed her eyes. "That makes no sense. Cindy cuts hair. She's more qualified than me." She tapped her front teeth with a fingernail. "Do you think perhaps they just wanted rid of me? If so, why manipulate me into cutting at all? They could have invited her to do the demonstration instead of me. I didn't want to do it, anyway."

Jerry frowned. "Then why are you doing it for a different chapter of the Women with Curls? Why not just lay low until it all blows over and then choose a group in your own time?"

"Does it sound as much like revenge to you as it does to me?" Kit poked out her bottom lip. "If there's one thing I've worked out already, it's that I don't like cutting hair under pressure. I think I've shot myself in the foot."

"I think you have." Jerry rested his chin on the top of her head. "And I aided and abetted you."

Kit yawned and closed her eyes against Jerry's chest. "You should say a Hail Mary when you get to work."

"I would." Jerry placed a kiss on her crown. "But I'm not a Catholic."

They slept for a couple of hours, squashed onto the sofa like a pretzel. The clatter of metal hitting the kitchen tiles woke them with a start, and Jerry pitched off the seat cushion backwards with a grunt.

"Sorry." Raki popped up from behind the counter. "Didn't mean to disturb you."

Jerry rolled onto his hands and knees on the floor and arched his spine like a cat. "Ugh," he groaned.

"This is new." Raki's eyes glittered as he waved a hand from Kit to Jerry. "I didn't guess a thing. Does Langdon know?"

"No." Kit sat up and rubbed her eyes. She pushed the bedspread away from her bare legs and rose, hauling her nightshirt over her thighs. "There's nothing for Langdon to know. I had a nightmare about Debbie's body and Jerry kept me company." She offered Jerry her hand and he took it, clambering upright like a pensioner.

Raki cocked his head. "Interesting. Is that like astral projection? Did Jerry enter your dreams to protect you against the corpse, or was it some other kind of shared experience?"

"Huh?" Kit leaned forward and cocked her head.

"Don't bother." Jerry bent to rub the blood back into his thighs and noticed the collection of cutlery in Raki's hand. "What are you doing with that?"

Raki scratched his head with a spoon. He still wore the same clothes from the previous day. Kit wrinkled her nose.

The pungent aroma of smoked noodle surrounding him suggested he had neither slept nor showered. "I'm taking a chemistry session for a group of school kids today." He waggled the cutlery. "I want to demonstrate the effect of sodium hypochlorite solution on stainless steel."

"You want to put bleach on our spoons?" Jerry snatched at Raki's fistful and missed. A teaspoon shot out of his hand, performed a backward somersault and landed in the sink with a clang.

Kit wrinkled her nose. "I'm more concerned that he wants to take them to a school and then bring them home again."

Raki and Jerry both turned to face her wearing identical expressions of confusion. "Why?" Jerry asked.

Kit shrugged and flapped her hand. Embarrassment flushed her neck. "You know, just kids." She jabbed her index finger at Raki. "Put them through the dishwasher when you bring them home. There are lots of bugs in schools."

"There are more bugs in shops." Raki shouted his helpful conclusion at the back of her head as Kit left the room. His mention of the shop reminded her of Mr Rashid. A dim light filtered through the fluffy cumulus clouds dotting the sky and she leaned her elbows on her bedroom windowsill and pressed her forehead against the glass. It seemed strange to watch the dawn breaking from home instead of catching sight of its striking colours through the shop window. A glance at the clock showed the time as just after six.

"So much for a lie in." Kit pressed her chin against her wrists and then shook her head. Her rumpled bed with its cold sheets offered no comfort. Staying at home and waiting for Lane to arrest her for Debbie's murder made the day seem oppressive and endless. She drifted to the bathroom and snatched up her toothbrush, jabbing it towards her reflection in the mirror. "You need to stop being a passenger," she told herself. "Sort out that haystack on your head, deal with Mr Rashid, apologise to Raj, fetch your car, and mend some fences with Piper." She sighed. "And if there's time after all that, find out who killed Debbie."

Chapter Thirty
Curly Conditioner

Kit arrived downstairs with her hair still damp. Raki smiled at her from behind a bowl of porridge. "Where are Jerry and Langdon?" she asked.

He shrugged. "Did you know oats are gluten free, but contain a substance called avenin which can activate gluten-reactive T cells?"

"No." Kit looked around the room for evidence of their presence. She wrinkled her nose at the absence of Langdon's jacket from the coat stand. "They already left?"

"Yep." Raki lifted a blob of porridge on the end of a fork. Kit closed her eyes and chose not to ask for explanations. A dull pounding at the back of her skull made her promise to run while she still had a working brain cell. He jabbed the fork towards a battered mobile phone sitting on the counter. "They left that for you. It's topped up with ten dollars' worth of credit. There's a pile of cash there too." He tapped the air with his fork. "You have to do something with your car. Jerry said you could pay him back later."

"Okay. Thanks." Kit stuffed it into her back pocket. She dug in the cutlery drawer and lifted a key from its hiding place beneath the tray. Each of the compartments held less implements than usual. Not a single spoon occupied the drawer. "I'm borrowing the spare house key." She waved it in Raki's direction as she closed the drawer. "Mine is still at the shop. I'm walking there now to fetch my car and then I'll run some errands."

"Key, shop, car, errands." Raki frowned at the blob on the end of his fork. "Errands." He savoured the word with more enthusiasm than his porridge.

Kit exhaled a sigh of exasperation. She snatched up the limp rucksack she'd used instead of her confiscated handbag the previous night and shook her head. A lip gloss, some hand sanitiser, and an emergency pump bottle containing lube jangled together in the bottom. Lane had taken everything; her handbag, purse and cash card, her phone, clothes and plimsolls. With a sigh, she dropped the rucksack next to the armchair and stuffed the spare key into her pocket with the cash and borrowed phone. "Damn you, Detective Lane," she hissed. She pushed her feet into a pair of old plimsolls hiding underneath Langdon's shoes in the rack and winced. The rugged innersoles were the reason for their consignment to the bottom in favour of her best and second-best pairs. Jerry had tried to wash the mud from her second-best pair, and they sat on the deck having taken on a gaudy orange hue.

Kit cursed Lane a dozen more times before reaching the end of her road. She avoided the grass verges and trudged along the edge of the gritty surface, stepping aside for passing cars. A reflective waterproof jacket covered her warm fleece and she sweated beneath their combined embrace. But the dawn walk cheered her and offered time to process the previous day's events. The rising sun dispatched the clouds to the south and promised a sight of the coming spring. Jackson's smouldering kiss in Debbie's garage heated her cheeks until another element crept into her thinking. She wondered if it formed little more than a distraction technique to stop her noticing something else. Or panicking. "A pity kiss!" Kit spat the words with disgust. Her enjoyment of the memory fizzled away, leaving bitterness in its place. It embarrassed her how she'd offered herself up like a flower to be trampled when he already had a girlfriend. "What a loser!" she hissed, not sure if she meant him or herself.

By the time she reached Mr Rashid's shop, she'd formulated a plan for getting some answers. She needed to stay off Senior Sergeant Jackson Delaney's radar. Forever. The only way to do that was to find out who killed Debbie. While many in the town might have possessed a motive, only a few had access to Kit's new matte black precision blades.

"Ah, you're here." Mr Rashid's head popped up from behind the counter as the bell jangled over the front door. "That tall bloke with the scary eyes said you weren't coming in today."

"Jerry." It offered Kit some comfort that Jerry had given Mr Rashid a taste of his own bullish behaviour. "Yes. A friend died yesterday, and I found her body." Kit flattened her lips into a line as she considered Debbie's role in her inner circle. Perhaps the label of friend pushed it too far.

"I'm sorry for your loss." Mr Rashid jammed an index finger into his left ear and twisted it round twice. After removing it with a pop, he waggled his head.

"Thank you." Kit waited for his punch line, almost disappointed when he just stared at her. "I came to fetch my car. I'll need it for the funeral." She frowned, not realising until she'd said the words that she entertained any thoughts of attending. "I'm not sure when it is yet."

"Okay." He blinked and still Kit waited.

"You're firing me, aren't you?" She glanced sideways at the neat display of baked bean tins she'd stacked at the end of the canned goods aisle. It had lost the point of its isosceles triangle since the day before and a sporting customer had played Jenga with three tins on the bottom row. A peculiar lightness spread up the back of her neck at the thought of never again having to make a food item look more appealing because it had reached its best before date.

"Nope." Mr Rashid steepled his fingers and tapped them together. He frowned. "Mrs Rashid likes you working here. It gives her more time to force me to do things upstairs."

Kit made a gagging noise at the back of her throat and closed her eyes. Images of a wrinkled Mr Rashid cavorting overhead in his Taj Mahal pyjamas burned itself onto the backs of her eyelids. "Right," she managed. "Thanks. Where are my car keys?"

"Upstairs in the hall." Mr Rashid tapped his top lip with his index finger and Kit set off towards the internal apartment door next to the counter. "The woman who died owed me money."

"Oh." She halted and turned to face him with a wince. "I'm not sure how you can deal with that. Perhaps you become a creditor against her estate. Have you told the police?"

"No!" His eyes bugged like boiled eggs in his brown face. "I didn't kill her!"

"I know." Kit took a step towards him. "And nor did I. But someone throttled her and then stuck a pair of scissors into her neck. If you know anything about that supply operation she ran from her garage, tell the police." She rested her hands over her hips and narrowed her eyes. "I thought you stopped dealing with her after the lube fiasco. You said you'd buy nothing from her again after that."

Mr Rashid's head performed a slow rocking motion on his neck as though activated remotely. "I know, I know." He exhaled in a rush. "But she offered to supply that special conditioner you buy. It retails at ten dollars a bottle and she could get it for a fraction of the price."

Kit's features scrunched into a mask of disbelief. "How do you know what conditioner I buy?" She spread her hands out either side of her.

"Your friend told me." He tilted his head back and stared at the ceiling. "It's in a blue bottle with a white pump lid." His black eyelashes beat a frenzied beat. "She said you would tell all your Curly people and they would shop in here." He wafted a hand around the store. "They'd come here for conditioner and then buy bread and milk and chocolate." He wrung his hands together in front of him and his tone took on a pleading whine. "She said the conditioner comes from Australia. And she promised me the customers could get hair advice from you."

Kit exhaled. She swallowed down the bitter realisation he'd intended to pimp her services for free. "It comes from

Australia. But it's made from plant materials and contains none of the usual chemicals. It's expensive to manufacture. I don't understand how she could get it so cheap. My mother ordered eight bottles last Christmas as a gift for me, and the company wouldn't give her a discount even for that many." Her eyes glazed as she remembered the products Debbie hauled from her bag during the committee meeting. Kit had recognised a few labels but not her favourite brand. "So, she took the money up front?" His slow nod sent a dart of fear snaking up the back of Kit's neck. "How much?"

Mr Rashid squirmed with obvious discomfort. He clutched at his heart and his eyes widened. "Don't tell my wife?" he begged. "She'll kill me."

Kit's shoulders slumped. "I won't but tell the police. Perhaps she did the same to other people and upset someone enough to make them kill her."

He scuttled beneath the counter flap and hurried to her side. His warm hands clasped her left wrist in a fluttering motion. "You can speak to that nice police officer who comes in here looking for you," he gushed. His head nodded as though of its own volition and a maniacal glint appeared in his eyes. "I gave her cash, so it would be easy to pretend that you paid her the money. That nice police officer will help you get it back and I won't have to tell Mrs Rashid that I did a stupid thing."

Chapter Thirty-One
Conditioner Custard

"Wait, what?" Kit swallowed and gaped at Mr Rashid. She shook her wrist free of his grip. "No! Absolutely not!" She turned away from him and walked towards the bean display. Anger burned in her chest, hot enough to incite her to give it a shove. Her fingers twitched and she veered around it, heading towards the toiletry aisle and the shelf of conditioner bottles.

"But you must!" Mr Rashid followed, wringing his hands in front of him. "Tell the police officer she owed you money."

"I can't believe you're asking me to do this." Kit spun on the spot and the worn soles of her old shoes obliged in a complete pirouette. She landed facing the back of the shop and had to edge herself the right way round to continue the conversation. The glazed look in Mr Rashid's eyes spared her his mockery. Guilt and fear consumed him.

Kit inspected the shelf of hair products, moving the bottles aside and taking stock of the brands. Her nose wrinkled and she saw nothing she'd put near her own curls. But someone had pushed two lone bottles of Curly Approved product to the back of the shelf. "Did she give you any of those?" She rapped out the demand and Mr Rashid gave a reluctant nod.

"That one and that one." He pointed to the pink and green bottles bearing a popular label among Curlies.

"Silicone and sulfate free." Kit read the claim placed around them in a bold banner. She lifted the green one down from the shelf and examined the price tag. "I didn't put these here."

"Mrs Rashid did it for me on Friday after you left for your awards ceremony." He gulped. "I'd sold most of them before the end of the weekend."

Kit tapped her fingernail against the bottle and frowned. "I don't remember selling any on Monday morning, but I left when Raj arrived. How much do they retail for in the supermarket?"

"A lot more than that." Pride entered Mr Rashid's tone before realising his eye for a bargain had landed him in a colossal mess.

"How many did you buy?"

"Twenty of each. Word went around that I had good quality conditioner at cheap prices." He punched the air with his fist. "Rashid's Superette takes care of your cents so the dollars can take care of you."

Kit exhaled in a rush. "Very nice." She sat the bottle of conditioner back on the shelf and withdrew her hand. "But I'm not lying to the police for you. I'm in enough trouble of my own for finding Debbie's body."

Mr Rashid bristled at her bland appraisal of his newest slogan. He returned to his role as hard-done-by employer to goad her into complying. "Raj is getting his van back tomorrow." His lips flattened into thin lines like railway tracks. "You got him an infringement notice for an expired warrant of fitness."

Kit snorted. "You're blaming me for him getting an infringement notice for not keeping his warrant up to date?" She frowned as the words left her lips at the memory of Jackson threatening her with one. "Damn. That's what I need to do next."

The bell jangled over the front door as a customer entered. Mr Rashid's eyes widened and he jiggled on the spot. Conflict produced frown lines on his forehead as he wavered between trying to convince Kit to perjure herself and protecting the cash register. But the customer spotted Kit and made a bee line for her.

"Hi, Danni." Kit's gaze coasted across the glossy ringlets bouncing around the other woman's face. "Wow. Your hair looks amazing."

"All thanks to you." Danni grinned and nodded to Mr Rashid. She turned back towards Kit. "I did what you suggested with the olive oil and it restored much of the condition. You were right. It needed moisture." She dug in her handbag and retrieved a bottle of conditioner. It matched the one Kit had just replaced on the shelf. "This is the stuff I bought. I haven't dared to use it again." She pushed it into Kit's hands. "I emailed the manufacturer and they've demanded the other three unopened bottles. They think the hairdresser damaged my hair, but I'm not so sure now. I think it was that stuff."

Kit frowned as she peered at the ingredients listed on the side of the bottle. She closed one eye and squinted to read the small print. "But I know this one is fine." She shook her head. "It makes no sense. Please, can I keep this and do some investigating of my own?"

"Yeah, sure." Danni lowered her chin and addressed Mr Rashid. "I bought them here on Saturday, but the company have offered me a refund. It's possible that my hair just doesn't like that brand."

Mr Rashid bristled like a hedgehog. He scurried back towards his cash register as another customer clanged the bell over the front door. Kit offered Danni a tired smile. "Your hair looks amazing. I'm relieved it worked out for you." She jerked her head towards Mr Rashid's retreating back. "I'm glad the manufacturer will give you a refund. He would make his own granny negotiate."

Danni grinned and followed her gaze. "Yeah. I got that impression. Oh, I almost forgot. I came here because I overheard someone saying you worked at this shop. This is for you." She pulled an envelope from her handbag and pushed it into Kit's hand. "Just a little something to say thank you. It's taken two months of hard work to get my hair looking half decent and one awful weekend put that in jeopardy. I know you didn't expect payment, but I needed you to know how much I appreciated your kindness."

Kit swallowed and stared down at the white envelope. The force with which Danni pushed it into her hand had bent it almost in half. "Thank you." She whispered the word, aware of a terrible weight landing on her shoulders and pressing her into the floor. "I don't deserve it." She blinked in surprise at the utterance, not aware of its existence before that moment. Danni patted her shoulder and hoisted her handbag over her forearm.

"You do deserve it. Right, must dash. I have a job interview in half an hour. Thanks for everything." She sailed away surrounded by a haze of floral perfume. The job interview explained her anxiety about her hair.

Kit stood in the aisle, staring at the envelope and too afraid to open it. Her words returned as an echo, a revelation of the fault at her core. She believed she didn't deserve payment for her hairdressing, placing no value on the skills she'd learned. Unless she changed her mind set and owned the natural talent recognised by the Queen of Curl, she would never succeed.

With a last glance at the shelf, Kit strode towards the front of the shop. She kept Danni's envelope and the bottle of conditioner in her hand. The door to the apartment opened after she entered the numbered code and she jogged up the stairs. Her car keys sat on a shelf above the Rashids' shoe rack.

"Hello, my darling. How are you after yesterday?" Mrs Rashid walked towards her, a smile on her face. A red sari wrapped her in a silken embrace, topped by a woolly cardigan. The carpet muffled her steps.

"Tired." Kit squeezed the bridge of her nose between finger and thumb. "I'm sorry about Raj's van getting seized and you having to work my shifts."

"It's never a problem." Mrs Rashid pulled Kit into an embrace and patted her shoulder. "You found your poor friend dead. Nothing is worse than that." She spotted the conditioner in Kit's hand and smiled with approval. "You're buying some of our new product? It's extremely popular. Mr

Rashid has big plans. He seems enthusiastic about curly hair all of a sudden." She clapped her hands together and laughed. "Your Curly antics must have rubbed off on him."

Kit corrected her smile from one of sarcastic tightness to a more genuine version. "Yes," she agreed. She lifted her car keys and dangled them in front of her. "I need to fetch my Bug."

Mrs Rashid nodded. "You're back on Thursday, aren't you? And then working this weekend."

"Yes." Kit's shoulders sagged. "See you then." She injected a fake brightness into her tone and clumped down the stairs to the shop. Everything in her nature rebelled. She didn't want to stand in a shop for nine hours a day, begging for bathroom breaks, making bean pyramids, and arguing with a cantankerous employer. An urge tugged at her, encouraging her to drive around in the sunshine, cutting hair and making another kind of difference to people's lives.

She burst through the apartment door with a spring in her step. The envelope in her hand galvanised her, offering courage and determination where she'd had none. It might contain a five dollar note or a fifty. Kit realised she didn't care which. It contained a hope for her future and she decided she'd take it.

Mr Rashid ducked beneath the counter and met her in front of the door. He resumed his attempts to make her lie to Jackson. "Help me." The hand wringing began in earnest, his knuckles just centimetres from her chest.

Kit tightened her jaw and faced him, anger bubbling beneath the surface. "I'm not doing it," she insisted. "And you can't make me. Ask me again and I'll quit."

Mr Rashid swallowed and his Adam's apple bobbed in his throat. "Oh, deary me," he murmured. "It's too late for that."

Kit narrowed her eyes and rested her hands over her hips. The envelope rumpled even more, and the conditioner bottle bumped against her waist. "What have you done?"

He squirmed on the spot, raking the shelves with his gaze to avoid looking at her. "I might have mentioned to your police officer friend that you paid for the supplies."

"You what?" Kit's whisper tailed off to a shout. She clapped a hand over her mouth and the envelope muffled her words. "How could you do that to me?" She backed away from him, nausea building in her stomach. In his effort to extricate himself from the frame, Mr Rashid had shoved Kit right into it.

Head first.

Chapter Thirty-Two
Curly Steps

"Don't leave in a rush." Mr Rashid tottered after her, his rubber soles squeaking against the tiles. For the first time in history, he ignored a customer waiting to make a purchase. An armful of junk food, a tube of sex lube and a dirty magazine tumbled onto the counter. Kit blinked and wondered who would eat the popcorn. Mr Rashid ran after her and tugged on her sleeve.

"Go away. I can't speak to you." She barrelled through the front door after fighting it open and stubbing her toe. She let it close behind her and Mr Rashid elbowed his way through the gap.

"I'm sorry." His shoulders deflated and he shot a cautionary glance at the upstairs windows of the apartment before lowering his voice. "I thought you wouldn't mind. You always help me out when I need you."

"Not this time." Tears of anger prickled behind Kit's eyelids. She ground her teeth together, causing her words to spit from her lips. "The police detective held me for six hours yesterday. He thinks I killed Debbie. You just gave him a motive."

Mr Rashid gasped and pressed a hand over his mouth. The whites of his eyes expanded and bulged in his olive face. "I'm so sorry!" He ran the fingers of his other hand through his shiny black hair. "It just sort of slipped out of my mouth last night." Rapid blinking accompanied his statement which betrayed the lie. "I think he likes you. He came here looking for you on many weekends while you were snipping hair."

"Whatever." Kit flapped a hand behind her and searched the gravel for her car. It took her a moment of shock to remember that Jerry had stowed it behind the shop. Avoiding Mr Rashid's twittering apologies, she stormed back through the front door and traversed the aisles before leaving via the rear. The customer at the counter watched with interest, his fingers already unwrapping the end of a Curly Wurly.

The rear door slammed behind Kit and she fought the urge to open and slam it enough times to dispel the fury building in her chest. She threw the conditioner bottle onto her passenger seat and stuffed Danni's envelope into her back pocket as she ran around the car. Her yellow Beetle started first time as though fearful of what might happen if it performed its usual coughing fit. She spun it in a tight arc and spat gravel at the metal rear door. The pebbles landed with a satisfying tinging sound and she wished Mr Rashid had shown enough courage to follow her and receive the painful gravel shower he deserved.

Her hand shook as she gripped the gear lever. She imagined Jerry's palpable anger when she explained what had happened, knowing he'd draw the same conclusion as she had. Mr Rashid resented Jerry's interference in his treatment of Kit and had exacted his revenge. She thumped the steering wheel and then apologised. "Sorry, Bug. It's not your fault." She suppressed a sniff of misery and headed straight for the vehicle testing station on the edge of Hamilton.

The harried receptionist slurped coffee from a stained mug while clicking on her keyboard. Kit tapped her foot while waiting for her to look up, hoping to beg for an early slot to avoid driving around without a warrant. The woman had scraped her muddy brown hair into a tight bun at the back of her head. Gel created a permanent wet look but the frizz at the edges had already risen in rebellion. Kit's fingers twitched with the urge to free the curls from repression, and she stuck them into her pockets and focussed her attention on a poster behind the desk. *It's an offence not to always carry your driving licence* it urged. Her chest tightened. The handbag and purse which Lane confiscated also contained her driving licence.

"I love your hair."

Kit shook herself free of the mental arithmetic required to add up her amassing fines. She curved her lips into an automatic smile and touched her red ringlets. "Thank you." The stock reply seemed all she could manage, but the receptionist knitted her brow and Kit tensed for the inevitable barrage of questions.

"How do you get it like that?" She lifted her fingers to her tight bun and winced. "I can't control mine."

Kit picked her reply with care from a list of possible answers. Sometimes, she took the trouble to explain the Women with Curls principles, depressed when the questioner's eyes glazed over and they lost interest after the first instruction. The explanation required effort and Kit weighed her energy pennies and decided she didn't have enough to spare. "It's called The Women with Curls Routine." She cocked her head and assessed the woman's interest before delivering any more. "We have a Facebook group you can join." The receptionist hunted for a pen and a scrap of paper, her eyes sparkling. Kit gave her the URL for the Hamilton chapter's page realising she didn't even know if Vanessa's group had social media. "It's a lot of work at the start," she advised, her tone stern. "But worth it."

The woman nodded and her gaze flicked to Kit's hair. "I want curls like that." She jabbed her pen towards Kit's head. "Can I get mine to do it?"

"Definitely." Kit's shoulders relaxed. Something about the woman's desperation struck a chord with her. She leaned her elbows on the counter. "Where there's a wave, there's always a curl," she promised.

A man waiting behind Kit gave a dramatic sigh of impatience and the receptionist ignored him. "My husband left me last year and I put on ten kilogrammes." She touched her bun again, self-care another casualty of a broken relationship. "I moved from a house with a rainwater tank to town water after the divorce. The chlorine turned my hair to frizz." Her eyelashes fluttered and she swallowed. "I'd love to do something positive for myself."

Kit took a deep breath and prepared to back her own dreams. "I just qualified as a Women with Curls hairdresser. I can give you a good rate on a consultation if you like?"

"What does that involve?" The receptionist leaned forward and her breasts pressed several keys on her keyboard.

The computer gave a worried bleep.

Kit read from a mental pamphlet in her head. Lilac edged paper shone from her imagination, gold scripted font displaying her service and costs. "I'll look at the condition of your hair and make suggestions. I can include a cut as part of an introductory package just for you and start you off on the WWC method." She pulled another idea fresh from her ass, one she hadn't even processed. "I'm setting up a monthly payment plan which will include a special Curly cut, advice, and my phone number on speed dial in case of any issues." Her words emerged in a rush and she stopped to deal with the knocking of her knees.

"A monthly payment plan?" The receptionist's azure irises sparkled with interest. "So, I can get regular cuts and spread the cost?"

"Yeah." Kit choked on the word, covering her nervousness with a cough.

"This isn't a hairdressing salon. Can you sign her up and have done with it?" The man behind growled his objection while inspecting his watch. "Some of us are in a hurry here!" He jabbed an index finger at his bald head. "Just shave it all off like me."

The receptionist rose from her chair and leaned her hands on the counter. "There's no need to be rude!" she snapped. "Try the other testing station in town. We don't have any slots left for today."

He released a groan of frustration and jerky steps took him to the door. He slammed it on his way out and stormed across the car park. Kit's shoulders slumped. "Is the other testing station still on Lincoln Road?" She glanced at her watch. "I'll try there too. My warrant ran out last week and I narrowly avoided an infringement notice. I was hoping to get a replacement driving licence and pay for my expired registration."

The receptionist's lips quirked into a grin. "You don't need to go anywhere else. Mike can take your car through now." She glanced around the empty reception with a nod of satisfaction. "And you can tell me more about this hairdressing business of yours."

Chapter Thirty-Three
Broken Curls

"I thought you wanted me to give you a ride to your car." Jerry's voice blared from the speaker to fill Kit's car. She winced and glanced sideways. A woman in the vehicle next to her at the traffic lights leaned forward to stare.

"Hang on." Kit grabbed the handle to close her window. The lights changed and the car behind her honked.

"What's all the grunting?" Jerry demanded. "What are you doing?"

Kit released the handbrake and scooted through the intersection just as the lights changed back to amber. She gave a wave of apology to the vehicle behind her now stuck at a red light. "This car doesn't have electric windows! You shouted so loud that half of Hamilton wanted to know why." She blew out a breath and reminded herself that Jerry was a friend and not an enemy. "Thank you for calling." She eyed the borrowed phone nestling in the cradle where hers usually sat. Her chest deflated. "I would have called you, but this phone has no numbers stored in it. I should learn yours and my mother's off by heart before Lane locks me up for good this time." Kit swallowed before telling Jerry of Mr Rashid's latest insult.

"He said what?" Jerry released a slew of expletives which told her Langdon must be out of earshot. "You need to speak to that cop. If he repeats Rashid's lie to Lane, then they'll come for you before the end of today."

"I know." Kit chewed her bottom lip and thought through her options. "But if I go looking for Jackson and try to deny what Mr Rashid told him, won't it look even more suspicious?"

"Maybe." Jerry no longer sounded sure. He exhaled. "I'm out of practise, Kit. We might need to bring my father in on this one."

Dollar signs rolled in front of Kit's eyes and she lost track of the mammoth cost of having an expensive defence barrister stepping in on her behalf. She sighed. "I can't afford him, Jerry. Mr Rashid just made it impossible for me to work for him again. I'm out of a job." Despite the fear ticking a warning in her chest, her lips curved into a shy smile. "Hey, guess what? I picked up a new customer today at the vehicle testing station. I'm giving her a cut and consultation tonight for fifty bucks. She's interested in taking out a monthly plan with me."

"Wow. That's fantastic." Jerry's tone changed to one of congratulations. "I knew you could do it."

"Thank you." Kit smiled at her reflection in the rear-view mirror. "I need to set myself up as self-employed with the tax office and work out if payment plans count as credit agreements. But it looks positive, doesn't it?" Pitting the negatives against the small win depleted her self-confidence.

The hurdles grew insurmountable in her mind's eye. "I'm doing the consultation tonight in case Lane locks me up tomorrow." All positivity left her voice. "Thank you for the loan. I got my car warranted and renewed my registration. The lady ordered my replacement driving licence for free. I'll pay you back, even if I have to wash saucepans in the prison kitchen."

"Over my dead body," Jerry growled. "We need to think of a way to prove you're not guilty." A voice echoed in the background, eerie and ghoulish in the deserted church. "Gotta go," he said. "Chin up, buttercup." A click heralded the end of the call and Kit ran a hand across her chin. She used the pause at the next set of traffic lights to Scrunch Out the Crunch on her curls, cracking the Cast created by the flaxseed gel and lube. Softer ringlets framed her face by the time she pulled up outside Piper's house.

Her hand shook as she lifted it to knock on the front door. A baby wailed from somewhere inside and Kit wrinkled her nose. Would she hold a vomiting child to earn Piper's forgiveness? "Hell yeah," she muttered under her breath. It seemed an age before the front door popped open. The woman standing in the gap glared at her.

"Oh, hi Pam." The wind in Kit's sails slowed to a feeble gust. "Is Piper here?"

Pam stood aside to let her pass, keeping her lips formed into a tight line. Kit hauled off her plimsolls and dumped them on the doormat. An innersole stuck to her left foot and she'd walked half way down the hallway before realising. She stopped to peel the cloth layer from the bottom of her bare foot and Pam walked into the back of her with a grunt of pain. "Sorry, sorry." Kit stuffed the innersole into her jeans pocket and straightened her shoulders.

Piper squatted on a dining chair with a pink plastic spoon in her fingers. Her daughter grizzled in a high chair, wearing most of her food. Kit gave them both a feckless wave and leaned against the kitchen counter. Pam's presence robbed her of all the things she'd wanted to say.

"I'm surprised you're showing your face here." Pam folded her arms and faced her. Blotches around her eyes showed where she'd cried.

Kit inhaled and tried to pick her words with care. "I didn't kill Debbie."

Piper turned in her seat and stared at her. She lifted her left hand and scratched at her crown. A faint frizz surrounded her head like a halo and Kit frowned. The baby snatched at the spoon and flicked a pale green mixture up the side of Piper's cheek. Then the child folded in half and licked crumbs from the tray attached to the high chair.

Pam released an exaggerated sigh. "I'm talking about your betrayal."

"My what?" Kit sifted the indictment without understanding. Piper's gaze slid to Pam and then back to her. She scratched the back of her head and gave an odd shiver.

"You set yourself up as the Curly Cutter for the Expo," Pam snarled. "For the Huntly chapter of WWC."

Piper released a groan as though hearing the news for the first time. "Oh, Kit," she sighed. "Why would you do that?" Her nails raked the curls above her left ear.

Kit stared at her bare feet and considered the answer. "I don't know." Flecks of red polish dotted her toenails, placed there months ago when she still had time for niceties. The borrowed mobile phone dug into her bottom from its position in her back pocket, reminding her of her predicament. She shrugged. "Jerry put me in touch with their group and when I got there, they'd already decided I'd do it." She spread out her hands either side of her. "You had Cindy. You didn't need me."

The accusation in Pam's eyes condemned her actions as childish. She shook her head and disdain dripped from her tone. "We've known you for years. I thought we could at least discuss it." Her voice rose and Kit's gaze tracked to Piper.

"Piper told me Cindy stepped in to help when I walked out the other night. I assumed you didn't need me."

Pam glared in Piper's direction. "We wanted both of you. Debbie thought we could take out the ultimate challenge if we had two people cutting."

"Right." An uncharacteristic hardness sealed Kit's heart. "So, having her there was always the plan. Not that she stepped in just to cover my overreaction." Kit stared at Piper with disappointment in her eyes. "I agreed to the Huntly chapter's request because I believed you didn't want me." She shrugged. "Miscommunication."

Piper scraped the green gunk from the inside of the bowl and pushed a dollop between the baby's lips. Kit looked away as it popped straight back out again with an added coating of saliva. The frosty atmosphere jangled her nerves and created such a stark contrast to Vanessa's all-inclusive vibe. She stood up straight and walked towards the kitchen door. "Thanks for everything." The words sounded final, and sadness tinged every vowel. She paused in the doorway and addressed both women. "By the way, where were you both around eleven o'clock yesterday morning?"

"What?" Piper gaped and her momentary confusion led to her daughter head banging the spoon. Her tiny lips opened and closed like a fish out of water.

"Where were you?" Kit rested her hands on her hips, trying to appear intimidating.

Pam let out a breath filled with venom. "At work!" She snarled the words, communicating her disgust.

"I took the baby to a mother and toddler group." Piper's bottom lip wobbled.

Kit's determination wilted. Her matte black precision scissors had cut more than just Debbie, they'd severed the best friendship she'd ever had. She gave a sniff and shrugged. "Well, someone stuck my scissors in Debbie's neck. Considering I haven't seen them since Saturday night's meeting, I'm guessing the detective will visit you both soon." She jerked her head in Piper's direction. "I can recommend tea-tree oil for nits."

Kit left them wide eyed and floundering. She let herself through the front door and pushed her right foot into its plimsoll. The cloth inner from the left shoe refused to go back into place and she abandoned it in Piper's dustbin. The inside of the plimsoll felt less uncomfortable without it. She dropped to one knee to tie her laces and her gaze fell onto Piper's doormat. Pam's sensible sandals sat to one side and their presence jarred a memory in Kit's brain. Her next stop was the police station.

Chapter Thirty-Four

Coffee and Curls

"How can I help you, Miss Maguire?" Boredom infused Lane's tone and he rubbed nicotine-stained fingers along his jaw. He glanced at his watch. The yawn he released told Kit to hurry.

She leaned back against the plastic chair and inhaled a fortifying breath. "When I arrived at Debbie's house, I saw two pairs of flip-flops on her front door mat."

Lane peered back at his notes and gave a slow nod. "Yes, you said. Where are you going with this, Miss Maguire? I have a murder to solve." He puffed out his chest and lifted his chin, exhaustion marring the attempt at importance.

Kit closed her eyes and imagined the scene as Jackson led her from the garage. They'd turned right and headed through the open front door to the waiting police car. Someone had wedged the door open and the spring from Debbie's husband's ingenious closing device hung limp like a broken wing from the architrave. "I told you there were two pairs, but when I left, we stepped over one. The other pair had gone." She opened her eyes and studied Lane's reaction. "I believe your killer has enormous feet and wears a pair of blue rubber flip-flops."

A sneer spread across Lane's thin features. It caused his nose to protrude from his face like a craggy rock. He threw his pen onto his notebook and leaned back in his chair until it pivoted on two legs. "How convenient." He raised one eyebrow. "How can I believe you when this is the first time you've mentioned it?" His front two chair legs thudded down onto the tiles.

Kit swallowed. "My lawyer made me lay on the couch and he did this thing to me." She twirled her finger next to her left temple. "He said it would help me remember."

Lane's eyes bugged in his face. His cheeks pinked with a flush which spread from the collar of his shirt. "I bet he did! But what you do with your lawyer in private is nothing to do with this investigation."

"But it is." Kit leaned forward and rested her elbows on the table between them. "It helped me remember what I saw. I heard the killer in the garage when I arrived. I bet you found no signs of forced entry. That's because Debbie knew them and she let them into the house. They drank coffee, then went into the garage with her and killed her there." She folded her arms and leaned back in her chair. "The question is why."

A grin spread across Lane's face and he lifted his hands. The slow clap echoed around the bare walls. "Wonderful, Miss Maguire. We discovered you at the scene of the crime and your scissors protruding from the victim's neck. You failed to call for the emergency services, offering some weak story about liking Senior Sergeant Delaney's bedside manner, and here you are with more information you forgot to mention." He used the index and middle fingers of both hands to draw air quotes.

Kit exhaled. "It's the truth." She stared down at her fingers. "We know the scissors didn't kill her. I don't think I could get my hands around Debbie's neck, not that I didn't sometimes want to."

Lane shot forward and his eyes narrowed. "I have told no one how she died." The staccato beat of his words acted as a knife blade in Kit's chest.

She floundered, her speech faltering as she dug a bigger hole and jumped in feet first. "But my lawyer said someone strangled her. He told me last night."

"Well, that's very interesting because I didn't tell him." Lane's jaw worked in his cheek, the stubble rising and falling like the spines of an agitated hedgehog. "I know your lawyer has connections, so I'll tell you this for free. The second coffee belonged to her husband. He said he only drank half a cup and that's what we found."

Kit rose on unsteady feet. "I just came to tell you about the flip-flops." She stuffed the borrowed phone into her back pocket and straightened her jacket. "He also said you found no evidence of blood on any of my clothes or property. I'd like them back now."

Lane's face creased as though he'd sucked on a lemon. He rose to face her. "The laboratory wants to run a few more tests on your belongings. I'll contact you if I'm prepared to release them."

As Kit's choices diminished, she made a dash for freedom and the unlocked door of the interview room. Lane didn't stop her, but she sensed his gaze burning into the back of her head as she exited. She stumbled through the police station, following the signs towards the exit. Closed doors covered each side of the corridor, interview rooms marked with a number and a digital sign displaying whether they were in use. Kit glanced behind her, wanting to see if Lane had turned off the sign over his door. She imagined the wording changing from 'in use' to 'guilty' and increased her pace.

Stretching out her arms, she pressed on the double doors ahead of her. Empty space greeted her palms and she stumbled forward, her face still pointing backwards in the direction she'd come from. Hot liquid doused her, accompanied by the powerful scent of coffee. It soaked through her jacket and shirt, burning as it hit her chest and neck.

"Oh geez!" a female voice shouted. Smashing crockery added to the chaos.

Kit gasped and pinched her shirt between her fingers, hauling it away from her burning skin. "Sorry," she hissed. Pain blossomed outward from every place the liquid touched. She stepped back and recognised the police officer who'd walked her to the bathroom. The woman's face scrunched in anger, brown coffee stains saturating her light blue uniform shirt. Biscuits swam in the puddle from the mug which hadn't fallen in the collision.

"Why don't you watch where you're going?" The officer's eyes narrowed and she cocked her head as though trying to remember where she'd seen Kit.

Eager to avoid talking to Jackson's love interest, Kit squatted and collected up the broken pieces of crockery. A shard cut her index finger and blood smeared across the handle she placed on the tray. "I'm very sorry," she repeated.

Embarrassment flushed her cheeks a vibrant red. Abandoning the soaked carpet and angry police officer, she pushed her way through the double doors and headed for the street.

"Kit!" A male voice shouted from behind her and her heart quailed. "Are you okay?" The concern in Jackson's tone paled against Kit's fear of his conclusion about Mr Rashid's lie. She picked up her pace, running through the front doors and tangling with two men trying to enter. Her heaving breaths cut across her apology and she ignored their stunned expressions, bolting to her car and performing a loud but perfect getaway.

Chapter Thirty-Five
Dead Ends

"I know you killed Debbie." Kit stood in front of Cindy and fixed her shaking hands over her hips.

"What?" Cindy's face creased into a frown and she lifted her left hand to touch her ringlets. "Why are you here?"

"Why am I here?" Kit raised her voice and repeated the question, not yet sure of the answer. She'd driven away from the police station after leaving rubber marks on the road and spotted Alec Roy's expensive Porsche heading north. For reasons not known even to herself, she'd followed 1ROY to the intersection with Pukete and then continued onto Wairere Drive. He'd led her to his new girlfriend without realising.

Alec appeared in the doorway behind Cindy. His face creased into a wide grin when he saw Kit standing on the garden path. His gaze drank in her dishevelled curls and the brown stain covering her white shirt and grey jacket. "What happened to you?" He stepped past Cindy and teetered on the edge of the threshold. "Come in. I'll lend you something else to wear."

"No, you won't!" Cindy whirled to face him. "Didn't you hear what she just accused me of doing?" Her voice rose to an unattractive screech.

Alec winced and jerked his head back on his neck. "No, I didn't. But Kit is an old friend and this is my house."

Kit's shoulders slumped. The fire of desire still burned in Alec Roy's eyes, undiminished by Cindy's manicured fingers winding around his wrist. She regretted following his car, not sure when she lined up her reasons that any of them made sense. "I'm fine." She waved a hand over her tee shirt as though to dismiss the stain. Lifting her index finger, she jabbed it in Cindy's direction. "But the cops are interested in your girlfriend. She gate crashed our WWC meeting, sat next to my open handbag and now, my brand-new scissors are missing. The cops found them sticking out of Debbie's corpse." Her hand shook as she dropped it to her side, but she saw the speculative glare radiating from Cindy's blue irises. Kit tipped her head for emphasis. "You have massive feet, Cindy," she mused. The other woman's stilettos shuffled against the carpeted hall as she placed the toe of one foot behind her heel. "And just for the record, I never touched the scissors. They won't find my fingerprints on anything but the velvet case." Kit jerked her head at Cindy. "Will they find yours?"

Cindy gave an involuntary swallow and Kit's eyes sparkled as awkwardness shrouded her opponent for long enough to indicate guilt. Victory burst in Kit's chest like a fanfare. "You did!" She shook her head from side to side. "You took the scissors!"

"No, no." Cindy stepped onto the path. "I didn't. The navy pocket looked familiar and I lifted it out and opened it just to see what brand you received." She pursed her lips and chewed the back-handed compliment before airing it. "Only the winners get the expensive ones now. I got some other ones when I finished my course." She flapped her hands. "But I put your scissors straight back where I found them. They were in your bag when you left Pam's house."

"Well, they're not now!" Kit shouted. She punched the air as though driving a blade into something hard. The tiny cut on her finger smarted. "They're in Debbie's neck!"

Alec Roy's healthy glow faded to a sickening grey. He edged past Cindy to approach Kit, holding his hands out before him. "Come inside, Katharine. Let's talk about this over a coffee." His gaze flicked to something behind her.

"No!" Kit backed away from him, aware of the audience gathering in her peripheral vision. A poodle squatted on a verge across the road, its owner transfixed by the drama outside Alec's house. The neighbour opposite stopped his electric hedge trimmer to watch. The suburban street boasted a low crime rate and lavish, two storey homes. Raised voices provided an exciting interlude from affluence and a taster of the kind of behaviour that went on across the river. The poodle owner nodded to the man brandishing his silent hedge trimmer as though to highlight their unanimity against the likes of Kit. She didn't fit in there and the realisation hacked at the edges of her confidence. "Ask her what she did yesterday around eleven o'clock." Kit's hands shook as she stuffed them into her jeans pockets. "Go on, ask her."

"I don't need to put up with this rubbish!" Indignation filled Cindy's tone and she bristled like a hedgehog. Marching across the grass to an expensive SUV sitting on the driveway, she deactivated the central locking and opened the door. The familiar branding of Roy's Garage wrapped around the bodywork.

"Aw, Cindy!" Alec's feet shuffled against the path but he didn't stop her. The engine fired and Kit held her breath as Cindy reversed the car off the driveway at speed, just missing the rear bumper of Kit's yellow Bug. She tore off up the road while connecting her seatbelt, the SUV veering across the centre line. Hedge-man and Poodle-lady continued to stare. The hedge trimmer lay on the pavement and the man had his phone in his hand.

"Come inside, Katharine." Resignation filtered through Alec's voice and defeat rounded his shoulders. He lifted his hand and waved to his neighbours, his expression impassive. Poodle-lady turned aside to chat with Hedge-man, and they conferred in lowered tones. The poodle continued squatting, its nose creased in a look of permanent disgust. Nothing emerged from between its straining buttocks.

Alec stiffened as the purr of a heavy engine drew up behind Kit. She half turned her head to see the chevrons of a police vehicle. "Oh, great!" she hissed.

"Just get inside the house!" Alec strode the three paces to her side and spun on the spot, slipping his arm around her shoulders. His forearm edged her up the path and over the threshold. Kit paused, hopping on one leg to remove her plimsolls but Alec drove her into a wide lobby and slammed the front door behind him. "Leave them on," he barked. "The floors are all wooden." He directed Kit to a kitchen on her left which faced the street. Venetian blinds showed a filtered view of the street and Jackson climbing from his patrol car. He slipped a police issue baseball cap over his hair and jabbed a finger at the poodle. Kit covered her mouth with her hand to prevent the nervous laughter as he reprimanded Poodle-lady for the sausage shaped dollop on the verge.

"Should I tell him he got the wrong dog?" A snort accompanied her sentence.

"No!" Alec growled. He clattered behind the counter, setting up a coffee machine and mugs. The activity involved every appliance in the fancy kitchen as he moved from the fridge to the dishwasher and back to the coffee machine. "It serves her right," he added. "Nosey woman."

Kit exhaled and watched Alec's neighbours waving their arms at the house. Jackson pulled out his notebook and turned towards Kit's car. In a moment of defiance, she hauled on the string and snapped the blinds closed. "I should leave." She shouted over the sound of Alec steaming milk with a wand attached to the machine.

He jerked his head towards a dining table with eight chairs placed around it. "Sit!" Two minutes later, he placed a perfect latte in front of her. He'd even drawn a wonky heart in chocolate powder in the froth. Kit grabbed the spoon he set next to it and scrubbed out the heart, not keen for another showdown with Cindy when she returned. She wouldn't go far, not wanting to risk leaving Kit alone in Alec's company.

"Now, tell me what happened." Alec slumped into the chair next to her and lifted a mug to his lips. White froth covered his top lip, no chocolate heart mingling with the milk. Kit lifted her mug and gave a quick slurp to hide the devastation of his design.

"Someone slopped coffee over me." She looked down at her shirt and groaned. "Do you think bleach will get rid of the stain?" She scratched at the dried coffee with her fingernail."

"I don't know." Alec pursed his lips. "My mother knows all that stuff." He studied Kit through narrowed eyes as though daring her to enquire after his mother's health. She didn't, slamming her teeth shut against the memories. His shoulders relaxed. "I meant what happened with us?"

Kit groaned and threw herself back in her chair. "I'm not going there, Alec! That's not why I'm here." She cast her gaze around the room, noticing Cindy's feminine touches dotted around the bachelor pad uniform of black and grey. Blue hyacinths stood like soldiers in a vase at the end of the kitchen counter and a furry mustard blanket hugged the sofa arm. She forced herself to look at Alec. "So, you and Cindy got together. I didn't think you'd want Paul's cast offs."

Alec frowned, thin lines crossing his proud forehead. "She threw herself at me." He offered no further explanation and Kit resented the flicker of sympathy which intruded into her thoughts. She'd never believed herself good enough for Alec Roy and his exploitation of Cindy's affection disturbed her. Cindy wasn't good enough for anything more than a stop gap either. They had more in common than they realised.

"She touched the scissors that ended up in Debbie's neck." Kit sipped the hot coffee, eager to have no more reason to stay in Alec's company. He oozed masculinity and sex appeal and it frightened her she might succumb to his charms like a desperate spinster. Only the certainty of regret in the afterglow kept her at arm's length from him. "Do you know what she did yesterday around the time Debbie died?"

Alec placed his mug on the table after pulling a coaster across the shiny surface. His fingers played with the hard edges. "She met me at the garage and stayed to fix an issue we had with the workshop computer. It took her most of the morning." He wrinkled his nose. "She didn't want to go back to working with computers, but I'm persuasive." His irises glittered like diamonds. "The usual company put us off until the afternoon. You know what it's like there." He looked up and his eyelashes fluttered. Kit remembered his devious brand of manipulative persuasion. "The mechanics couldn't update the jobs on the system. It caused chaos in the office with the invoicing." His eyes narrowed. "You should come back to work for me. Everyone misses you."

Kit drank the rest of her coffee so fast, it burned the back of her throat. "I'm good, thanks." She rose and offered Alec a lacklustre smile. "Thank you for the coffee. The cops will come for Cindy so at least you can give her an alibi. It's great that she'll get something from this relationship."

The front door shook with the force of the knuckles rapping against the glass. Alec jumped and slopped coffee over his expensive shirt sleeve. Kit strode towards the lobby and called over her shoulder, "That will be them now. I'll let them in."

Chapter Thirty-Six
The Curly Choir Girl

Jackson stood on the front doormat with his notebook still in his left hand after issuing Poodle-lady with an unfair warning for her constipated pooch. He raised his right eyebrow as Kit threw open the door. She beat him to the punch, lifting a hand to silence him. "Let me guess. Poodle-lady and Hedge-man called in a disturbance in suburbia. As you can see, there's nothing exciting happening." Kit jerked her head towards the lobby. "Alec is inside waiting to see you. His coffee is terrible." She breezed past him and didn't give him time to respond before jogging to her car and unlocking the door. Hedge-man had returned to butchering his camelia and a brown smear remained where Poodle-lady had collected the anonymous poop. Kit patted the Bug's steering wheel as the engine turned over first time. "I don't deserve your loyalty," she crooned and pulled away from Alec's street.

Jerry called again as she turned onto her mother's road. Kit answered and his lyrical tenor boomed throughout the car.

"Where are you?"

Kit blew out a breath and looked around her. "I just got to Mum's house. I thought I'd break the news to her about the scissors. Lane will start looking for whoever owns those fingerprints and I need to make sure she has an alibi for the time of Debbie's death. He'll find Cindy's too, but I don't care what happens to her." She crossed her fingers in her lap after pulling on the hand brake. "Kenny has a job now, so I'm hoping Mum went to one of her Bitch and Stitch groups. I'm not in the right frame of mind for a confession."

Jerry made a sound like a humph. He cleared his throat. "I spoke to my father and asked his advice. He doesn't think you need a barrister yet. For now, he advised that we just sit tight and do nothing to draw the cops' attention. Stay home, behave and wait."

Kit stared at the Bug's ceiling and exhaled. "I can't stay home, Jerry." She remembered the unopened envelope in her pocket. "Danni came to find me. She gave me an envelope with cash for cutting her hair."

"Nice. How much?"

"I don't know. Maybe you could open it for me." Kit gnawed on her lower lip. "I'm scared to see my worth in dollars."

Jerry grunted. A click in the background muffled his voice. "Actually, I need a favour. Langdon booked me to speak at a school assembly at twenty past eleven. I need a helper."

Kit made gagging noises and shook her head from side to side. "That sounds like the fourth level of Hell."

Jerry lowered his voice to a whisper. "Please. I'm desperate. The little rug rats terrify me. I need a rear-guard."

Kit stared at Marian's empty driveway and groaned. "Mum isn't here and I do kinda owe you for all your unofficial legal help." She gnawed on the edge of her thumbnail before dropping it into her lap. "Okay. I'll meet you there. But I spilled coffee on my shirt. Please can you find something to cover it."

"Yep." A whoosh of relief burst into Kit's ear. "I'll just knock off this wedding and meet you in the vestry."

Kit closed her eyes and pictured the primary school right next to Langdon's church. "Okay. We can walk there. The fresh air might take my mind off things. Like a cold shower but without getting wet." She exhaled. "Wedding." Kit repeated the word as her mind flicked back to Alec Roy's handsome profile. She likened the sense of dismay to picking the scab from a healed mosquito bite. "Tell me about the wedding." She leaned her head back against the head rest and closed her eyes.

Jerry sighed. "It's difficult to describe. I'm hiding in the vestry because the groom's mother already pinched my bottom through my cassock. Now I know why Langdon handed it off to me with such enthusiasm."

"Vicar abuse. Wow. I didn't know it was a thing." Kit frowned at her reflection in the rear-view mirror. "I look like a harpy, otherwise I'd offer to stop by and protect you. It might do more damage to your reputation if I came out swinging."

Jerry grunted. "Vicar abuse is a thing. Langdon calls it cleric fondling." A knock echoed in the background of the call and Kit stared at her mother's front door.

"You need to go now. But just before you do, I've discovered that Piper, Pam and Cindy all had alibis for

Debbie's death."

"I hope you're not investigating!" Jerry's whispered hiss made Kit jump and press the volume control button on her speaker.

"I thought you were hiding in the vestry. Why are you whispering?"

"I'm in the cupboard." Jerry's voice strained as he attempted to stop its characteristic boom. "Gotta go." The call ended and silence enveloped the car.

Kit looked down at her shirt before starting the engine. The dashboard clock showed she didn't have enough time to get home and change. She hoped Jerry didn't raid the second-hand stash again or she might look even worse. It amazed her how he could perform a full wedding in the time it would take her to drive across the city.

The bride and groom emerged onto the front steps of the church as Kit dumped her Bug in the car park. Jerry posed for a photo with the family, a pained expression on his face. A woman with purple hair clung to his left arm, pink spectacles balanced on the end of her nose. When Jerry jumped sideways to avoid her obvious manhandling, the blushing bride almost fell off the steps. Her new husband performed a rough but well-intentioned rescue, and her veil fluttered away on the breeze. It took an essential hairclip with it and her updo collapsed, cascading her hair around her face like a disintegrating umbrella. Kit pressed herself against the Bug as a wail of fury sent non-essential members of the happy family scattering.

Jerry disappeared and emerged from a fire escape, clattering down the metal stairs to the car park. He patted his dishevelled curls with gentle palms. "Why do middle aged women think it's acceptable to sexualise males?" The first words from his mouth accompanied a lot of spit. Kit stepped away from him and wrinkled her nose.

"What are you eating?"

"Mint." Jerry fumbled beneath the white surplice covering his black cassock. He withdrew a tube of mints from a hidden pocket. "Want one?"

"No thanks." Kit frowned and did the mental arithmetic of sugar to carbs ratio. "And nor should you."

Jerry shrugged. His eyebrows knitted into a line at the sight of her shirt. "Ah yeah, I have an idea about that." He jerked his head towards the fire escape and waggled his hand to indicate she should follow him up the stairs.

The church echoed with the voices of the departing wedding guests as Kit arrived on an upstairs landing. Jerry closed the fire escape and pressed his index finger to his lips. A balcony ran along the nave and she peeked over it to see a frocked verger closing the main doors. He leaned against them and ran a hand across his forehead. Kit pulled her head back before he could glance up and notice her scurrying after Jerry. She trotted along a corridor flanked by rooms, panicking as he took a sharp left and descended another set of stairs. Toys and books lay on the carpet of one room and biscuit crumbs trailed towards the door. Kit hurried enough to see Jerry disappear around the curve of a spiral staircase.

"Wait!" Her voice echoed around her as a hiss as she ran straight into Jerry's bulk.

"Ouch!" he complained. "I did!"

Kit gripped her ribs and followed him to a heavy wooden door, holding her breath as he pushed it open and vanished. Tentative steps took her over the threshold and into an office. Jerry closed the door behind her. The life of Jesus played out on the walls surrounding a pair of impressive wooden desks. Angels heralded his baby form before the images fast forwarded to a man handing out bread and then preaching to a group of seated children. Kit gulped at the bloody wreckage of a man hanging from a cross behind the desks. She wrinkled her nose. "I can see why you keep that one behind you." She lifted her index finger and pointed at the bloody Jesus.

Jerry hauled open a wooden cupboard door and metal coat hangers jangled against his hand. He glanced back at the image of the crucified Christ and a gentle serenity settled over his olive features. "I often turn the chair around to face it," he admitted. "It helps me think."

Kit closed one eye and examined the blood spilled onto a dusty floor in the painting. Poor Jesus looked like he'd been for a Saturday night drink at the Fairfield Arms. "At least he still has his halo," she whispered. "I bet that would sell for a few dollars on Trade Me."

"Got it!" Jerry jiggled in the cupboard, appearing to joust with the coat hangers. He gave a hefty yank and a white dress slithered into his arms. "Slip this over your clothes."

"No!" Kit backed towards the door. "I don't want to be the Virgin Mary."

Jerry snorted. "Bit late for that. This is a choir tunic." He frowned at the neck of her shirt. "Remove your jacket and shirt but keep your jeans on underneath the tunic." He glanced down at her third-best plimsolls and wrinkled his nose. "They'll have to do for now."

Kit pressed a hand to the top of her head where the day's stresses had caused frizz to rise. Mr Rashid's bombshell, a coffee shower, a fight with Cindy and an escape from Alec and Jackson had tested the limits of her hair skills. "Is there a hat to go with that?"

Jerry frowned and shook his head. "No, but I read an online article that said you can refresh by misting water from a plant sprayer." He cocked his head and twisted his lips as he thought. "Put the tunic on and I'll see if I can find one. Mrs Abernathy mists the flowers with a pink bottle. I'll find it." He examined his watch. "We need to get to the school. The children go straight from morning tea to assembly."

He left to retrieve the bottle and Kit peeled off her coffee-stained clothing. She slipped the tunic over her head and the heavy robe settled on her shoulders. A pink lipstick stain on the right cuff made her recoil and she lifted the hem to wriggle back out of it. Jerry's muffled voice sounded to the right of the door. "What are you doing?" Agitation laced his tone.

Kit popped back through the ruffled neck and scowled at him. "This is dirty!" she protested. "It's got lipstick on the sleeve."

"Oh, it's Melinda's." Jerry dropped his chin in a definitive nod. "She started singing in the choir last week, so Langdon lent her the spare tunic. Choir members don't get their own until he's sure they're serious." He leaned sideways to close the cupboard door, but a box stopped it shutting. He tutted and shifted the cardboard further inside, wincing as glass tinkled.

"Is that your secret stash of gin?" Kit sniffed the sleeve again and flattened her lips.

"No. It's the empty bottles from communion. I'm hiding them from the thief."

Kit rose onto her tip toes to watch him shuffle the box to the back of the deep wooden cupboard. Brown bottles rocked together like excited football fans. A waft of perfume drifted into her nostrils. "This is Melinda's?" She pressed her hands over where she thought her hips might be hiding and narrowed her eyes. "Is there anything Melinda hasn't got involved with at church?"

"No." Jerry's curls moved on his head and his guileless smile produced a wave of protectiveness in Kit's icy heart. "She's trying everything."

Kit straightened the tunic on her breasts and smoothed her palms over her thighs. "She certainly is," she murmured.

"I found this, anyway." Jerry strode across the carpet bearing a metallic pink bottle with a pump nozzle at the end. "I filled it with warm water." He flapped his other hand at Kit's head. "I think it's called spritzing."

"I know what to do with it." Kit grabbed it and squeezed the handle, sending a few puffs of mist into the air. She leaned forward and sniffed. "Are you sure it's just water?"

"Positive." Jerry examined his watch. His robes rustled as he spun across the room and grabbed a cardboard box from the desk. "Let's go."

Kit lifted the bottle and doused her head. She used the mirror on the back of the door to separate her ringlets from the frizz and tease them into something presentable. The water activated the conditioner, lube and flaxseed gel in her hair and eased the process. With the frizz eliminated, Kit heaved a sigh of relief. She turned to Jerry with a smile. "Let's go Vicar." She punched the air with her fist. Her face fell as she remembered the task before her and realised Jerry hadn't yet told her what he expected her to do.

Chapter Thirty-Seven
Curly Creativeness

The choir tunic flapped around Kit's shins as she tried to keep up with Jerry. He strode through the school gate after acknowledging a woman strolling around with children clinging to her hands and her skirt. His long stride carried him across the playground before Kit had taken decent stock of her surroundings. Children milled everywhere, eating, gesticulating and screeching about an invisible disaster. A group of miniature people jogged in a circle for no particular reason. Three children clopped past on imaginary horses and a chunky girl neighed at her.

Kit's confidence shriveled in her chest as many turned in her direction, pointing and whispering behind their hands. She spun and pressed her finger against the gate latch. Jerry liked food. She could pay off her substantial debt by cooking for him. Her finger froze on the cool metal. She hated cooking, but not with as much ferocity as she hated bogey wielding midgets.

Strong fingers closed around her wrist. "Oh, no you don't!" Jerry tugged her around to face their growing congregation and jerked his head towards the school's main door. "You owe me, remember?"

"Haircuts and free styling advice." Kit sent her weight into her feet and braced her plimsolls against the pavement. "I don't like kids and they don't like me."

"Same." Jerry's angular features softened. "I find it's easier to get in and get out. Like a SWAT raid."

Kit gulped. "I've never been on a SWAT raid. Will I get hurt?" Her gag reflex activated. "I can't do vomit, pee or poo."

"We shouldn't see any of that. They seemed quite civilised when I visited with Langdon. I saw one pee, but it was accidental. Just don't let anyone sit on your knee and you'll survive." He tugged Kit's wrist and his bulk outweighed her resistance. Her hips bent and her torso shot forward before she unglued her feet from the floor.

"Is she being naughty?" A boy stood by the path with chocolate around his mouth. He lifted a brown stained index finger and pointed it at her choir surplice. "Is she an angel?" His eyes widened. "Is she an evil angel? Oh, no! She's a devil." He clamped his jaws in a grimace, and a strange palsy gripped his body. Sticky brown fingers balled into fists. By the time his mouth opened again in a scream, other children surrounded him and Kit and Jerry had made it to the reception desk.

"Hello, Vicar." The lady behind the counter regaled them with a sunny smile. "Here for your assembly?" Kit rose on tiptoes to see her. The desk and the woman seemed much lower behind the counter than she'd expected. Poker straight blonde tresses pointed in ironed spikes towards the floor, remaining static despite the breeze from the open door.

"Hello." Jerry maintained his grip on Kit's wrist. "I've brought a member of our choir with me." He nudged her with his hip, and she managed a grunt.

"How wonderful." Smiling white teeth glinted at her. "Are you going to sing?" The receptionist spun on her office chair to address a group of minions sorting envelopes behind her. "Make sure you go into assembly today, everyone. This lady's singing for us."

"I'm not singing. I can't sing!" Kit spoke through gritted teeth to Jerry. She pressed her right plimsoll hard over the instep of his shiny shoe. "Tell them, I'm not singing."

The door clanged behind her, and Kit jumped. She turned to see the boy from the front playground. He clung to the hand of a frowning woman, who wiped her sensible shoes on the mat before steering him towards a corridor on the left. He stared at Kit's plimsoll stamping on Jerry's foot, and his eyes widened. Another piercing wail left his lips. "I want my mum!" he screeched.

Kit clamped her left hand over her ear. Jerry still clutched her right wrist. "That kid wasted most of his chocolate." Her carbohydrate craving brain cells hated him for his negligence, and the sentence emerged with a jumbo-sized bar of disgust. "You do think that was chocolate, don't you?" Her voice wavered.

The receptionist leaned over the counter as though scaling Everest and slapped Kit's left breast. She gasped and lifted her hand to defend herself before Jerry nudged her again. She read the word *Visitor* upside down on a yellow sticker where her left nipple hid beneath the tunic. "The children mustn't bring chocolate onto school premises." The receptionist had risen from her chair and kneeled on the seat to gain additional height. "We're a healthy school. No chips, chocolate, lollies, fats or sugars. They can have bread and fruit." She nodded her head once, as though punctuating her sentence with the seal of approval.

Kit wrinkled her nose. "You're still filling them with carbs." She yelped as Jerry extracted his shiny shoe and kicked her ankle. Then she remembered the brown stuff on the boy's face and gagged. He'd either smuggled something in or found his own alternative. "Berk." She clapped a hand over her mouth, and Jerry released her wrist and fixed his fingers around the back of her neck.

"We'll wait in the hall." He steered Kit towards a set of double doors on the other side of the lobby. He mushed her face against his ribs, and she registered a flash of yellow in her peripheral vision. She turned her head to see his visitor's sticker at a jaunty angle on his surplice. The miniature receptionist with the teeny desk had only managed to slap it over his belly button. They passed through the double doors, and Jerry released Kit from his stranglehold.

She bounced up like a rubber ball and came out swinging. "I didn't agree to this!" she snarled. She jabbed a finger at his chest. The hem of the tunic became airborne as she swung back towards the exit and tripped. Jerry caught her arm as the parquet floor rose to meet her.

"Twenty minutes of your life to help a friend," he growled. "Behave!"

"They don't need us!" she complained. "Kids go to heaven, anyway. It doesn't matter what you say to them, they get to go and we don't."

"Speak for yourself!" Jerry pulled the cardboard shoe box from beneath his right arm and cast around for a surface. "The Lord takes a very dim view of people being mean to his mini flock."

"Mini flock!" Kit's lips turned down in a sulk. "I bet even he won't want that one with brown stuff around his mouth." The memory of the boy's coated lips and fingers made her grateful she'd missed breakfast. She sniffed the air. "It smells in here." She tossed her curls, and the strange scent grew stronger. "It's this tunic. It stinks of something." Kit spun in a circle to sniff her armpit. Jerry laid his box on an ancient overhead projector. Kit marched across the hall to him and raised her arm. "Sniff this," she demanded.

Langdon would have refused, but in the spirit of camaraderie, Jerry obliged. He gave a decent inhale and frowned. "It's weird but familiar."

Kit sniffed again, and they bumped heads. "It is," she agreed. "I know what you mean."

"Stop sniffing your armpits and help me with this." He lifted the lid and pulled out a tube of toothpaste, a knife and a fork.

"Are they from our house?" Kit narrowed her eyes at the leaf design at the top of the cutlery.

"Yes." Jerry gave a dramatic sigh. "I wanted spoons but Raki borrowed all of them."

Kit grunted in disgust. "I'm counting the entire set tomorrow morning and they'd better all be back in the drawer. What are you doing with them?"

Jerry grinned and waggled his black eyebrows. A wicked sparkle turned his irises to onyx. "Wait and see," he whispered. He laid out his props on the lid in a particular order and then held it out to her. "Hold this and I'll tell you what to do." He pushed the box lid at her stomach and forced her to take it. Her eyes widened as the double doors opened and a line of silent children filed into the space.

"These are bigger than the ones outside!" she hissed. She sidled closer to Jerry's arm, and the lid tipped. The toothpaste slid to one end and crashed into the knife. "You didn't tell me there were big ones!"

Jerry leaned sideways to whisper in her ear. "We came in through the playground for Years 1, 2 and 3. The older children play on the field. These are Year 8s." He gave a dramatic sigh. "Apparently they do this incredible thing called *growing* between entering and leaving."

Kit blinked at the array of knobbly knees and budding breasts. She averted her gaze, leaning in to whisper to Jerry. "That one's hairy. He's done too much growing. He shouldn't be here." Her voice wobbled. "I shouldn't be here. Please, don't make me do this."

"Too late." Jerry mouthed the words instead of saying them out loud. He folded his arms across his stomach and clasped his fingers together, standing like a sentry at the front of the assembled crowd. More children filed in, getting tinier with each group. His robes hid his body from his neck to his shiny toes, and Kit sidled close enough to use his muscular shoulder and flouncy sleeve as a partial shield. She stared at the odd contents of the box lid and practiced her yoga breaths.

"Is this Langdon's toothpaste?" She peered at the expensive brand label responsible for Langdon's pearly white smile.

Jerry hissed through the side of his mouth. "I put it back after my practice, and he didn't notice. It has a better nozzle."

Kit fixed her gaze on a mural of a zoo on the far wall to avoid catching any particular child's eye. The last class trooped into the room and sat at the front. They required more help and direction to sit cross legged with their arms folded. They fiddled and shuffled like fruit flies on a forgotten apple. Their teacher walked to the side and sat on a tiny chair. She clasped her arms around her knees to create enough ballast to stop her from ending up on the floor.

A man stepped into the room and a hush fell. The children sat up straighter. A maniacal grin split his face in half and the items rattled on Kit's makeshift tray. He stood taller than Jerry and built from a variety of the wares from local fast-food stores. She waited for him to pull out a weapon and the school to dissolve into lockdown chaos. Piggy eyes squinted from behind enormous pink cheeks. "Good morning, children." His voice boomed to the back of the hall, and the ropes on the wall apparatus swayed.

"Good morning, Mr Westerfield." The children chorused their reply as one, stumbling over the selfish monopolising of vowels in the man's name. His gaze cast over Kit until it fell on Jerry. "Let's welcome these special guests from our wonderful church next door."

The children murmured a salutation which had less coordination than their greeting for him, and Kit held her breath. Jerry stepped forward and spread his arms. "Thank you, Headmaster." His left hand slapped Kit in the face and the tray shot sideways, scattering the cutlery and Langdon's toothpaste at the headmaster's giant feet.

Chapter Thirty-Eight
Kid's Curls

Laughter spread through the hall, echoing towards the vaulted ceiling like tinkling bells. With a frantic glance at Jerry, Kit knelt to collect the items back onto the cardboard lid. She mouthed a silent apology, and he brushed it off, resorting to his experience as a barrister to carry the crowd. "Apologies to my glamorous assistant." He affected a dramatic bow. "Never hit your friends." His finger wag drew another round of giggles. A child at the front used the moment as an opportunity to dissolve into exaggerated hysterical laughter until a teacher raised her finger to her lips. He silenced, as though she'd pulled his plug. Kit rose and reordered the props. She placed the toothpaste to the left and the cutlery to the right before frowning and switching them around again. Her thumb kept the tube in place and nerves increased her pressure. An agonised look in Jerry's direction offered no help as he waxed lyrical about friendships and reached for the New Testament bible app he kept on his phone.

Kit's pounding heartbeat droned out the reading and the words which followed it. Most of the children watched Jerry, but a few studied her. Discomfort sent a flush of colour soaring up her neck and into her cheeks. The ruffled collar of the tunic made her itch and sweat trickled down her spine. She battled an overwhelming need to rip the heavy cotton from her body and hurl it into the crowd. With only her bra and jeans underneath, her striptease would get Jerry fired, and her arrested.

Kit balanced the cardboard lid against her stomach and slipped a finger between the collar and her neck. The tiniest draught snaked inside to offer a tantalising coolness. She tilted her head back and closed her eyes, repeating the exercise with more rapid movements and generating enough air to calm the uncomfortable flush. The funky but familiar smell grew stronger, and she grimaced, caught between needing to waft air or breathe. A titter of laughter sent her eyes flicking open to discover the front two rows of children beaming at her. She hadn't intended to steal the limelight from Jerry, but as his story flew over their immature heads, they settled on her to provide the entertainment.

Jerry turned to face her, his robes swishing as he moved. The white surplice over his black cassock gave him the appearance of a giant magpie. He held out his hands. "My beautiful assistant will help us with our experiment. Can I have a volunteer?"

Hands shot up across the room. Index fingers pointed high in the air and children rose onto their knees to gain extra height. Kit stifled a snort behind tight lips, amazed by their childish desire to make exhibitions of themselves in front of their peers. She couldn't imagine anything worse.

Nervousness busied her fingers, and she pressed the toothpaste tube with her thumb, bunching the contents towards the lid and flattening out the vacant space.

Jerry chose a boy from the back row. The child took his time to come forward, picking his way over bodies to find a channel through the crowd. He arrived in front of Kit, sturdy and almost as tall as her and pushing his spectacles up his nose. "What?" he demanded, glaring at her as though she'd singled him out for a public flogging. He put enough insolence into the single word to make the hair rise on the back of her neck. She gripped the cardboard lid until her hand left a dent in the rim. Her right thumb rubbed the plastic tube, and it grew warm.

Jerry reached for the toothpaste and struggled against Kit's resistance. His eyes widened at the dangerous glint in her hazel irises. "Violence isn't the answer," he whispered. Moving her thumb aside, he lifted the tube for the audience's benefit and the fingers of his right hand closed around the lid. "I'm going to squeeze a little toothpaste onto the cardboard," he announced. "Then this young man will put it back into the tube using the knife and fork." He waggled the tube in his fingers, holding onto the empty, flattened end. "The toothpaste represents our words and actions. Let's see how hard they are to put back into the tube once we've said or done them."

With her escape in sight and the most interesting part of the talk imminent, Kit released a sigh of relief. Jerry's fingers worked the lid loose with a quirk of his eyebrow and a gratified smile.

Langdon's expensive, organic, striped toothpaste ejaculated from the end of the tube and kept going. The jiggling around, coupled with Kit's inadvertent warming of the plastic, had encouraged the paste into a runnier consistency. Red, white and blue dots speckled the boy's glasses as an airborne dollop continued over his left shoulder and plopped onto the parquet floor. The audience gasped and then howled.

Kit held her breath and studied Jerry's reaction. It created a question mark over his integrity and made her desperate to see the result. His eyelashes fluttered as three potential scenarios moved through his brain. He could abandon the demonstration and apologise. He could continue and replace Langdon's toothpaste with a new tube. And apologise. Or he could continue, replace the toothpaste in Langdon's special Batman mug in the upstairs bathroom and say nothing.

Jerry's shoulders slumped. "Oops," he said. "That belonged to my boss."

Laughter continued around the hall, and the youngest children squealed. A few rose onto their knees for better vantage and the teachers patted their heads and shoulders to get them seated again. The adults moved through the rows like frogs, dropping low as though believing it hid them and creeping with little hops and shuffles. Kit narrowed her eyes and clung to her personal decision not to bear offspring. It seemed clear they reduced those around them to bowed, hunching, nervous wrecks.

Jerry straightened his shoulders. He leaned forward, and the boy gave a sullen reply to his whispered question. The room silenced with a clap of Jerry's hands. Another jet of toothpaste escaped and created a three-tone streak across the floor. "Barry will attempt to place the toothpaste back in the tube using the knife and fork."

Kit cocked her head with interest. Jerry had dismissed the first option and moved on to the second or third. The cardboard lid jabbed her stomach as Barry lifted the knife and fork and chased the toothpaste streaks across the floor. His activity appeared torturous, and Kit struggled with the heat from the tunic and the odour which surrounded her like a fog. Funky but familiar. She wracked her brain to identify the musky, nauseating blend as Barry smeared toothpaste in a five-metre radius.

Kit hoped Jerry let him suffer just enough for his insolence, but the kind-hearted cleric released him long before she would have. He handed an ungrateful Barry a red lollipop for his efforts and dumped the toothpaste and cutlery into his box. Kit leaned sideways and noticed a packet of neon lollipops nestled against one corner.

Jerry concluded their guest appearance as the village freak show with a moral. "Once our words are out in the open, it's impossible to take them back or cancel out the hurt they cause." He pressed his palms together and bowed his head. "Let us pray."

Kit dipped her head but squinted from beneath her eyelashes. A tiny child at the front stared at Jerry, his index finger pushed far enough up his nose to require a surgical removal. She let her gaze move over the rows of curls and ponytails and wondered how she'd fare as a children's hairdresser. A memory of Lottie rose to the fore, and she gave an involuntary shiver. She'd stick to adults.

Jerry's prayer pushed her thoughts towards her conduct with the Hamilton chapter of the WWC. She could have handled things better.

"Dear God,

Help us think how what we say will make others feel.

Help us not to do things we wish we could undo.

Amen."

The children moved and shuffled, eager to leave the crowded space and run around like maniacs to disperse their pent-up energy. Mr Westerfield took charge and relayed a notice about litter and a warning about bullying. Then he raised his hand to silence the rising volume and reminded them of the rules regarding the exclusion of anything tasty from packed lunches. Those weren't his exact words, but the remaining options offered little hope of excitement or sustenance. With a straight face. Kit turned her head to stare at him. A walking example of overindulgence, he epitomised society's hypocrisy and lack of self-reflection.

His next announcement made her forget her indignation. "There's no recorder club after school today," he boomed. "Mrs Reedy will be back next week. Mrs Rogerson made some wonderful cards with her lunchtime art club and I drove them around to Mrs Reedy's house last night. She said to thank you all for your kindness and she misses you."

"Reedy." Kit whispered the name under her breath. "Pam Reedy." She looked around her through a fresh lens. Pam worked here. A prickle worked its way up the back of her neck and caused her spine to tingle. Pam worked here and everything stopped at a quarter to eleven for morning tea. Pam could have done it. She could have stabbed Debbie with Kit's scissors.

Chapter Thirty-Nine
Curly Confession

Kit accepted the head teacher's handshake and tolerated the fascination of the smaller children. A line of girls took it in turns to hug her around the hips, pressing their cheeks to her stomach as though farewelling a long lost aunt. She patted them on their heads, muttering, "Bless you, my child."

"You don't need to say that." Jerry's black eyebrows drew into a line. His height and flowing robes intimidated the smaller children, and they dodged his offered handshake with wide eyes.

"Bless you, my child." Kit patted another hugger. "They like it."

Jerry grimaced. "You're not Catholic."

As though to illustrate his point, a tiny boy tugged on her tunic. "Can you hear my confession?" His thin voice piped from rosebud lips.

Kit snorted. "Sorry, dude. I'm in enough trouble." At the startled expression widening Jerry's eyes, she recovered. "Did you kill anyone?" The child shook his head at the same moment as Jerry's fingers fixed around Kit's wrist. She bestowed a beatific smile on the guilty waif. "How about I just forgive you for whatever you did. Let's call it quits."

A smile curved the boy's lips into a bow. His enthusiastic nod almost overbalanced him, and Kit lifted her hand for a high-five. He skipped into the air and slapped her palm, drawing the attention of his teacher and the rest of his class. "Yes!" His triumph echoed around the hall. "I'm forgiven."

"What did he do?" Kit frowned and addressed a girl with half her escaped ponytail hanging over her face.

She removed her thumb from her mouth for long enough to answer. "He flushed the class goldfish down the toilet." Her thumb went straight back into position.

Kit gasped. "Hey, you!" She tapped the boy on the shoulder. "You said you didn't kill anyone." He jammed his fingers into his ears and jabbered to himself in a loud voice.

"Time to leave." Jerry used his bulk to edge her towards the door. The sharp corner of his cardboard box dug into her spine as he herded her away from the crowd gathering around the fish flusher. Kit glanced back to find him grimacing. "That funky smell is worse. We need to get you out of that tunic."

"Vicar! I beg your pardon?" The head teacher blinked, his cheeks flushing pink. He looked from Jerry to Kit.

"Oh." Jerry hissed in a breath, and awkwardness shrouded him. He gave a feckless wave with his hand. "I meant nothing inappropriate." His cheeks super-heated like two tomatoes grafted onto his square jaw.

"He means because it stinks." Kit lifted the flowing sleeve to her nose and inhaled. A floral scent drifted from the fabric, and she halted in the doorway. "That's weird." She sniffed the sleeve again. It smelled like a woman trying to impress a potential partner and not like something left in the bottom of a fishmonger's fridge. She ran her nose along the fabric to her armpit and the funky but familiar odour grew stronger.

Jerry stayed behind to discuss something related to the church hall and Kit wandered into the sunlit playground to wait. The smell gave her a headache, and she needed space to consider her theory about Pam. Empty of children's shouts and laughter, the play area missed something she couldn't define. It lost its raucous energy as a lonely swing creaked on its frame. The breeze pushed the rubber seat back and forth, but the activity lacked its earlier attraction without a child holding on for dear life and another one pushing with a glint in its eye.

"How was your singing?" The tiny receptionist appeared from an adjacent building and paused in front of Kit, her arms clasping a ream of paper. She jerked her head towards the lobby.

"Great thanks." Kit released the lie without guilt. It seemed kinder than a lengthy, pointless explanation.

"I love your hair. How do you get the ringlets?" The woman stared at a point above Kit's eye line, an uncomfortable experience for the recipient of her scrutiny.

"It's the Women with Curls method." Kit studied her reaction for signs of disinterest before continuing.

The receptionist hefted the paper higher against her chest but cocked her head as though listening for the secret to eternal youth. "I straighten mine." She lowered her voice and dipped her head forward to create a bubble of confidentiality. "I wish I had the courage to just rock my curls."

Kit exhaled and nodded. "I know. It's a huge decision and lots of hard work establishing a routine that works for your hair. We use alternatives to shampoo and conditioners without sulfates and silicones."

The receptionist gave a wistful smile. "I'll look into it. Where can I find more information?"

"There's a WWC group on Facebook. The Hamilton chapter is very active." Kit glanced up as Jerry strode towards her. The sleeves of his robes blew out from his body like wings. An idea surged into her mind. "Pam Reedy is the group's chairperson. You should speak to her."

"Oh." The receptionist's blonde brows waggled, and her eyes widened. "That's the hairdressing group she's part of?" She paused and bit her lower lip. "You must be friends with the woman who died in her garage. I'm so sorry, it's terrible."

Kit feigned concern. She placed her fingers over her mouth and tilted her head. "Poor Pam. Did someone break the news to her at work? Her and Debbie were so close. I bet it devastated her."

The receptionist tilted her head back and stared at the clear blue sky. A single cumulus cloud puffed across it like a late-night reveller stumbling home. "I don't remember how she heard about it." Her brow furrowed. "Mr Westerfield gave her the rest of the week off and asked me to process it as sick leave. That's how I heard about it." She pursed her lips, realising she'd said too much but irritated that she'd found herself out of the gossip loop. "Mrs Mace covered her class, so she must have already been here. We phone her when we need her, but she won't come in if she's already started her day." She glanced at Kit's hair again. "Pam's curls are lovely, but perhaps I could contact you about it. I don't have Facebook."

Kit nodded as Jerry reached her side. "I don't have my phone on me at the moment, but you can always reach me via Jerry." She looked up at him, her eyes sparkling. "Is that okay with you?"

Jerry nodded his affirmative and slid his sleeve back to check his watch. "I'm afraid I must dash to another meeting now." He smiled at the receptionist. "Phone me at the church office and I can put you in contact with our star hairdresser."

"Hairdresser?" The receptionist's eyes glinted, and she turned her feet to face Kit. "You didn't mention that."

"Oh yes. She styled mine." Jerry patted his curls with his left hand and beamed at her. "She won the award for stylist with the most flare." He dipped his chin and edged Kit nearer to the gate, using the box to administer covert jabs to force her into motion. She reached around him to wave to the receptionist.

"Jerry, Jerry!" She rounded on him as soon as the gate clicked shut behind him. "You'll never guess what I found out."

Chapter Forty

Curly Conscience

Jerry wrinkled his nose. He leaned forward and sniffed her hair. "I think the stink is you."

"What? Really?" Kit snorted in her armpit again.

"Yes." He glanced over his shoulder at the retreating receptionist and urged Kit along the pavement. "And I think I know what it is."

Kit's feet pattered along the path and up the front steps of the church. A round woman with wobbling hips barrelled towards them as Jerry stepped into the nave. "Ah, Vicar!" she called. "Have you seen my bug spray?"

"Bug spray!" Kit whispered the words and grabbed her head.

"Mrs McAvoy, how great to see you." Jerry shielded Kit with his body. "I borrowed it and left it in the vestry. Apologies. My meeting at the school came around faster than I realised."

The woman skidded to a halt in front of him and rested her hands on her hips. She peered at him over her spectacles.

"Why did you need bug spray?"

Jerry spread his arms out wide. "I thought you used water to mist the flowers. I made a mistake."

"This is the water bottle." Mrs McAvoy pulled a blue metallic bottle from the bag at her side. "The pink one is bug spray. I thought Mrs Harper borrowed it." She used a set of pudgy fingers to emphasise her accusation the other woman had carried out a bottle heist, without saying the actual words.

"What's in it." Kit lifted a shaking finger and pointed at the bottle.

"Just water." Mrs McAvoy lowered her head to inspect her. "Who are you?"

Kit ignored her question. "What's in the other one?"

Mrs McAvoy bristled at her demanding tone. "Neem oil!" she snapped. "I want it back right now. We have greenfly in the azaleas Mrs Roberts dropped off for the funeral this afternoon. I need to spritz them."

Jerry positioned his body at right angles to Mrs McAvoy, shielding Kit from her fiery glare. "I'll fetch it for you." His voice remained calm, but Kit recognised misery in the straightening of his lips. She stepped behind him and skirted Mrs McAvoy, desperate to touch her curls but resisting. Jerry followed her along the corridor to the vestry and closed the door behind them.

"Neem oil! Yuk!" Kit made retching noises and hauled the heavy tunic over her head. "I need to go home and wash my hair with dish washing liquid."

"I'm sorry." Jerry's furrowed brow communicated his regret. "Whenever I think I'm helping at the moment, I get it wrong and make things worse." His shoulders slumped, and he clapped his hands over his eyes as Kit emerged from beneath the tunic. Sweat trickled down her spine and into her jeans and she dumped the wretched shroud into an armchair.

"It's just a bra, Jerry." Kit reclaimed her stained shirt from the back of Jerry's office chair. "You won't go blind."

"I have seen a naked woman before, thank you." He spoke from behind his hands and irritation accompanied the grinding of his teeth.

"Sorry." She hauled the shirt over her head and straightened the hem. Too hot and bothered for the jacket, she flopped it across her forearm. "I'm decent. You can look now."

Jerry gave a snort of derision. "You, Kit Maguire, are never decent." His lips quirked upward in a reluctant smile. "Sorry about the bug spray."

"Funky but familiar." Kit shrugged. "At least it's natural. I'd need to visit the emergency room after spraying myself with a chemical insecticide, so I'm grateful it just stinks."

"What did you want to tell me?" Jerry glanced at his watch and sighed. "I hope Langdon gets back in time for the funeral. I've had enough for one day."

Kit snatched up the borrowed phone and her car keys. She tapped the toe of her left plimsoll on the polished wooden floor. "Pam told me this morning she spent Monday morning at work. She seemed quite indignant about it. But she works at the school next door and the receptionist couldn't recall Pam hearing about Debbie's death at school."

Jerry slumped into his office chair with a sigh. "Maybe she checked her mobile phone at lunch time or during the afternoon. Why would the receptionist need to know?"

"Because Mr Westerfield asked her to put in a sick leave application for Pam. And a woman called Mrs Mace covered her class."

"So?"

"The receptionist said she must have already been at school. She's a relief teacher and won't come in part way through a day. Maybe it's a money thing." Kit pursed her lips. "I need to get this funky smell out of my hair. Do you think there's any point telling Lane to look harder at Pam's alibi?"

Jerry ran a hand across his scratchy stubble. "It should come out as part of his enquiry. He'll interview the woman who covered her class on Monday morning to enable her to slip out and stab Debbie. An alibi is only as solid as the person who verifies it. Your argument sounds weak to me. She might have answered a text in class or checked Facebook. Not everything comes via the main switchboard anymore."

Kit shook her head, resisting Jerry's cold water on her desperate theory. "School receptionists know about everything. Yet she didn't know about Debbie's death until the principal told her. That site is like a concentration camp. Pam couldn't leave without walking through that front gate and I reckon that receptionist would have seen her. I arrived at Debbie's house just after ten past eleven. Someone stabbed or strangled her, perhaps even both. I believe they were in the garage when I arrived. They escaped through the front door as I came in through the back and that's why the door had so much drag on it. I figured she had a window open elsewhere, but it's because the front door takes time to close. The killer shot outside, grabbed their flip-flops and left me to take the blame."

Jerry blew out a breath. "You think Pam killed her?" He winced. "Lane won't go for that. There are too many variables." He lifted his hands in the air and waggled his fingers. "Do you realise how much strength it takes to throttle the average person? The assailant might have enough experience to know what they're doing, but it's very hit and miss. It can take as long as five minutes for the victim to die unless you use a garrotte."

Kit shuddered and turned away from him as the image of Debbie's prone body resurfaced. "I know Pam had something to do with it." She stared up at the ceiling and blinked a few times as though that might clear her mind. "Finding the truth might keep me out of jail."

Jerry rose, already shaking his head. "Leave it alone, Kit," he stressed. "You need to go home and stay out of trouble. I forbid you, as your lawyer and your friend, from visiting Pam or investigating on your own."

"I won't." Kit tapped the pocket containing her car keys and the spare one for her house. "She and Piper made it clear they wanted nothing to do with me again." Her shoulders slumped. "See you later, Jerry."

Before she had taken two paces towards the door, she stalled at the loud hammering which shook it on its hinges. "Vicar! Vicar are you there?" Mrs McAvoy's voice echoed in the corridor. "Mrs Rogerson brought carnations for the wedding later this afternoon. She's arranging them on the altar but she's not on the roster. It's my day! I'm doing the flowers for that." Her wheedling tone reminded Kit of the children she'd seen in the school assembly.

She turned to Jerry, lowering her voice to a whisper. "It's like kindergarten. Is it always like this?"

Jerry shrugged. "Some people just need a little more love than others."

Kit twisted her features into a grimace. "At least you're getting paid to have people treat you like crap."

Jerry barked out a laugh. "This is nothing. If you want to see people treated like crap, visit a law firm and speak to the fresh graduates. At least my dreams are still intact." He took a step forward and wrapped Kit in a fortifying embrace. She pressed her cheek against his solid chest and listened to his heartbeat thrumming in her ear.

"Vicar! I know you're in there Vicar!" Two heavy raps punctuated Mrs McAvoy's rebuke. Undaunted and filled with entitlement, she turned the brass door handle and marched into the room. Her rubber-soled shoes screeched against the floorboards as her gaze fixed on Kit snuggled against Jerry. "Oh my!" she exclaimed. Her sensible shoes caught against the rug and she stumbled.

"See you later, Jerry." Kit kept her voice level, subduing a giggle at the indignant flush on Mrs McAvoy's face. She exited the vestry and found her way along the corridor to the nave. A moment of bitterness entered her thoughts that even if she showed an interest in Jerry, she'd never be good enough for the likes of Mrs McAvoy.

Chapter Forty-One
Stuck in a Curl

Kit found it difficult to drive past the end of Pam's street without parking in front of her house and demanding answers. She drove through a rain shower and pulled into her own driveway just as Raki exited the front door.

"Hi Kit." He stood in the gap to stop it from slamming. A box of glass test tubes tinkled in his arms as Kit locked her car door and bounced up the front steps. She stopped and gaped at Raki's head.

"What did you do?" Lines and patches of scalp showed through the tight crop of black fuzz. He shrugged and wrinkled his nose.

"I used the nose hair trimmers to draw a chemical formula on my head. But I forgot it looked backwards in the mirror. I found Jerry's clippers and tried to make it better." He stared up at the remains of the hair he no longer owned and winced. "It looks like someone dipped me headfirst in a piranha pool, doesn't it?"

Kit considered her reply with care. She placed a hand over Raki's wrist and gave it a light squeeze. "That's one hell of a side parting. Where are the clippers?"

Raki's lips drooped and his almond-shaped eyes sagged at the corners. "You're putting them in the bin, aren't you?"

Kit nodded in the affirmative and jerked her head towards the hallway. "Come back inside and I'll give it a tidy."

"Thanks, Kit. I'd love to take you up on it if the offer still stands for later today." He tilted his wrist to read the hands on his watch. "I'm giving a lecture on the periodic table after lunch. I can come straight home." His sentence held a veiled plea.

Kit nodded. "I'll do you a favour if you do one for me? Someone gave me a bottle of hair conditioner. It's meant to be silicone and sulfate free, but a woman's hair behaved as though she'd soaked it in both those chemicals. Is it possible for you to analyse the contents of the bottle?"

"Easy peasy. I'll do it in the lab." His shoulders dropped as the tension left his spine.

Kit unlocked her passenger door and retrieved the bottle of conditioner from the seat. She handed it to Raki, and he added it to his box of test tubes. "I have an appointment this evening, but I can sort out your hair if you come home early enough."

Raki pulled a woollen hat onto his head one handed and tugged it over his ears before giving her a wave and a smile. Kit stood on the porch and watched the road until long after he'd left. The evidence ricocheted around her brain like a bouncing ball, and she couldn't escape from the knowledge that Pam had lied about her alibi. She needed to find the owner of the large blue flip-flops, sensing they held the key to something important.

The ringing of the house phone drove her inside, and she closed the front door behind her with her foot. "Hello?" She spat the word into the handset, not in the mood for sales people.

"Is that Kit?" Vanessa's voice contained a muffled quality, as though she held her hand over the microphone. She swallowed, and Kit braced herself.

"Yes. What's wrong?"

Vanessa sniffed and paused. Then she cleared her throat, her voice still sounding thick and strange. "Bronwyn's son died. His friend is in an induced coma." Her ragged inhale covered Kit's gasp of shock. Before she could respond, Vanessa continued. "Anyway, she can't help at the Expo. She's pulled out of everything. We'll all have to muck in and cover her shifts. I'm sorry."

"Okay." Kit couldn't think of a sensible reply other than that. She paused, hoping that Vanessa would give her some clue as to the group's expectations. A faint sob from Vanessa's end of the call indicated it wouldn't happen. "Is there anything we can do for her?" she asked.

Vanessa sniffed. "That's kind of you. The church has a committee which takes care of food and cleaning for bereaved families." She exhaled. "Just pray for her when she comes into your thoughts. It's a tragedy."

"How did it happen?" Kit's mind tracked back to the night of the group meeting and Bronwyn's hasty exit. "She said he'd been drinking. He couldn't have died from that, could he?"

Vanessa's voice tightened, as though she spoke through pursed lips. "It depends on what he drank. The police are looking for whoever supplied the alcohol. There's something wrong with it." Her words shuddered through the phone. "It's just tragic."

"Why don't we pull out of the Expo?" Kit suggested. "We can redouble our efforts next year and make sure we're better prepared. I've come to this too late to do my absolute best. Let Auckland take the win again just this once."

"No!" Vanessa's reply blasted into Kit's ear. "We have to win this one! I convinced my sister to wait one more year before shutting down the New Zealand operation. We've worked too hard to lose all our support."

"Why does it matter so much? If we all own the book she wrote and follow the method, it doesn't mean we can't continue spreading the word and meeting as a group, does it?" Kit realised she'd asked the wrong question as Vanessa's tone became hard and unyielding.

"My sister owns the brand name, Women with Curls. She pays for all the advertising. If she goes back to Australia and forgets about us, we're finished. This organisation is nothing without her."

"Right." Kit's mind mulled over Vanessa's foreboding. She imagined Women with Curls without the reverential presence of the Queen of Curl. Though most group members had never met her in person, her existence through social media images and videos of cutting courses provided them with an example of how their hair could one day look. Stunning grey ringlets framed the older woman's face, her smiling brown eyes and elfin features making the most of every photo opportunity. Kit had seen her from a distance during the cutting course and shaken her hand once. It had been more than enough to galvanise her and give her courage for her Curly future. Her shoulders slumped. "You want me to do this alone?" She heard the dread in her loaded question.

As though sensing Kit's uncertainty, Vanessa lightened her tone. "You can do this. We're counting on you."

"Okay then, what's next?" Kit held her breath and waited for Vanessa's response.

"We proceed with the same plan as before, but you'll do all the cutting, including the ultimate competition. I'll make sure the other girls step up to cover the stall, but you need to be there to give advice and consultations. We'll be right behind you. The committee believes in you, Kit. We won't forget this." A click signified Vanessa ending the call. Kit clutched the phone in her fingers for a long time after silence cut the air between them.

"You can do this, girl," she whispered. "She said they believe in you. Now, you just need to believe in yourself."

She hung up the phone and sank onto the bottom step leading to the upstairs level. An enormous sigh rocked her body and as she leaned forward, something crinkled in the back pocket of her jeans. Kit rose and extracted the envelope Danni handed to her. Her altercation with Mr Rashid seemed like days ago instead of hours. Kit gritted her teeth and pulled open the flap of the envelope. Twenty-dollar notes fluttered onto the carpet at her feet. Reaching forward, she lifted them in shaking fingers and counted them. Amid the notes, she found a handwritten letter.

'Thank you for stepping into the breach last night. Fifty is for cutting my hair, and Lottie's mum contributed the other

thirty. We are both incredibly grateful. A few of the other girls asked for your details after you left. Vanessa gave your phone number to them but they're having trouble getting through, so I figure they filled your voicemail. I'm compiling a list of girls and phone numbers, but I'll give it to you when you're not working. Hope I didn't get you into trouble handing this to you in the shop.

Kind regards Danni.'

Chapter Forty-Two
Crash Curls

Kit washed her hair and gathered her clean curls into the green scarf she used as a Plop. She tidied the house and sifted through the contents of her hairdressing bag. The Plop came off after ten minutes and damp curls dangled next to her cheek. She relaxed, using the time to clean her scissors and comb ready for her evening appointment with the lady from the vehicle testing centre.

Raki returned home early, eager for her to fix the mess he'd made of his hair. Kit used the techniques she'd learned on her hairdressing course to cut his hair as short as possible. The gouges over his fringe area proved harder to disguise. "I can't do anything about this," she soothed, resting her hands on Raki's shoulders. "Your hair grows fast, so it'll mask the bald patches in less than a week. Until then, I'd wear a hat to cover it. At least now, it will grow at the same rate as the rest."

Raki seemed happier, returning from his shower with a smile on his face. He clattered around in the kitchen with a packet of his favourite noodles to celebrate. Kit sat on a stool at the counter, transferring contact numbers from Raki's phone into her borrowed device.

"I hate not having my own," she grumbled. "It makes life harder." Her fingers tapped in Jerry's number and she saved it.

"What will you do for work now?" Raki hunched over his noodles, stirring in cheddar cheese and ham.

Kit squinted at the phone screen and winced. "I don't know yet. I'll make the mortgage payment and keep my unemployment a secret from the bank for now." Her mood brightened as she remembered the envelope filled with twenty-dollar notes. "My hairdressing business might succeed of its own accord. I got paid eighty dollars for a couple of hours of work last night. The going rate seems to be fifty dollars per cut but I'm sure I could increase that with more experience."

"Ah!" Raki turned and wagged his fork at Kit. "I asked an undergrad to test that bottle of stuff you gave to me. He said it's full of sulfates and silicones." He dropped his fork into the noodles and disappeared into the hallway. Kit heard him rummaging in his rucksack. He returned bearing a printed sheet. A list of chemicals lined one above the other. She winced at seeing two names beginning with the letter 'M' and shook her head in disgust.

"This explains why Danni's scalp looked so dry. She'd rammed her hair into a ponytail, but spent all day scratching her head. There's no wonder she felt so miserable. Her conditioner contained the Itchy M's."

Raki nodded, his expression sage. "Methylchloroisothiazolinone and methylisothiazolinone.

They're safe as preservatives, but some people react to them." He shrugged. "Then again, many don't."

Kit tapped the sheet with her index finger. "The Women with Curls handbook advises against any products containing those. As soon as you stop using the sulfates contained in shampoo, it's difficult to wash out the Itchy M's." Her shoulders slumped. "I don't understand. I use that brand and it doesn't contain any of these things. It's organic and plant based." She exhaled and covered her eyes with her hands. "This makes no sense."

"Email the manufacturer." Raki spoke around a mouthful of noodles. Kit looked up to see him eating at the counter. His eyes glazed in thought. "Perhaps your friend got a faulty batch."

"Maybe," Kit mused. She studied him as he dipped his fork toward his bowl and missed. His mind played through a field of chemical formulae and their combined effects. He jumped as the fork clattered against the side of his bowl. "Thanks for checking it out, anyway." She narrowed her eyes. "Please, can we have our spoons back soon? I don't have the cash to replace them."

"What?" Raki blinked and nodded at the same time.

Kit sighed and nudged her phone with her finger. "This doesn't have much data left on it. I'm hoping Lane gives mine back soon and then I'll email the company."

"Yep." Raki lifted the fork and missed his mouth. His brow furrowed. "That girl who cleans our house is a student at the university. She came to my lecture today."

"Melinda." Kit rested her chin on her wrists. "I thought she liked the vicars but perhaps she's after you."

"Not gonna happen." Raki's mind flicked him back into reality. "I don't want her here. She hid my bum flannel, and she saw my underpants."

Kit blinked. Raki's legendary bum flannel haunted the shared bathroom on the first floor. His tendency to leave it hanging over the bath led to arguments. She focused on the underpants-sighting to avoid dwelling on the flannel's whereabouts. "How did she see them?"

"I left them on my bedroom floor." Raki's wrist twitched, and a string of melted cheese hung from his fork. "I suspect she vacuumed round them."

"Then stop leaving them there." Kit sat upright with a gasp, and her stool tipped backward with the force of her movement. "Oh, my goodness!" She glared at Raki. "Piper didn't have nits. She used the same conditioner as Danni."

"That's terrible." Raki shrugged. "You should borrow my laptop and email that manufacturer. There are laws against misleading product information." He waggled his eyebrows and pushed the fork into his mouth. His teeth worked as he nibbled dried cheese from its prongs. "It's on my desk. Just open a new window and don't close the screen with the tables on it."

"Thanks. Did you keep the conditioner bottle?" Kit closed her eyes as she waited for the reply. "I bet they'll want me to post it back to them."

"I'll ask the undergrad tomorrow." Raki picked up his bowl and walked towards the dining table, signifying another bout of distraction. He tripped over the edge of the rug and walked into a dining chair, moving as though blind.

Kit ran up the stairs, taking the steps two at a time. She grabbed her bottle of conditioner from her ensuite and went in search of Raki's laptop, finding it where he said. She opened another window and logged into her Gmail account. Emails from the Rashids filled her inbox. One contained her payslip, and Kit heaved a sigh of relief. After four begging letters, Mr Rashid had set his wife on her, though it seemed clear he hadn't told her the truth about their disagreement. Kit's fingers twitched to delete them, but she sensed she might need them as evidence if Lane came after her because of Mr Rashid's lie. In his second email he'd confessed to panicking and misleading Jackson. She figured she could always use it in her defence.

After double checking the ingredients listed on her bottle, Kit used the contact details beneath the company's logo to send them an enquiry. The three-hundred-character limit forced her to give a concise account of what she'd discovered, so she left the house phone number in case they wanted more. She sent the email, forwarded Mr Rashid's messages to Jerry's personal account, and then closed the window on the screen. Raki wandered into his bedroom as she finished, blinking at her presence as though surprised to find her there.

"Thanks, Raki." Kit moved past him to the doorway. "I've sent the email." She waved her conditioner bottle in front of her. "The ingredients on this are different to the one you tested. I'll check later to see if they've replied. Is that okay with you?"

"Yeah, sure." He ran his palm over his stubbly head and exhaled. "I can't find my lunch."

"Right." Kit kept walking, used to his moments of absence. She imagined the places he might have ventured to after he left the kitchen and smiled as she threw the bottle from the doorway where it landed on her bed. "Check the dishwasher to see if you already ate it," she called over her shoulder. She set off down the stairs, her feet pattering a staccato beat. "I'm just nipping to town. I need to tell Piper to stop using the conditioner."

"Call her!" Raki's voice sounded stern. "Aren't you meant to stay home?"

"I can't remember her number without my mobile phone." Kit let go of the banister rail to move faster. She missed a step and jumped onto the next. "Try the back porch. Sometimes you eat with Jerry. You might have forgotten he's at work."

A clatter followed her scream as her left foot landed in the bowl lying on the bottom step. Her ankle rolled, and the bowl slipped out from beneath her, planting her on her backside on the hall floor. Her head hit the edge of the second step and bright spots filled her vision.

Then nothing.

Chapter Forty-Three

Bowl Cut

Kit woke to find Langdon standing over her. Raki ran to the front door and back again on a continuous loop, his phone clasped in front of his face. His bare feet pattered against the carpet, deafening beneath the painful hum in Kit's head. Langdon squatted on his haunches and pressed his palm against her forehead. "Do you need an ambulance?" His soothing tone cut through the hum and it shifted to the periphery of her mind.

"No." Kit closed her eyes. "I want to lie here for a minute." Her backside rested on the hall floor, but her crown registered the hard edge of the second step pressing against her scalp.

"Place the patient in the recovery position." Raki ran back to Kit. "There's a diagram. Move out of the way, Langdon and I'll do it. I need to bend her arms and legs like this." He shoved the phone screen in Langdon's face.

"If he bends any part of me, I'll hurt you both!" Kit pushed herself to a sitting position, pressing her spine against the bottom step. "I'm fine," she lied. Her hand shook as she passed it in front of her face.

"The patient must not watch TV or read." Raki continued his pacing. "Check for bright flashing spots in front of the patient's eyes." He swerved near the front door and scampered back to Kit. "I can't see any." He elbowed Langdon's shoulder. "Do you see any spots in front of her eyes?"

Langdon pursed his lips and shook his head. "Can you stand? If I help you to the sofa, we can see if anything falls off on the way." His lips quirked upwards as he spoke.

"Falls off!" Raki dropped his phone and pressed his hands against his eyes. "This is all my fault. I want nothing to fall off her. What can I do? How can I make this better?"

Langdon blew out a breath filled with exasperation. "Perhaps start by not leaving your lunch on the stairs." His lips tightened into a line.

Kit gripped his fingers and relied on his strength to haul her upright. The narrow hallway spun in her vision. "I need to stand here just for a minute." She rested one hand over Langdon's forearm and the other gripped the banister rail.

Raki bent over and retrieved his phone, staring at the screen as though it held enlightenment. "I'm so sorry, Kit." His hazel eyes squeezed shut as he issued his heartfelt apology. "It's the lecture on the periodic table," he sighed. "It got me thinking. I know there are more elements to find and I'd love to be the one to do it."

"That's very noble." Langdon spoke through gritted teeth. "Try not to kill your flat mates in the process."

Kit winced. Despite the pain, she experienced a moment of sympathy for poor Raki. "Accidents happen," she conceded. "He didn't leave the bowl there on purpose."

Langdon's left eyebrow inched higher, and the bridge of his nose wrinkled. "He left chocolate mousse in the bathroom yesterday." He gave a visible shudder.

Raki's eyes widened. "I was in a hurry and couldn't eat all of it! It seemed quicker to put it down the toilet than run downstairs. I took the bowl down later."

Langdon's cheeks paled. "But you knew it was chocolate mousse. I however, walked into the bathroom and imagined a grenade went off in your bowel."

"Oh." Raki lifted his left hand and scratched at the stubble covering his head. "I didn't think about that."

"Can we salvage the bowl?" Kit peered around Langdon to see fragments of her crockery dispersed along the hall carpet. "Maybe not." She sighed. "Raki, as of this morning, I have no job. You're emptying our kitchen for your experiments faster than I can replace things. We need the spoons back and soon."

"I'll do whatever you want. I'll replace the spoons and the bowl."

Kit released her grip on the banister rail, testing her ability to stand without assistance. "Just bring our spoons home," she said.

"There's a bit of a problem with that." Raki turned his bottom lip inside out in a grimace of pure discomfort. "They sort of melted."

Kit's audible groan echoed in the hall way. Langdon supported her as she made her way to the sofa in the lounge. Twinges sparked along her spine, but apart from the headache, she'd escaped without too much damage. "Where was I going?" She pressed her finger and thumb against the bridge of her nose. "Why did I run downstairs?" It flooded back to her like a tsunami, washing over her in a wave of misery. She sighed. "That's right, I was driving to Piper's house." Her shoulders slumped. "I bet she won't open the door."

"So, why go?" Langdon settled next to her on the sofa, his long fingers teasing the tassels of a cream cushion. "You can't drive after a bang on the head. You need to stay here this afternoon."

Kit turned to face him, and a spasm erupted to engulf her spine. "I need to tell her about the conditioner," she urged. "There's something wrong with a whole batch. I emailed the company from Raki's laptop, but they'll take ages getting back to me. When I saw Piper this morning, she scratched like she had nits. I think the conditioner caused it, like it did for Danni."

Langdon's eyes glazed. "Is this more Curly business?" His tone held scepticism. His fingers strayed from the tassels to the luscious waves gracing his blond head. He frowned before deciding. "I'll drive you," he offered. "Let me phone Jerry and tell him where we're going, otherwise he'll wait for me at the gym."

"I'm coming." Raki shoved his phone into his back pocket and helped Kit up from the sofa. Between them, the boys treated her like a geriatric. She sat in the passenger seat of Langdon's car and took stock of her injuries. A cut stung inside her mouth, an egg formed at the back of her head and her spine felt like someone had run a cheese grater up and down it.

They'd reached the city limits when Raki let out a groan. "Oh no! I remembered my phone but forgot my shoes."

Chapter Forty-Four
Curly Clues

Langdon knocked on Piper's front door, and Kit waited just behind him. She used his bulk to shield her from her friend's expected wrath, standing sideways and holding her breath. Raki hopped around behind her on the cold concrete, his toes reacting to the roughness. He grumbled about the periodic table and noble gasses, great sighs leaving his body in whooshes of disdain.

"No, thank you." Piper half-opened the door and gave a wave of her hand. "I don't want to become a Jehovah's Witness. Thank you for calling. Please, have a nice day."

Langdon jammed his foot in the gap and grunted in discomfort as Piper trapped it between the door and the frame. "I'm not a Jehovah's Witness!" Disgust leaked from his voice. "I'm an Anglican!" He peered down at his black clerical vest and white collar before reaching behind him and grabbing Kit's wrist. "She needs to speak to you." He hauled her forward, wincing at the groan of pain Kit released as she tripped over his right foot. Winded, she bent at the waist and rested her palms on her knees as though she'd run a marathon.

"Sorry." Langdon patted her shoulder. He released his foot with a wiggle and stood square on the path. "Let me take you to the emergency room."

"No!" Kit rose and the front of Piper's house shifted to one side and then righted itself in a visual earthquake. She exhaled through pursed lips.

"What's happened?" Piper stepped over the threshold and cocked her head. "Why do you need the emergency room?"

Kit waved away her concern with a flapping hand. "I'm fine. But you need to stop using your conditioner."

As a reflex, Piper's left hand lifted and her nails scratched the scalp beneath her fringe. She frowned. "I used a nit comb." Defensiveness entered her tone. "I don't have nits."

"I know!" Kit exhaled in frustration. "It's your conditioner. Raki tested a bottle for me after it wrecked another girl's hair. It contains sulfates and silicones when it's meant to be Curly Approved." Kit swallowed. "And the Itchy M's."

"What?" Piper's voice rose to a screech. She grabbed a handful of hair and tugged. Her eyes widened like boiled eggs in her delicate face. "No! I can't start again! I can't go through another Transition Stage!" Her complexion grew waxy and Langdon took a step away from her, as though afraid of catching her ailment. He looked to Kit for help.

"Transition Stage?" He ran a covetous hand over the blond curls flopping over his ear. "Will I need to endure a Transition Stage?"

"No!" Kit stamped her foot and groaned as pain shot through her ankle, traversed her spine and blossomed in her head. She jabbed her index finger at Piper. "Get inside and let me explain! You as well." She dragged on Langdon's sleeve before turning to look for Raki. "What is he doing?" she hissed.

Raki squatted in a flower bed with a handful of soil. He held it up to his nose and sniffed. "Not enough potassium," he muttered. Langdon reached him in two strides and hauled him upright by the scruff of his tee shirt. Raki kept the soil in his hand and staggered sideways on the path.

Piper seemed reluctant to let them inside, but gave way as Kit hustled her through the doorway. Langdon stood over Raki as he washed his hands at the kitchen sink.

"What's going on with him?" Piper leaned sideways as Raki splashed with the water like a child.

"I don't know." Kit exhaled and grabbed her ribs. "He gets like this when he's cooking up some weird chemistry experiment. He finished his PhD and I think he's a little lost."

"Right." Piper itched her head, using both hands to reach two different places. Her face fell as she remembered Kit's warning about her conditioner. "I can't start again," she whimpered. "It took ages to repair my curls."

"It isn't like the first time." Kit rested her hand on her shoulder. "It's a Blip. Remember? One quick wash and then carry on as normal."

"But I don't understand." Piper's voice changed to a whine. "I use the same brand as you." Her gaze flicked to Kit's head. "Why are you not itching?"

"I don't know." Kit glanced at the kitchen table and eased herself into a dining chair. "It's interesting, though, because that's the same brand Danni used. I've emailed the company because I think it's a faulty batch. Raki tested it for me and it contained heaps of nasty stuff. The other lady bought her bottle from Mr Rashid's shop. Where did you get yours?"

"Debbie." Piper's nostrils flared as she said the dead woman's name. "She ran a scheme where you could take your old bottles to her and she offered a discount. It's helped with us going down to a single income." Piper pursed her lips, and Kit winced at the memory of her friend's momentary lapse of decency. Alec's kiss resulted in an ultimatum from her husband, abandon the job or leave the marriage.

Piper rallied and placed a unique spin on Debbie's scheme. "It helps the environment too. Less plastic packaging floating around the planet."

"Right." Kit frowned. "Did you always buy the same brand?"

Piper shook her head and ratty frizz moved against her shoulders. She lifted her hand and gave an involuntary scratch behind her ear. The scrape of her nails raking her scalp made Kit clench her teeth. "She started doing the Australian stuff a month ago. It's the Natural brand you use. She bought it in bulk and filled our bottles."

"When?" Kit blinked. "Why did no one tell me about this scheme? "

Piper shielded her eyes with her hand and stared at a stain on the ceiling where water leaked through the roof the previous summer. "She asked us not to tell you."

Kit gaped. "Why? I work part time in a dairy! I'm not a millionaire. Didn't you consider I might like a discount?"

Piper shrugged. Her chest deflated as a baby wailed from upstairs. "She said you'd make trouble and find some loophole to stop her helping us." Her brow furrowed into fine lines. "You must admit, you like detail. You'd want to know where her stock came from and check it all out properly before you let her sell it. Besides, you've spent the last six months either at work or in Auckland. You haven't stood still long enough for me to tell you anything."

Kit exhaled. "Fine," she conceded. "I'm here now and I'm listening."

"I'm here too." Raki slumped against the counter, drying his hands on his tee shirt. "And Langdon." He tapped the vicar's shoulder as though Piper hadn't noticed the six-foot-tall vicar in her kitchen. He released a sigh. "My phone is here but not my shoes."

"Right." Piper widened her eyes at Kit in a moment of shared confidence. Perhaps they could salvage their friendship from the brink of destruction. "What else do you want to know? I need to feed the baby and wash my hair."

"Tell me about refilling the bottles." Kit leaned forward, and the bump at the back of her head sent a dart of pain into her nerve endings. She gasped and raised her hand to her curls. "Did you give the empties to her at meetings?"

"No." Piper shook her head, the motion conveying certainty. "We called at her house on Monday mornings. She didn't make appointments."

"Did you watch her fill the bottles?" Kit rested her left arm on the table and discovered another bruise.

"No. She opened the front door, took the empty one inside and came out with a full one."

"Your bottle, or someone else's?"

Piper shrugged. She paused for a moment, her expression blank. "My own, I think. Does it matter?"

Kit wrinkled her nose. "Maybe not, but if you switched bottles, they might have contained other chemicals."

"No." Piper shook her head. "I washed mine before I took it and it looked like my bottle when I brought it home. The itching only started a few days ago. I used up the last of the old bottle and switched to the new one."

"Why Mondays?"

"What?" Piper winced at another wail from upstairs.

"Why could you only go on Mondays? What was the significance?"

"Oh." Piper's fingers drifted to her scalp, and she fingered an itchy spot above her fringe. "I assumed it was because she got a delivery from a bulk store every Friday night. I only know that because I dropped off the accounts one week and saw the van."

"What van?" Kit leaned forward, an intense light making her irises glint. "Do you remember the name?"

Piper groaned. "No." She stared around her kitchen as though for inspiration. "It had a logo of a bin with grains tumbling into it." She waved her hand in the air. "There's one on the other side of town, but I can't remember the name."

"Did you go to Debbie's last Monday?"

Piper swallowed and her colour heightened. Her daughter wailed from upstairs again, the sound angrier and filled with more urgency. She glanced up at Langdon and then at Kit. "I didn't." She shook her head and lifted her hand in a wave. The fluff edging her slippers wobbled as she rose and walked towards the stairs.

A baby monitor on the kitchen counter echoed her movements upstairs as she retrieved the baby. She gave no sign of returning to the kitchen. Kit's shoulders slumped. "We should leave."

Raki inhaled. "Ah well," he concluded. "She didn't go to Debbie's house on Monday."

"Do you believe her?" Langdon raised a blond eyebrow.

"Yes." Kit faced them, easing herself off the chair. "I've known her long enough to understand when she's lying. She didn't visit Debbie last Monday."

They trooped out to the car and Kit hauled the front door closed behind them. She settled into the passenger seat with a groan.

"So, what's the problem?" Langdon reached for the ignition key. "You sounded uncertain about something."

Kit rested her chin against her seatbelt. "She didn't visit Debbie. But I think she knows who did."

Chapter Forty-Five

Bulk Curls

"You can't go round to Pam's house!" Langdon edged Kit towards his car, blocking her as she tried to dodge sideways. Her injuries pinched, and she released a groan of pain.

"But I know she visited Debbie on Monday morning!" She pleaded her case to the back of Langdon's head. He unlocked the car and got into the driver's seat. Raki skipped into the back and inspected the soles of his feet.

With a sigh of exasperation, Kit hauled open the door and slumped into her seat. The belt stuck as she yanked on the catch. "Please, will you take me to the police station instead, then? I can tell Lane my suspicions."

Langdon started the engine but killed the flicker of hope burgeoning in her chest. "No. Jerry needs to give permission. You can't expect him to advise you and then blindside him." He tapped the clock on the dashboard. "He's driving home instead of going to the gym, but he thinks you have an appointment somewhere."

Kit's eyes widened, and she clapped a hand over her mouth. "My consultation with the lady from the vehicle testing station!"

Langdon drove at a sedate, funereal pace through the growing volume of traffic. SUVs appeared on the route, enormous, off-road vehicles driven by women collecting children from school. The driver of a black Ford gave Langdon the finger as she turned across him. He jammed on his brakes to avoid a collision, and Kit snorted with laughter at the look of horror on the woman's face as she noticed Langdon's dog collar. The bite of the seatbelt across her chest and stomach wiped the smile off her lips. "Do you ever feel the world is out to get you?" she mused.

Langdon raised a knowing eyebrow. "All the time, my friend." He sighed and eyed her sideways. "Jerry said you quit working at the dairy. What will you do?"

Kit puffed out a long breath. "I don't know right now. People want me to cut their hair and will pay for my help. I'll see if it's enough to cover the mortgage and if not, I might get another part-time job to plug the gap." She closed her eyes and leaned her head against the seat. "Unless Detective Lane locks me up for murdering Debbie. He seemed rather keen yesterday."

"Jerry thinks Lane knows you're innocent." Langdon gave her writhing hands a comforting pat. His lips tightened. "Debbie's husband contacted the church. He's asked me to lead her funeral once the coroner releases her body."

Kit pursed her lips. "That's nice. I can't imagine a WWC meeting without her flogging her wares." She paused and sat up straighter. "We have time for one tiny detour." She pressed her index finger and thumb together to emphasise her promise to keep the visit short.

"Where?" Scepticism entered Langdon's tone. "Jerry wants you to go straight home. He's driving you to your consultation and waiting outside until you finish."

"There's no need for that." Kit screwed up her features. A shopping centre loomed in the distance, rising from the residential street like a leviathan. She jabbed her finger towards it. "I want to pop in there."

"I want to pop too." Raki leaned forward so his face pressed between the front seats. "Can I pop with you?"

"What for?" Langdon demanded. "You can lose a day in there!"

Kit turned sideways in her seat. "Not the mall. I want to visit the bulk buy store across the street. Please, can I run in and out if I'm quick?"

"I'll go with her." Raki unfastened his seatbelt, and a bell chimed from the dashboard. With a growl of exasperation, Langdon made the turn into the correct lane and fought his way across the traffic to the car park in front of the store.

"Two minutes!" He held up two fingers to make his point, and Kit seized his hand.

"Wrong way around," she hissed. A woman unlocking the car next to them kept her mouth open in a wide 'o' of shock at the sight of a vicar making a rude gesture. "That doesn't mean two of anything."

She pushed open her door and followed Raki across the car park. His bare feet slapped against the cold concrete. "Please, can I use the data on your phone?" She grabbed his wrist as he barrelled towards the entrance.

"Yeah, sure." He hoisted the device from his back pocket and unlocked it. Kit's fingers flew across the keys as she logged Raki out of his Facebook account and entered the username and password for her own. Within seconds, she'd found the secret Women with Curls page and located the relevant photograph.

While Raki strode to the back of the store and raided the chocolate aisle, Kit queued at the checkout. She waited her turn and smiled at the middle-aged man behind the counter. "Please, can you tell me if this woman buys bulk hair products here?" She turned Raki's phone screen to face him and he jerked in surprise at the question.

His eyes narrowed. "Why do you want to know?" He glanced at the overhead security camera. "I'm not meant to give out customers' details."

Kit patted her hair and switched to a gushing tone. "I don't need them. She's a friend of mine. She raved about a conditioner brand she picked up at a local bulk order store. I wondered if it was this one and wanted some for myself."

"Oh." His demeanour changed, his shoulders losing their tension and his chest puffing. "That's different. That lady used to come in every Friday."

"Used to?" Kit cocked her head, her eyes narrowing. "She doesn't anymore?"

He shrugged. "She bought so much of it, the boss gave her a better deal and he delivers it by the barrel."

"By the barrel?" Kit swallowed as she repeated the sentence. Another customer pushed a trolley into the side of her knee and apologised. He couldn't see over the top of a biscuit tower.

The cashier raised an eyebrow and put his hands on his hips. "Are you buying anything today, miss? Do you have a membership card?"

"I need a membership card?" The moot question left her mouth before she could stop its escape. "Yes, sorry. Of course, I need one." She leaned forward and lowered her voice. "Where do I get one of those?"

"Hello Vicar." The man's irritation evaporated, and he stared at a point above Kit's head. Langdon's heavy hand rested on her shoulder.

"I think your two minutes and mine are on a different time line." He spoke the rebuke while smiling at the man behind the counter. "Hi, Dan. Busy day?"

"So-so." He turned his palm over and back to indicate his indifference. "I didn't realise this lady came with you." He turned to Kit. "You can make purchases on the reverend's church account, but you need to pay for it yourself."

"Okay, thanks." With a grin at Langdon, Kit spun from beneath his grip and jogged along the nearest aisle. She scrambled at an intersection until she located a sign for hair products. A plastic barrel of shampoo sat next to one with a conditioner label. A list of generic chemicals clung to the front. Kit snatched up an empty plastic bottle marked with a dollar price tag and filled it from beneath the conditioner spout. She cast around to make sure she hadn't missed another container in her haste.

"Is that all you're getting?" Raki peeked from behind a pillar of chocolate tins. A familiar logo ran around each rim.

"Yes." Kit frowned at his teetering pile. "Why do you need eight cake sized tins full of last year's Christmas chocolates?"

Raki shrugged, and his tower leaned at a dangerous angle. "Storage." His expression remained impassive, and Kit almost believed him. Almost. She laughed.

"You're such a liar."

He grinned. "I might share one or two." He noticed the container in her hand and frowned. "Why are you buying that stuff? I bet it contains all the nasties you hate."

Kit nodded and waved the bottle in front of him. "I know. Could you analyse it and see if it's the same as the last sample I gave you?"

"I don't need to; I can read it right there." Raki squinted and dipped enough to scrutinise the label on the side of the barrel. "The order of each ingredient is proportionate to their ratio. It looks identical, so I'd say it's from the same manufacturer." He stood up straight and sighed at his chocolate steeple. "Do you have a membership card for this place?"

"No, sorry." Kit let him offload the top two layers into her arms. "But Langdon does. He's at the checkout and he's not happy."

"Oops." Raki's mischievous smile showed no remorse. He jerked his head towards the myriad tins. "Party in my room tonight then."

Chapter Forty-Six
A Curly Clientele

Kit slammed the passenger door and stomped onto the footpath. A neat 1950s villa hugged a wraparound section of lawn beyond a white front gate. Jerry wound down his window and called her back to the car. "I'll wait here until you're finished." He drummed his fingers on the sill as her animosity shrouded them like fog.

"This is a hair appointment! You're treating me like a child!" She stamped her foot to emphasise the point, and Jerry grinned.

"Can't imagine why," he murmured. He shook out a giant newspaper with the title, '*The Anglican News*' emblazoned above a headline screaming, '*Chairs or pews?*' A cool breeze rippled the paper, and Jerry wound up the window. Kit stomped through the gate and up the crazy paved path to a red front door. She glared back at Jerry once more in silent protest, before rapping on the glass window in the centre of the door. Light shone from behind it and shapes moved around in dashing motions.

The door eased open like the gate to a penitentiary. The woman from the vehicle testing station stood on one leg, the other holding back a tan-coloured Great Dane and a white Labrador. Wagging tails thudded against the wall and alternately whipped their owner's thigh. "Sorry," she gushed. "I forgot to warn you about my girls."

Kit kicked off her plimsolls and left them under the porch. She stepped over the threshold and skirted both woman and dogs with equal wariness. Her scissors dug into her ribs from the ferocity with which she clutched her hairdressing bag, and she pressed her spine against the wall.

"They're friendly." The woman gripped a collar in either hand as she wrestled the giant dogs. Blonde fluff dotted the chocolate carpet in every direction as though one had chased the other and ripped out tufts of hair. "I hope you don't mind dogs." She snorted an embarrassed laugh. "I remembered after you left, I forgot to tell you my name or anything about me other than my address and phone number."

"It's fine." Kit blew out a nervous breath and sent a sideways glance along the wide hallway. "Where do you want me to cut your hair?"

"Kitchen. And my name is Margaret." She jerked her head at the dogs. "The Dane is Ellie, and the Lab is Flora. If I can just let them sniff you, they'll settle down and then we can get to work."

"Sniff me?" Kit's eyes widened in horror. "One at a time or both at once?" She didn't catch Margaret's reply as the woman released her grip on their collars. Kit squealed as the Dane rose like a goliath and set its weighty paws on her shoulders. Pain radiated from the bruise on her head as it pressed her against the wall. She held her breath and turned her face aside to avoid the wet nose pushed against her cheek. A scent like rotten meat engulfed her head as the giant maw opened to reveal sharp yellow teeth and a line of dribble which dangled like a cobweb.

"Get down, Ellie. That's rude!" Margaret hauled on the dog's collar and it ignored her. But the Dane's impropriety didn't compare to the indecency exhibited by the Lab. Kit shrieked as a hard nose appeared between her thighs and she found herself shunted almost off her feet. "I'm so sorry." The great Dane in Kit's face muffled Margaret's voice. "Get in your room, both of you!"

Both dogs ignored her squeaks as though she hadn't spoken, but grew bored with Kit. The Great Dane's pointy ears flicked back and forth before she put her front paws on the floor and ambled into a side room. The Lab sat on her bottom in front of Kit and looked up at her with a wide doggy smile. A trail of slobber coated the front of Kit's jacket from the Dane's onslaught. She tamped down the urge to dash for the front door and make an excuse to leave, instead, formulating a mental note to ask more questions before she did home visits in the future.

The Labrador flanked Kit's every move as she followed Margaret to the kitchen. She plonked her bottom on a stool to avoid another embarrassing body search by the enthusiastic canine. Margaret made a pot of coffee and jerked her head at the dog. "She doesn't like everyone," she commented with her back turned. "You must use the Naturals range of shower gel. She can't get enough of that. I had to give my last lot away to my sister."

Kit gave the dog a covert sideways glance, but found her gaze returned by unblinking eyes the colour of copper pennies. Flora's tail wagged at its tip, leaving a wide swathe of loose hair on the carpet. When Kit's foot slipped from the foot rail of the stool, the dog's body dipped forward as though waiting for an invitation to perform round two of her disgusting sniff test. Anxiety budded in Kit's chest at the thought of having to get off the stool and stand unguarded with scissors in her hand. The heady sage and eucalyptus scents wafting from inside her shirt made her wish she'd arrived without having a shower. Her shoulders sank, and her head dipped lower. Why did she think she could make a go of this?

Margaret served coffee and enticed the dogs into a rear bedroom, where she corralled them with food bribes. Kit relaxed without the constant threat of a canine weggie hanging over her. She stationed Margaret on a dining chair in the middle of the kitchen and waited for her to untie her frizzy locks. It took an hour to separate the dead ends from the healthy hair and instil neat layers into the overall shape. Kit kept up a commentary about the Women with Curls principles as she worked, gratified by Margaret's growing enthusiasm. It took her mind off her various body aches and the sharp pain in her ankle from standing.

"Look." Kit took a hair from the collection on the floor. She pulled it until it stretched to over twice its original length. "It needs some protein. This is just a basic test, but it's a good indicator. Another significant thing to understand is your hair's porosity. It makes an enormous difference to what products you choose and your ongoing routine."

Margaret bit her lower lip and avoided shaking her head. Kit kept her scissors still. "I didn't expect it to be so complicated." She sighed. "Do you think I can manage this routine?"

"I know you can." Kit inhaled a yoga breath and released it by degrees. "It's like everything else in life. There are no short cuts, and you need to want it more than anything." Her mind wandered as Margaret's frizz fell to the floor like brown snow. It occurred to her that she pushed her own dreams and desires before her in a covered wheelbarrow, too afraid to lift them out and allow herself to want them. She gave a groan of realisation. "I'm a fine one to talk. My life is a series of mishaps and disasters."

"Disasters?" Margaret gave an audible gulp. "Not hair disasters I hope."

Kit shook her head and attacked the layers above Margaret's eyebrows. "No. My hair is the only thing I get right in my life. It's all the other stuff that crashes and burns. I should have gone to university but figured I wasn't good enough yet and got an office job instead. I bought a house because the landlord wanted to sell, and I didn't want to move. The office job started as a stop gap, and I stayed there for over ten years. I fell out of that job and into my current one and now I've fallen out of that one too."

"What about the hairdressing?" Margaret squinted up through one eye. She kept the other closed as Kit snipped off the dead ends next to her cheek. "Your hair is an amazing advertisement."

"Thank you." Kit stood back to admire her work. "I'd love to do this full time, but I'm not sure where to start. The course ended last Friday, and I'm lost."

"How many cuts have you done this week?" Margaret ran a hand through her soft hair. "Ooh, this feels much nicer."

Kit frowned and stared at the ceiling. She added up the involuntary haircuts she'd performed since the previous Saturday. "Six, including yours. But three of them were my flat mates. They got into a pickle with a set of rusty clippers. The other two people attended a Women with Curls meeting and I hadn't planned on styling either of them."

Margaret turned on the chair and narrowed her eyebrows. "It's Tuesday."

Kit cocked her head and confusion crossed her features. "Yes." She answered as though replying to a question.

Margaret waved her hands in front of her. "But don't you see? You've performed six cuts in four days." Her lips curved into a smile. "You sound like a hairdresser to me."

Chapter Forty-Seven
Curly Shenanigans

Jerry drove Kit home in the dark, his mood upbeat but his fingers frozen. "I'm glad it went well for you." He smiled sideways at her through blue lips.

"You didn't need to wait for me," Kit grumbled. She clutched her hairdressing bag to her stomach and sighed. "I don't need a bodyguard."

"You have such a hard job accepting help and affection, don't you?" Jerry raised a speculative eyebrow and turned onto a rural road. He glanced in the rear-view mirror and frowned. The lights of the city suburb twinkled behind them.

Kit shrugged. "No." But her protest sounded futile even to her. "Maybe a little." She flattened her lips into a reluctant smile and patted Jerry's thigh. "You're a good friend. I'll admit I enjoyed knowing someone waited outside for me. I loved cutting Margaret's hair, but I should try to schedule most of my appointments during the day. This whole thing could eat into my life even more than working for Mr

Rashid if I don't organise it. Working every night will be as bad as getting up at four every morning to open the shop." She left her fingers on Jerry's thigh and he covered them with his cold palm.

"Schedule at least one day off every week and work within a structure. Otherwise, you're right, it will eat you alive." His gaze flicked again to the road behind them.

Kit leaned forward to stare through the windscreen at the Milky Way. It soared over them like a motorway speckled with headlights. "I don't want to get ahead of myself." She sighed. "I've had one proper customer so far. It doesn't make a business, does it?"

Jerry squeezed her fingers. "I disagree. If that person has a fantastic experience and spreads the word among her friends, this thing could catch fire for you faster than you realise."

"Maybe." Kit leaned her head back against her seat and closed her eyes. "I'm tired and my feet ache."

Jerry put both hands on the steering wheel to guide the vehicle onto their street. He cleared his throat. "Mr Rashid called the church today. He wants to speak to you."

Kit sat up straight. She inhaled, anger seizing her heart in a vice. "What he did to me is as bad as Cindy knowing the cops arrested me for Mr Roy's murder and keeping quiet." She turned in her seat. "Do I have *idiot* written on my forehead?"

"No." Jerry bounced his car onto the driveway and nestled it next to Langdon's station wagon. He tapped his fingers on the handbrake. "But it still leaves us with the issue of what to tell Lane. I'm surprised he hasn't come looking for you after Mr Rashid handed him a motive."

Kit blew out a breath which took with it all the satisfaction from her successful evening. "Should I try to see him first and explain what Mr Rashid did? Jackson will have already told him." She bit her lip after saying Jackson's name. Confusing, cheating, gorgeous Jackson.

Jerry wrinkled his nose and released the central locking. "My father suggested we just face what they throw at us for now. Putting other things into the mix isn't helpful. If it comes up, we'll deal with it. Your bank account won't show any payments to Debbie or large cash withdrawals, will it?" He dipped his head as he asked, peering at Kit from beneath his eyebrows. The shadows merged them into a single line across his forehead.

Kit gulped. "Mum transferred the course money to me in March. The administrator let me pay in six instalments. Lane will see large amounts going out on a regular basis." She groaned. "I paid in cash."

Jerry lifted his chin, but practice as a barrister and a vicar meant he kept the sigh of dismay contained in his chest. "It's okay," he soothed. "Lane can contact the course administrator. She'll verify the payments unless she embezzled it." He realised the error of his throwaway comment as Kit inhaled with enough force to make herself cough.

She sat up straight and her eyes became white orbs reflecting the interior light. "What do you mean? Oh, no! If she pocketed it, it won't be there." She raised a shaking hand to her mouth. "She didn't give me a receipt." Her hand strayed to her chest and pressed against the heartbeats thudding through her ribcage. "Jerry, I need to find Debbie's killer before Lane locks me up for it!"

"Not your circus, not your monkey!" He exited the vehicle at speed and hauled open her door. His gaze raked the road as an SUV passed their driveway. "Lane will work it out, but you can't risk being next on the murderer's list. Go inside and eat. Raki made something strange with noodles for dinner and saved some for us."

Kit entered the house with slumped shoulders, her appetite fleeing at the sight of Raki spinning noodles and grated cheese in the microwave. Jerry remained outside on the porch for a moment. When Kit passed the open front door, she saw him leaned on the front rail deep in thought. "What's wrong?" she asked.

"Nothing." Jerry's smile appeared fake, but he left his position after a last glance at the street and followed her into the house.

Avoiding the carb feast, she laid on her bed and stared at the blank ceiling as though it contained hidden clues. Debbie used unapproved product to make fast cash from the Women with Curls, passing it off as an approved conditioner.

Kit closed her eyes and allowed her mind to take her back to the crime scene. Boxes surrounded her, robbing her of oxygen as she studied them in more detail. Each bore the familiar logo of a branded alcohol, the name scored with a diagonal black line to suggest something else nestled within the cardboard folds. She exhaled, wishing she could text Jackson and glean tidbits of information from the handsome cop.

Reaching for her borrowed phone, she opened the contacts' folder and wrinkled her nose at its sparseness. It contained only her flat mates' names and numbers, unlike the bursting list on her own device. She'd added Margaret as *VTNZ lady*. Kit rolled onto her stomach and rested her chin on her wrists. Sifting through her limited information felt like digging her fingers into broken glass. She couldn't get past the fact that Mr Rashid gave her a motive for killing Debbie, coupled with her unreceipted cash payments to the course administrator.

"Pam knows something." She exhaled. "I lost my scissors at her house and she didn't stay in school on Monday morning."

"No." The voice made her jump and Kit squeaked. Jerry leaned against the door frame, his silhouette backed by the hall light. He folded his arms and tilted his chin down in rebuke. "You're not going to Pam's house at this time of night." He tilted his wrist to check his watch. "It's late and I don't want you out on your own." His sharp features acquired the same thoughtful expression as earlier. "It's not safe."

Kit groaned and pushed herself to a sitting position. "But she knows something." She thumped the bed with her fist and left a dent. "And Cindy admitted to touching my scissors. Why are guilty people so happy to let me take the fall every time?"

The mattress tilted as Jerry sat next to her on the bed. "Because that's what guilty people do. It's possible the killer saw you at the victim's house. I don't want you out on your own." He paused. "Do you know someone who owns a dark coloured SUV?"

Kit thought through her motley group of Curly friends and shook her head. "No. They all have mum mobiles with seven seats and puke on the upholstery. Why?"

"No reason. Get some sleep," he urged. "We'll sort everything out in the morning. Can you phone the course administrator tomorrow and ask for receipts?"

Kit's bottom lip poked out like a shelf in her misery. "Not unless Lane returns my phone. Her number is on it." She sighed and rubbed her eyes. "I'll borrow Raki's laptop again tomorrow and check my emails. I can contact her that way but she'll take a few days to come back to me. She's part time."

"Okay." Jerry squeezed her shoulder and rose. "Get some sleep. Enjoy not waking up at four o'clock." His lips quirked upwards into a grimace and he pressed a hand to his stomach. "Nice pass on the noodle surprise."

Kit gave a visible shudder. "I smelled the cheese and couldn't face it. What was the fishy aroma?"

Jerry's eyes watered and he gulped. "Shrimp. Noodles, shrimp and what he called, '*an accent of melted Gouda.*' He said he saw the recipe on TV, but I suspect he saw it in a dustbin and reverse engineered it."

Kit wrinkled her nose. "It's best to avoid Raki's experimental cooking, especially when his mind is sifting chemical processes. He's rambling about the periodic table at the moment and that's how I fell down the stairs." She lifted a hand and pressed careful fingers against the lump on the back of her head. A yawn accompanied the movement. "You're right, I need sleep." She reached behind her and fluffed her pillow. Jerry gave a cursory wave and moved towards the door. Kit sensed him pause as she snuggled against her favourite silk pillowcase, knowing he wanted to warn her not to sleep in her clothes. She released a sigh and smiled. "I'll just lie here for a minute," she murmured.

She remembered nothing after the click of her bedroom door and Jerry's receding footsteps.

Chapter Forty-Eight
Curly Confusion

Kit woke in the early hours, still clothed and on top of the bedspread. Her minute's snooze had lasted six hours. A glance at her digital clock showed she'd woken at the exact moment her alarm usually roused her from a beautiful slumber. "Damn and blast it!" she cursed.

By five o'clock, she'd showered, styled her curls and dressed, taking the time to apply flawless makeup and remove her Plop. She tidied the empty kitchen after Raki's impromptu cooking spree and scraped noodles off the hob. At six o'clock, she pushed her feet into her third best plimsolls and left the house, starting up her Bug with her fingers crossed. It fired first time, the gentle whisper of its Volkswagen engine behaving in the frigid air. She reached Pam's house to find lights shining through gaps in the curtains. Her insistent rapping on the front door ensured everyone in the street knew of her visit.

"Go away, Kit!" Pam opened the door to reveal a fluffy dressing gown, and a Plop made from a man-sized tee shirt.

"I've nothing to say to you." She leaned back and called into the hallway. "It's just for me, Brian. WWC business. Don't worry."

"Well, I've a lot to say to you!" Kit snapped. "You either speak to me now or I'll make sure Detective Lane hauls you out of your class to answer his questions. We both know your alibi doesn't stack, don't we?"

A hand shot from the gap and fingers closed around Kit's lapel. Pam yanked her through the doorway and clapped a hand over her mouth before she could object. "Keep your voice down, please?" Her eyes widened beneath the stained fabric of the Plop. She glanced along the hallway and jerked her head towards the rear of the house. "Come in here. Swear you'll hear me out and then say nothing to anyone?"

Kit swallowed and gave a shallow nod. The conversation hadn't gone as she expected and she'd arrived with only one plan of action. Pam removed her hand and set off towards a closed door. After a moment of hesitation, Kit followed. To her surprise, Pam led her through the kitchen and outside into the garden. She whipped off her Plop and flopped it over her shoulder before bending herself in half and running her fingers through her curls in the Rake and Shake method. Kit put her weight into her right hip and waited.

"What a bloody nightmare!" Pam grumbled as she stood up straight and flipped her hair backwards. "Why can't you just leave things alone?"

Kit snorted. "Because the cops found my matte black precision scissors sticking out of Debbie's neck. That's why! I'm five minutes away from a prison cell."

Pam folded herself onto a bench outside the back door and pulled her fluffy dressing gown tighter around her stomach. A cloud of condensation surrounded the women as they breathed in the freezing air. "I'm so sorry, Kit. This has got way more complicated than I ever intended."

Dawn stole across the inky sky as streaks of azure and a breeze snatched away her anger. "What's going on?" Kit demanded. "Did you see Debbie on Monday morning? Were you in the house when I arrived?" She cocked her head and regarded Pam's glossy curls through narrowed eyes. "Wait, you're not using that rubbish she passed off as the expensive stuff, are you? Did you see the way Piper scratched her scalp?"

Pam blew out a breath through pursed lips. "No and yes. I bought nothing from Debbie. And I confronted Piper after you left. She phoned me last night. She didn't have nits but suffered a reaction to one of her products."

"The conditioner she bought from Debbie." Kit slumped onto the bench next to her and relaxed. She rested her elbows on her knees, blowing on her fingers to stop them freezing. "I know."

Pam nodded. "I didn't know Debbie held those drop-in sessions at her place. I didn't want to be chairperson again and everything got away from me in the last few months. She started doing her own thing, like inviting Cindy to the committee meeting and nominating her as a cutter."

"I know you visited Debbie on Monday." Kit lowered her voice. "Did you stick the scissors in her neck?"

"No!" Pam's voice rose to a shriek. Her eyes widened as she glanced back at the window. "You're wrong! I didn't visit her house." She leaned forward to whisper in Kit's ear. "I told my boss I lost a filling and needed an urgent dental appointment. He got Mrs Mace to cover my class until after morning tea, but then I heard about Debbie and I couldn't go to work after that." She closed her eyes and paused a moment before continuing. "What happened was I got a last-minute appointment at the clinic in Frankton." Kit's expression remained blank. Pam groaned. "The plastic surgery clinic. I got a boob job."

"A boob job?" Kit shot backwards. She couldn't stop herself staring at the mounds turning Pam's dressing gown into Mount Ruapehu and her sister Ngarahoe. "But you already had big ones."

"I know!" Pam hissed. "I had a pre-op consultation, and the surgeon found a space for me yesterday. If you tell my husband before they're healed, I'll never speak to you again." She closed her eyes and exhaled. "I shouldn't speak to you, anyway. What possessed you to agree to a cutting demonstration on behalf of the Huntly group? You dropped us in a right pickle."

Kit shook her head and rose. "Debbie did that for you when she invited Cindy to the committee meeting. There were ways to reintegrate her, and that wasn't it."

"I know. I'm sorry." Pam hung her head. She flicked her wrist over and checked her watch. "I need to get dressed. My husband thinks I'm working today."

"Won't he notice something is different when you get undressed?" Kit wrinkled her nose and peered down at her own tiny mangoes.

"Nope. I'm keeping them hidden." Pam released a shuddering smile and sighed. "I spent fifty-five years hauling those mismatched melons around. Yesterday, Podgy Pam morphed into Perky Pamela."

"Good luck." Kit gave her a nod. She clicked her fingers and paused. "How did you find out about Debbie? It didn't make the news until dinnertime."

"The police visited her husband at work to tell him and check his alibi. They took his clothes." Her nose wrinkled in sadness. "Her husband and mine work together at the council."

Awkwardness descended with Kit's imminent departure. She exhaled a cloud of white smoke. "I'm sure I'll see you around." She fixed a fake smile on her face as a lump lodged in her chest. Her haste would cost her more than she wanted to pay.

Pam tutted. "Be careful, Kit. The Huntly crowd are an odd bunch. They didn't need to enlist you to demonstrate for them. It was plain mean when they knew we needed you."

"You have Cindy." Kit backed towards the side gate shaking her head.

Pam rose and settled her hands over her hips. She rolled her eyes. "Cindy can't cut curls!" she snapped. "She says she did the refresher course in Australia but forgot to bring her certificate to the meeting." She used her fingers and thumbs to draw air quotes around Cindy's omission. "I don't know why Debbie invited her. Sharon asked if she'd trim her dead ends and she made an excuse and shot off home like a cork out of a bottle. She left just after you. The woman's all talk."

"Right." Kit's shoulders slumped. Not for the first time, she regretted allowing exhaustion to beat her into the wrong corner. "Tell Sharon to call me and I'll sort out her hair. She'll need to ring the land line as I don't have my mobile phone."

"Okay." Pam inhaled through her nose. She jumped as a male voice shouted her name from inside the house. "My boobs must remain sacrosanct. I'm trusting you to keep my secret."

"I will." Kit strode towards the gate and her fingers closed over the latch. She paused, a frown creasing her brow. "What did you mean about the Huntly group not needing me to demonstrate?"

Pam waggled her eyebrows. "That whole committee is certified to Curly Cut. The Queen of Curl used them as guinea pigs for her experimental course a few years ago. Any of them could do it if they wanted. She gave them all scissors at the end. But she didn't run the course again for another five years, and she extended it to two weeks intensive training as a refresher for qualified hairdressers. She also moved it to Melbourne and only brought it back to New Zealand this year. Rumour has it she didn't rate them. The Huntly group stopped entering the Expo competition after losing six times in a row and they boycotted it until now. They just don't have your flare and even the Queen of Curl knew it."

Chapter Forty-Nine
Curly Conundrum

Kit sat at the junction with the Gordonton Road as headlights danced past her in the silent stream of work traffic. She rubbed her thumb over a dent in the leather steering wheel and sighed. So, it wasn't just Bronwyn, Ronnie and Vanessa who could cut Curly hair but all the women on the Huntly group's committee. She gnawed on her top lip and pondered their enthusiasm at her appearance when they didn't really need her. Jerry's chance phone call with Vanessa had kicked off a chain of events outside her control. She'd become their reluctant human grenade intended to blow up the competition.

Kit pulled onto the main road during a break in the traffic. The waiting vehicle behind her slid out and turned right. The blast of a horn made her jump, and she glanced in her rear-view mirror to find the third car had also made a break for it and almost tangled with a truck heading north. "Idiot!" she gasped. It rode her bumper as the truck exorcised its angry driver's temper by tailgating it. The height of the windscreen above her Bug's rear window meant she couldn't see the embarrassed face of the driver.

Unhappy with being at the front of the potential vehicular sandwich, Kit took a hasty left turn, indicating at the last minute. The SUV and the truck barrelled north towards Gordonton. Kit found a cul-de-sac, turned around and stopped next to a children's play park. She buried her face in her hands and contemplated her altered life. Friday night's celebration had faded to the back of her memory like a movie reel belonging to someone else. One minute she was the star of the show and the next, accused of murder, jobless and without the support of her usual crowd of Curly friends.

She leaned back in her seat and rubbed her eyes. Black mascara coated her fingers. She found a cleaning wipe in her glove compartment and patched up the mess. A glance at the dashboard clock showed the stupidity of her mission. At twenty to seven, even Jerry would still be asleep and not coherent enough to bounce ideas around with her. She released the handbrake and set off for home.

And drove right past the end of her road.

Instead, Kit made another early morning visit to someone who possessed answers of a different kind. She drove to Vanessa's house, hoping to catch her before she left for work. On the way up Vanessa's footpath to the front door, Kit took back her autonomy and formed some conclusions. She hadn't planned to enter the competition at the Expo but found herself forced into it by two different groups. Her personal circumstances coupled with Debbie's death made her less ready to exhibit her skills to a hostile audience.

Kit balled her fingers into a fist and rapped on the leaded glass of the front door.

"Can I help you?" A tall man whipped it open, already yanking a jacket over burly shoulders. Yellow light flooded around him to bathe the porch in a buttery glow. He spoke to someone inside the house and his sharp features relaxed into a smile. "It's for you, Nessie," he shouted, squeezing past Kit. A briefcase occupied his left hand, but he pointed at her head with the other. "I can tell by the curls." He hauled up his jacket collar and bounced down the stairs, long legs moving in a hurried pincer movement. Kit watched him stride towards a vehicle parked on the grass. He reminded her of someone, familiarity in his appearance.

"Hey, Kit." Vanessa appeared in the doorway. Dressed in a frock with blue and red checks, she cocked her head. Chocolate ringlets cascaded down her back and covered her shoulders. They appeared damp but not soaked, a testament to a successful second day refresh without starting from scratch. "Hey, come in, come in." She stood back and waited for Kit to kick off her plimsolls. Heat hit her like a wall from the warm interior.

"Do you have a few minutes to chat?" Kit stood on the doormat, her fingers writhing behind her.

Vanessa frowned. "Problems?" She waved a hand towards the kitchen and moved across the carpet in feet encased in pantyhose. Kit followed, her feet leaving imprints in the deep pile. "Tea or coffee?" Vanessa filled the kettle and grabbed two mugs. Kit opted for coffee and slumped onto a stool at the counter. She picked through her chosen words while Vanessa poured their drinks.

She swallowed as a mug of steaming coffee appeared in front of her. "I need to talk to you about the Expo." She opted for ripping off the plaster instead of delaying the inevitable. "I'm not ready for the competition." The words slipped free, giving her a view of the next ten days without stress bowing her shoulders. It offered her a clear run at proving her innocence and getting her fledgling business off the ground. Kit blew out a ragged exhale. "I'm sorry." She reached for the mug. "I realise it's disappointing for the committee and I'll definitely do it next year. Right now is a terrible time for me."

Vanessa's facial muscles twitched. Her hazel irises seemed to harden. "There won't be a next year." She swallowed, and the words seemed to choke her. "We explained the situation and trusted you with the information."

"I know." Kit leaned back on her stool. The warm air grew cloying, last night's dinner still adding its muted, second hand scents. "I'm deeply sorry. Debbie died and I've lost the special matte black precision scissors The Queen of Curl awarded me." Her shoulders sagged. "Then, I lost my job, and the cops think I killed the woman from the Hamilton chapter."

Vanessa blinked but her body remained static. "You didn't kill her. The detectives will work out what happened. It doesn't matter what scissors you use. Borrow Ronnie's again. I think they're still here somewhere and I'm sure she won't mind right now." She exhaled and leaned her palms on the counter either side of her mug. "Cut hair for a living. The committee can help you with a business proposal and perhaps a loan. We've done it before with other start-ups."

Kit swallowed as the possibilities ran through her mind. The idea of sharing the burden with other women who had business experience attracted her. But she'd need to compete at the Expo to access their help. She sipped her coffee, burning her tongue on the boiling liquid. "Can I think about it?" Exhaustion laced her spluttered words.

Vanessa pursed her lips and drew her brows into a line. Her nonchalant shrug didn't fit with the venom in her stare. "You'll need to decide before the end of today. Jen already entered you and paid the fee. You'll owe the committee two hundred dollars if you don't do what you promised."

Kit choked on her drink. She aspirated liquid and the ensuing coughing fit stole her air. "There's a fee?" Fear forced her chest to cave as though Vanessa had punched her. "I've lost my job and don't have two hundred dollars." She slid backwards off the stool, bumping her mug so that coffee spilled over the counter.

The pursing of Vanessa's lips betrayed a smugness which roiled Kit's stomach. "Then win the competition." She lifted her hand and pulled back her sleeve to examine her watch. "I need to get to work. We can discuss tactics and do a practice cutting session at the next meeting. We've told everyone there's an extra one on Monday. There's a new girl who might make a suitable model, so I'll phone her and see when she's free. Jen pulled her name from the hat after you left." Her brow furrowed. "The way you bolted seemed very odd. I thought we'd made you welcome."

Anger bubbled in Kit's chest. Both groups seemed determined to bend her to their will. She'd escaped one trap only to fall head first into another. Vanessa had her pinned, and she knew it.

Kit turned, her gaze raking the counter behind Vanessa as her mind emptied. She'd think of clever answers later, but not right when she needed them. A familiar bottle caught her eye, and she stilled. Vanessa witnessed her face freezing in a mask of confusion and followed her gaze. A translucent, generic bottle from the bulk buy store sat next to a stainless-steel toaster. Kit swallowed. Her cheeks flushed, and the air crackled with danger as Vanessa turned and shifted an air fryer in front of it. She made the movement appear casual, but the stiffness of her shoulders betrayed the lie. Kit sensed the older woman ahead of her in working out what caused the Curlies to have terrible hair.

Kit decided to leave. She needed time to process the rambling pattern of thoughts. She edged away from the counter before turning, curiosity and a need for exoneration driving her foolishness. "Did you know Debbie?" She asked the question and studied Vanessa's expression as she turned.

"I knew of her." The words left Vanessa's mouth without her lips moving.

"Right." Kit reacted to the sparkling light behind the other woman's eyes, tasting the sense of threat from across the room. She scrambled to cover her error. "I didn't know if each group needed to send a representative to the funeral."

Vanessa took a step forward and Kit jerked, clattering with the stool next to her. "I don't want to see you hurt," she hissed. "Just forget what you think you know." Her chin wobbled above the collar of her dress and her fingers writhed in front of her ample stomach.

Kit held her breath, afraid to say anything to trigger Vanessa's tension into something more threatening. She backed towards the front door. Her feet moved in slow motion as her brain scrambled to make sense of the confusion. Everything had seemed fine with Vanessa until it wasn't. It turned sour from the moment Kit backed out of the competition.

She kept tracking towards the door, too wary of turning her back to do more than edge her heels backwards on the carpeted floor. Fear rolled off the older woman in waves, an unpredictability in the jerkiness of her actions as she reached for a nearby bread knife. The back of Kit's right knee pressed against an armchair and the clanking of bottles marred her silent progression.

She exhaled and glanced sideways, noticing the cardboard box tucked between the chair and the wall. Empty brown bottles nestled together like soldiers, alongside plastic recycling and crushed cardboard toilet roll holders. Kit frowned as a memory of the boxes in Debbie's garage crossed her mind. The same black line scored through the brand name printed on the cardboard. The bottles matched the ones Jerry stashed in the vestry. She lifted her chin to counteract the icicle sliding down her spine as puzzle pieces slotted into place. Vanessa knew Debbie because she'd bought something from her. If it wasn't conditioner, it had to be alcohol.

Her taste buds reminded her of the foul whiskey she'd struggled through on the night of the meeting. Whoever made the alcohol stole the empty bottles from the church. Vanessa formed the link between the church, the alcohol and Debbie. Kit's shoulders slumped. Jackson must have felt like he'd won the lottery when he catalogued the contents of the crime scene. He'd found his dodgy hooch supply and Kit had found Debbie's murderer.

She reminded her feet to move, simultaneously tapping her jacket pocket to check for her keys. "I'll see you at the next meeting." She lifted her hand in a feckless wave, knowing she wouldn't.

The sense of threat emanating from Vanessa seemed to trickle away like flood water. Her body sagged, and she leaned against the kitchen counter, the bread knife clutched flat against her stomach. Her lips snarled as though she'd sucked on a lemon. "See you." Her brittle voice carried across the dining room as her breasts shuddered together like bowling balls. Vanessa's relief at Kit's imminent departure confused her. Surely, she realised Detective Lane would pay her a visit sometime soon.

The front door clicked behind her and Kit paused only to snatch up her plimsolls. A prickling sense of peril surrounded her. "Put them on in the car," she instructed herself in a hiss, coaching her bare feet across the damp, slippery deck. Gripping the banister, she bounced down the stairs, almost falling off the second to last step. Her spine jarred as she skidded to a halt and gasped. A single blue flip flop rested in a camellia bush, its thong caught on a branch. With the sole worn down in the same place, she knew in her heart she'd seen it on Debbie's doormat the day she died. Kit peered over the rail to see its mate lying on its side between the woody twigs and the deck. They appeared as though cast there by a strong wind. She fumbled in her jeans for her phone, not regretting the loss of her contacts list for her next call. The screen opened as she prepared to dial the emergency services.

Chapter Fifty
Outraged Curls

Kit barrelled across the lawn while keying in the digits to unlock the phone screen. The laces of her plimsolls impeded the movement of her fingers and the soles bumped against her thigh and spread grass stains over her jeans. She glanced up as the screen activated, finding herself stepping off the lawn and into a flower bed. A branch attacked her shin through her jeans, and she stopped. She hadn't needed to activate the screen to dial the emergency number but once it lit up in the dirty grey dawn, she realised her near mistake.

Kit exhaled and tramped back across the grass to the front steps. She pressed the camera icon and snapped a picture of each flip flop in turn, nodding with satisfaction at her foresight. Lane believed nothing she said, but images didn't lie. A bright light emitted from the flash and she gritted her teeth and hoped Vanessa would mistake it for passing headlights.

Kit spun to face the road, dropping a plimsoll into the bush. Cursing, she hauled it free by its lace and rose, pushing her phone into her jacket pocket.

"Oops." The familiar female voice caught her by surprise and she jumped and clutched her chest. "Dropsies."

"Jen! Hi." Kit blew out a breath filled with panic and forced her jarred nerves to settle. Jen stood close enough to kiss her, one hand resting on the banister. She'd tied her chestnut curls into a ponytail and perfect ringlets bounced against the collar of her fleece. Khaki combat pants sported multiple pockets.

Kit tried to edge past her, but Jen remained stationary. "I've snapped a couple of pictures of the camellia blooms." She pointed at the pink petals nuzzled between a wall of green leaves. "My mother loves them."

Jen glanced down at Kit's filthy toes and the plimsolls dangling from her fingers. Her expression didn't change, but her tone conveyed disgust. "Liar!"

Kit inhaled and shook her head. She added a lightness to her voice. "No. She prefers the pink ones." She used her shoulder to push between Jen and the bush, but the woman's body formed an immovable obstacle.

A spiteful smile spread across Jen's lips, the gloss glinting in the light from Vanessa's front windows. Kit looked up at the house and considered screaming for help. Jen's dismissive snort stopped her. "Don't bother. She only sees what she wants to see." She lifted her free hand and gave one of Kit's damp curls a tug. "A bit like you, really."

Kit recoiled, almost overbalancing as soft soil claimed her feet. "I don't know what you're talking about." Her poor footing and Jen's height put her at a disadvantage. The air crackled around her, filled with latent danger. Her yellow

Bug sat on the road, waiting with patience and blind to her plight.

"I know you saw me." Jen wrinkled her nose and rubbed a manicured finger across her top lip. "That's why you ran away from the meeting. I heard you tell Vanessa you didn't want to take part in the competition. That's why, isn't it?"

Kit exhaled and shook her head. "I don't know what you're talking about," she protested. Her heart beat its way from her chest cavity and into her throat. The blood swishing through her eardrums deafened her. "I'm leaving now. Jerry's waiting for me."

Jen cocked her head to one side. "The vicar?" She wrinkled her nose. "Bit too pious for me, but my sister-in-law likes the notoriety that comes with church committees and parish council meetings." She shrugged and pressed hard fingers over Kit's wrist. "I live in the annex behind the house. Let's go for a brief chat."

Kit yanked her hand free. "No. I don't want to go anywhere with you. Get out of my way!" Her voice rose, and she hoped it carried to Vanessa's ears. Coins dropped into place in the slot machine of her mind as she recalled snippets of sentences and facts she'd glossed over in her confusion. She took a step back into the depths of the bush. Her ankle smarted at the uneven ground. Bark and twigs cut into her soles as she worked to make it harder for Jen to come and get her. She dropped her plimsolls. One landed next to the lone blue flip flop. "You're related to Vanessa." The dullness in her tone conveyed her acceptance of her peril.

Jen pressed her palms together in an irritating clap. "Clever girl. She's married to my brother." A line appeared between her eyebrows. "Nothing is more important to me than the Women with Curls." She shook her head and her ponytail bounced. "That stupid woman promised to sell the conditioner to her own group, not ours." Her jaw showed through her cheek. Condensation rose like a white cloud from her lips as Jen spoke. "I gave her the idea when I met her at a charity event run by the council. Her husband works there." She flapped her hand in the air. "She tried to flog me lube out of her garage and I gave her a contact at the bulk buy store. Then she got greedy."

Kit's lower jaw dropped in horror. She blinked, icy droplets cascading from her lashes. "You told her to replace genuine brands for chemical crap? Why would you do that?" Anger drove her to take a step forward. "You know how hard it is for the women of WWC! Why would Debbie do anything you said?"

Jen laughed. "I joined your group's Facebook page. I set up a fake profile years ago because it's easy to watch all the groups that way, to listen to your futile prattle and your plans for taking over the Curly world." She cocked her head and pressed a hand to her chest. "Hi, I'm Jennifer from Glenview. I can't get to the meetings because I'm a solo mum with three children." She fluttered her eyelids and Kit recoiled in disgust.

Ice lodged in her throat. "You've been watching us, pretending to contribute and all the time just spying." She pressed a shaking hand against her forehead. "This makes no sense. Debbie ruined women's hair. Why would she do that on purpose?"

Jen spread her hands either side of her, palms upwards. "I told her the stuff from the bulk buy store was safe." She flipped her ponytail with her hand. "I told her I used it all the time and my hair is fine."

Kit swallowed. "You told her it was safe, but the list of ingredients said otherwise."

Jen took a step forward and jabbed her index finger in Kit's chest. "People see what they want to see. I told her it was safe, so she never checked for herself." She fluttered her eyelashes and placed the tip of her index finger between her lips. "Somebody help me. I'm in the hair care aisle of the supermarket and I need someone to check this product for me." The reedy inflection in her voice mocked the hundreds of new Curlies who posted in the group desperate for help.

"You're disgusting!" Kit's fingers balled into fists as rage lit her from the inside and blossomed as a flush across her cheeks. Myriad women's faces floated past her vision, women hating their appearance and sick of fighting the frizz on top of their heads. Her own teenage face joined the crowd, urging her to act.

She leapt from the bush with no poise or grace. Pure temper drove her actions as she punched Jen in the face with every ounce of strength she possessed. Jen gasped as her elbow hit the newel post of the banister. Her brow furrowed in pain. As Kit drove her backwards, Jen used her other hand to scrabble in the pocket of her combat pants. She hauled a knife free in the seconds before they both landed on the soggy lawn.

Righteous anger burned behind Kit's eyes. Instead of rolling sideways and out of range, she scrambled onto Jen's chest and delivered a heavy punch to her nose. She barely registered the sharp scratch of the blade as it tangled in her jacket and nicked the soft flesh over her ribs. "You make me sick!" Kit rammed her knuckles into Jen's cheek for a third time, adrenaline forcing power into her muscles.

Jen tried to cover her face, keeping the knife in her hand as she dragged it past Kit to press her palms over her bleeding nose. The blade opened a gash along Kit's jaw and their blood mingled in a red sticky mess.

The air left Kit's lungs as her chest tightened. She lifted into the air like a child, her knees still bent and her arms flailing. As she twisted against her assailant's powerful grip, she glimpsed Vanessa standing on the front porch. Tears speckled her eyes, and she clasped her hands in front of her chest as though praying.

Chapter Fifty-One
Foolish Heads

Kit whirled like a banshee, writhing and twisting as her body clattered against hard limbs.

"Stop!" The familiar cadence of the voice sucked the air from her lungs, and her arms and legs turned to jelly. He held her around the waist as she registered his presence and ceased struggling. When he set her down on the grass, her knees collapsed and her fingers dug into the loamy soil.

"She attacked me." Jen rolled onto her stomach, blood sputtering from her nose and mouth.

"She killed Debbie." Hatred radiated from Kit's eyes as she glared at Jen's prone body.

"Rubbish!" Jen spat grass chippings and blood from between her lips.

"You're under arrest!" Exasperation hissed through Jackson's words as he strode to the steps and used his handcuffs on Jen. He kicked the knife away with his foot. "I don't want to hear another word from either of you."

Kit closed her eyes as she exhaled. Arrested again for something she hadn't done. Sirens screeched their muffled approach in the background, and Jen glared up at Vanessa. "I won't forget this!" Her shout echoed off the windows and bounced back against the shocked hush of the dawn.

Jackson recited her right to remain silent, getting her to her feet but keeping a hand over the cuffs, pulling her arms behind her. Kit sat in the damp grass, a prickling sensation working its way through her jeans and underwear. She'd look like she peed her pants by the time she got to the squad car.

Blood dripped from her cheek onto her jacket sleeve, but efforts to stem the flow coated her fingers and resulted in a sticky mess. The open wound stung like a paper cut. Her auburn hair and porcelain toned skin would make sure she kept a battle scar forever. She sniffed and hoped it hadn't destroyed the rest of her flagging confidence. She snaked her right hand inside her blouse and blood smeared her fingers as she pulled them free. The knife had nicked the sensitive skin over her ribs, but the volume of blood indicated a scratch rather than a stabbing.

An ambulance pulled up behind a police car and doors slammed as they disgorged uniformed personnel onto the scene. One police officer took Jen to the car while another bounced up the steps to speak to Vanessa. A paramedic questioned Jen while supporting her chin with a gloved hand. She spoke with a high nasal voice, and Kit wished she'd hit her harder.

After collecting the weapon into a bag without touching it, Jackson scrunched across the grass to Kit's side. She kept her gaze on the lower levels of the camellia bush and held out her wrists for him. A pink bloom drooped from within the forest green leaves. "Idiot!" He squatted down in front of her and placed the bag and knife on the grass. "I only carry one pair of cuffs when I'm not on duty." Blue denims met tan Timberland boots at the ankle. Kit shrugged, unable to think of a suitable reply. She tilted her head and wiped her nose on her jacket sleeve. The action spread blood across her chin and a line furrowed in Jackson's forehead. "Come and sit in the car so the paramedics can assess you." He rose and offered her his outstretched fingers.

Kit ignored them and leaned on her right arm. She twisted her torso and tried to rise, realising every muscle in her body had gone on strike. She made it onto all fours and then got stuck, opting instead to crawl a few paces towards the flashing lights. Jackson gripped her beneath the armpits and hoisted her upright. Her jellified legs protested with a dangerous wobble, and she yelped as his fingers closed around the injury to her ribs.

The second cop finished with Vanessa and clattered down the stairs. He called to Jackson as he reached the bottom. Spotting the bag, he bent down and snagged it between finger and thumb. "I'll take this to the evidence locker. Can you do the paperwork when you get to the station? There's another car on the way."

"Thanks." Jackson nodded and offered a half smile.

"You all good with this one?"

"Yeah.

"No." Kit turned towards the other cop, a mute appeal in her eyes. "I'd like to come with you." She held out her wrists and glanced at the handcuffs attached to his belt.

The man frowned, black brows knitting into a line above his sharp olive nose. He looked at Jackson and then back at Kit, his brain whirring with suspicion and confusion. "What's going on here?" He lowered his voice and glanced across at his colleague as the officer bundled Jen into the back of the police car. He'd released her cuffs, and she held a wad of gauze below her bleeding nose.

Kit's phone rang in her pocket, the pathetic bleat muffled by the fabric. She pulled it free and glanced at the screen. Jerry's number strobed, the smiley face he'd added next to his name inducing an attack of longing for the sense of safety he exuded. Before the cops could stop her, she pressed the flashing green icon and lifted the device to her ear. Her fingers shook and a sob cut across her words. "Jerry," she choked. "Jerry."

"What's wrong?" On instant alert, tension entered his tone. He waited, but when she didn't reply, he delivered his message. "One of your friends just phoned the house. Her son found your hairdressing scissors stuffed down the back of her sofa. I called Detective Lane."

"Thank you." Kit's whispered reply suffocated beneath a disgusting sniff. "Jen killed Debbie. She stabbed me in the face and Jackson arrested me." Her chest heaved and her brain switched off in disgust at her display of pathos.

Jackson rolled his eyes at his colleague and the man strode towards his car. Leaning forward, he plucked the phone from her fingers. "Officer Delaney here," he said to Jerry, his tone clipped. "It's a flesh wound. Paramedics are here and we'll head to the station after they've assessed her." He exhaled a ragged sigh. "Okay. See you there."

"You all good?" The paramedic shouted to Jackson from the edge of the lawn and jerked his head towards Kit. "We've got another call." He frowned and tilted his head sideways, squinting to see her injuries. "How bad is it? I should at least take a look."

"We're fine." Jackson pocketed Kit's phone. "It's a flesh wound. The doctor at the station can fix it."

"If you're sure?" He didn't sound sure, but he left, anyway. The ambulance rolled off down the road for a few metres before its flashing lights began strobing the world with a red haze.

"I didn't kill Debbie." Kit sniffed again, the guttural sound an unladylike tribute to her single status. She backed away from Jackson, flapping her hand. "Charge me for this and then let me leave."

Another police car slipped in front of her Bug. Her gaze flicked to the one containing Jen, finding the other woman glaring at her from the rear window of the retreating vehicle. She turned in her seat to maintain eye contact until the patrol car slid away, carrying her to her fate.

Jackson gave the officers emerging from the new car a wave, and Vanessa appeared on the porch again. She locked the front door behind her. A tan handbag dangled from her forearm, clashing with her blue sandals and the purple jacket overlaying the checked dress. Kit stared at her wide feet and her shoulders slumped. Some people were immune to the cold weather, and it seemed Vanessa was one of them. She pointed towards the fallen flip-flops. "They're in the bush," she shouted to her. "The shoes you wore when you went with Jen to kill Debbie."

Jackson blinked in surprise, and his gaze followed the line of Kit's jabbing finger. "You strangled her, and then Jen stabbed the scissors into her neck. Did you realise she was using Jerry's bottles from the church? Was it that or the dodgy conditioner?" She lifted onto her toes and set off running towards the stairs. Jackson took two giant strides and caught her before she reached Vanessa's descending figure, grabbing her around the waist with one arm and turning her in a dizzying circle. Kit found herself facing the camellia bush.

Vanessa's chin wobbled as she reached the bottom step, and Kit screwed her head around to see her. "It wasn't like that." Her soft voice met with Jackson's raised palm as he wrestled Kit to his side with a muscular arm.

"Not here," he advised. "Officer Davies will caution you before you say anything." He jerked his head towards the approaching cop. "I think this is more than just a public order offence. It might link to the Flagstaff death. Take her to the station and hold her until Lane arrives. Don't let her speak to the other woman."

His colleague arrived at the bottom of the steps and offered Vanessa his hand. She took it and transferred her fingers to his forearm as they walked across the lawn to the waiting car like they'd gone out for a stroll. Grass brushed the exposed toes of her pantyhose and spread droplets across her sandals, darkening the fabric in a series of dots. She climbed into the back of the police vehicle and it slid away from the curb.

"Get off me!" Kit snarled her demand and as Jackson released her, she lurched for her plimsolls.

"No!" He grabbed her wrist. "It's obviously a crime scene of some sort, which is why you're here. What do you know, Kit? What have you discovered?" He increased his grip as she strained towards her shoes. "Touch nothing."

"They're my third best plimsolls!" She stamped her bare foot on the grass and balled her fists. "You have all my shoes!" In a fit of unbridled temper, she snatched off her jacket and hurled it into the camellia bush. "Have everything!" she screamed. Buttons popped as she dragged off her shirt, getting the collar stuck beneath her chin. She whirled in a circle, losing her arms and unable to release herself.

Jackson's voice held restrained laughter. "Much as I love your second-best bra, you're killing me." Soft fingers plucked at the hem of her shirt and hauled it down over her shoulders. He grabbed Kit's head and squashed her face against his chest. "You're bleeding and you're freezing." His other hand rubbed her spine. "And you're messing up your hair." Blood spread across the emblem of his grey sweatshirt. "I'm taking you to the station so you can make a statement. You're not under arrest. I promise you can keep all your clothes."

Kit sniffed again, and he produced a handkerchief from the back pocket of his jeans. It smelled of male deodorant as she accepted it and pressed it to her nose. She crooked her index finger and pointed to her jacket. "Can I have that back, please?"

Jackson cocked his head and stared at the jacket clinging to the fringes of the bush. Another patrol car stopped at the end of the driveway. "I guess so." He leaned over the flowerbed and lifted the fabric by the zipper. "It will only confuse matters if it stays here." He handed it to Kit, and she clutched it to her chest. A single officer climbed from the vehicle and settled his hat on his head. He closed the door and ambled across the lawn. His eyebrows rose at the sight of Kit's dishevelled appearance, and he turned his gaze to Jackson.

"What do you want, boss?"

Jackson used his finger to create a circular, all-encompassing motion. "Bag up what you find." He pointed to the plimsolls and one of the blue flip-flops. "The blue ones are evidence, but the dirty white ones aren't. Photograph them where they are."

"I heard most of the details on the radio." The officer removed his hat to scratch at his scalp. Kit's eyes widened as he replaced his hat, wondering if he also had a case of the 'Itchy M's.'

"I'm heading to the station." Jackson pressed his hand against Kit's shoulder. "See ya later." He led her across the lawn to avoid the grit lurking on the driveway. Kit's feet swished across the wet grass. Her bare toes chilled to the point of numbness.

"My car." Kit stared at her Bug, waiting patiently for her and tapped her jeans pocket. "Jen might come back and vandalise it."

Jackson clasped her elbow. "Jen's going nowhere," he soothed. "We'll come back for it. Right now, I need your statement and a doctor should assess those cuts. I'll drop you back here later, I promise." He jerked his head towards a navy SUV sitting outside the front of the neighbouring property. "Please, Kit."

Kit pressed her palm against the bright yellow chassis of her Bug and released a sigh. "Isn't this all a bit much for a little assault?"

Jackson shook his head. "It's more than that. There's something else going on here and you know it. Please get in the car."

Her wobbly legs rebelled against the thought of driving through town in her Bug. "Okay," she conceded. "As long as you promise to come back for my car."

Jackson touched his chest. "I'm a terrible liar."

Kit gave a snort of derision. "Really?" Her features hardened into sharp lines and contours. "You had me fooled." A swallow bisected her sentence. "You kissed me in Debbie's garage to stop me from noticing the counterfeit alcohol. You're a better liar than you think."

Chapter Fifty-Two

Straight Lies

Kit's feet slid on the runner board, and Jackson gripped her waist to hold her steady as she clambered into the passenger seat of his SUV. Grass clippings spread from her bare toes to the immaculate interior. He climbed into the driver's seat and fiddled with settings on the dashboard. A comforting warmth filtered through the leather seat to Kit's damp bottom. "Seatbelt." He jerked his head towards her, and she frowned.

"I'll make everything bloody." She held up her hands to show him the sticky mess. "I already put grass on the carpet."

"It doesn't matter." Jackson leaned far enough across the handbrake to seize her writhing fingers. "Let's go to the station."

Kit turned to him, her stomach roiling hard enough to make her sick. She blinked back tears. "Did I ever tell you why I'm single?"

Jackson swallowed. "I never asked. It's none of my business."

She released a ragged exhale and stared at the rear of her yellow Bug. It offered a haven of honesty and would take her home instead of to the police station and certain incarceration. "I fell in love with a liar." The words seemed to crackle in the air between them. Kit pulled her sleeve over her bloody left hand and clasped the door handle. "One is enough for a lifetime."

Freezing air pushed into the vehicle like a greedy river as she opened the door. Grit bit into the soles of her feet as she ran to the Bug. The fob which should have disconnected the central locking ignored her and forced her to use the key on the driver's door. She fell into the seat and locked it behind her as Jackson rived on the handle.

"Open this door!" He issued the command as a snarl, darting a glance at the police officer leaning over the camelia bush to grab a flip-flop. Kit stabbed her key into the ignition and gunned the engine. Jackson dipped his head to her eye level, a frown bisecting his forehead. "I've never lied to you," he shouted.

"Whatever!" Kit released the handbrake, and the Bug jolted forward, just missing his toes as he jumped out of range. It bounced through the gears, burning oil in its excitement and adding grey streaks to the white cloud of condensation emitting from the exhaust. The soles of her feet smarted against the rubber foot pedals as she drove her car towards Hamilton. Jackson followed, his SUV a carbon copy of the one which almost rear-ended her on her earlier drive. She fitted the puzzle together in her mind. He'd been following her, and she wondered for how long. It fitted with Jerry's nervousness and his questions about a dark coloured SUV.

The realisation drove home another bitter shard of betrayal and instead of heading to Gordonton or to the police station at the bottom end of town, she veered off on a side road and left Jackson scrambling to follow in the heavy school traffic.

"You came back!" Mr Rashid's delight carried him across the shop floor to greet her. A pricing gun dangled from his fingers. His complexion paled as he noticed the blood on her cheek and hands. "What happened?" His gaze tracked to her bare feet and back to her frazzled hair.

Familiar faces appeared from behind shelves, customers feasting on gossip alongside their pot noodles and peanut purchases. "This!" Kit held out her blood-stained palms. "This is what your lie caused." Her voice shook with rage and disappointment. "You and Debbie were the same. It was all about the money and you didn't care who got caught in the crossfire."

The doorbell tinkled as Jackson burst into the shop behind her. If he'd needed a clue to her location, she'd left her Bug slewed across the car park and the driver's door open. His boots screeched against the floor tiles as he halted.

"Tell the truth!" Kit lifted her right hand and jabbed her index finger into Mr Rashid's face. "Tell the police how much money Debbie owed you. Tell them how you purchased counterfeit hair products from her." Her voice wavered and reduced to a hush. The customers ventured from the aisles, not hiding their enjoyment of the scene. "And then tell me why I meant so little to you that you'd set me up to take the blame."

Mr Rashid's eyes rolled until his lids crashed over them to cover his turmoil. He clutched the plastic gun hard enough in his fingers to crack the casing. "I didn't know it was counterfeit," he whispered. "She was one of your Curly friends and so, I trusted her. I apologise for giving you a motive. It was never my intention." He jabbed the gun at Jackson. Another kind of gun would have elicited a different reaction from the police officer.

Jackson's feet moved, and Kit heard him sigh as he edged next to her. He faced Mr Rashid. "You don't think I believed you, did you?" His tone held scorn. "I bought two bottles of whiskey while I listened to your concerns about Kit's relationship with the victim. One went to the laboratory and the other to the manufacturer. Both confirmed it's not what it says on the label. The alcohol proof is much higher than described. I hope for your sake the teenager who died didn't get it from here or you'll face a manslaughter charge."

The gathered customers gasped in shock. Mr Rashid pressed his hands over his face and smacked himself in the forehead with the pricing gun. "But what about my liquor licence?" His wail drifted along the aisles to summon other customers from the rear of the store. The tension left Kit's shoulders as the situation engulfed her. It was bigger than she ever imagined.

"Please, tell the truth about me," she urged. Sadness laced her tone. "I hope you don't lose your liquor licence or your shop. But I quit."

Her feet slipped against the cold tiles as she walked towards the door. The bell jangled overhead like the serenade of an old friend as she walked beneath it for the very last time.

CHAPTER FIFTY-THREE

Follow Through

"Stop running around like a barefoot vigilante!" Jackson caught Kit's arm as she stomped across the car park. Grit dug into the tender soles of her feet, and he dragged her around to face him. Lifting his fingers, he dangled her car key in front of her face. "Did you want your car stolen?"

Kit grabbed for them and missed as he lifted them up and out of range. His brow furrowed. "I don't want to arrest you, but you need to make a statement at the station now. No more unscheduled visits!" He jerked his head at her yellow Bug. "Get in the car. I'm driving."

He'd locked it and the button on the remote refused to cooperate again, forcing Jackson to use the key on the passenger and driver's doors. His lips tightened, but he offered no derogatory comment on the age or temperamental nature of the vehicle. The Bug displayed its disgust at his driving skills by bouncing like a kangaroo for the first half a kilometre. Kit fastened her seatbelt and stared down at her bloody fingers. "Is it bad?" she asked, eventually. She turned to face him. "The cut. Is it bad?" Wiping the back of her hand across her cheek produced another streak of blood.

Jackson frowned. "You don't need stitches, but the doctor uses medical glue." He stopped for a red light and gripped her chin in his left hand. He tilted her head to the side and inspected the cut. "It's still bleeding." He released her and put his hands back on the steering wheel. "You don't want scars like mine." His knuckles whitened, and his fingers twitched. Kit sensed him resisting the urge to touch the myriad of lines dotting his neck. Glass shards from a broken windscreen on a teenage Jackson left their indelible marks.

Kit held onto the ineffective platitude. Instinct told her to reassure him, but she didn't feel much like offering him anything. She blew out a breath and stared through the windscreen at the traffic, a lack of energy robbing her fighting spirit. "You didn't tell Lane what Mr Rashid said." She pursed her lips and winced.

Jackson gave a snort of derision. "I've been a cop for a long time. Give me some credit, Kit. Why would you give the victim a massive amount of cash when you drive a car like this?" As if in response, the Bug gave an indignant lurch and backfired loud enough to make the car behind swerve.

Kit gave a shocked inhalation. "How dare you! I love my Bug. Even if I earned a million dollars, I'd keep him."

"See, right there." Jackson wagged his index finger at her. "If you *earned* it, not if you won it or invested it or stole it. If you earned it."

"I just quit my job. I'm unlikely to ever earn that much." She pressed the bridge of her nose between thumb and finger. "I can't even make my next mortgage payment."

"You're a hairdresser. I'm confident you'll make it work." He winced at another monumental backfire and shook his head. "Besides, your scissors just turned up at the back of someone's sofa."

Kit's face contorted as though she'd sucked a lemon. "I don't want them!" Her irises darkened. "Cindy lied about putting them back into my handbag. She hid them to stop me cutting at the Expo." She closed her eyes and leaned her head against the seat. "I've done nothing to warrant her need to sabotage me every time there's trouble."

"Is that the argument I witnessed a few days ago?" Jackson's lips twitched. "Alec Roy is a player. Rethink your friendship group."

"My friendship group just imploded." Kit flicked at a strand of grass in the foot well with her big toe. She sat up straighter as a memory caused her lips to twist into a pout. "Piper threw shade at someone. I asked her if she'd visited Debbie to get her conditioner bottle refilled and she said no, but her behaviour suggested she knew someone who did. I went after Pam, but she had an alibi."

Jackson rolled his eyes. "You think we didn't know that?" Irritation burgeoned in the set of his shoulders. He fought the Bug to a stop outside Hamilton Central Police station. "You must believe we're amateurs."

"Why did you follow me?" Kit gnawed on her lower lip. "You were outside Pam's house on the night of the showdown and minutes away when I found the body. I saw you at the fast-food restaurant with your girlfriend and then you turned up at Vanessa's. How long?" She studied Jackson's chiselled features for signs of an imminent lie. His expression remained impassive.

"I live in the same street as your friend, Pam." He shrugged. "Coincidence." He lifted the index and middle fingers of both hands to perform air quotes for his next sentence. "My *girlfriend* and I posed as a married couple to help Lane catch people selling stolen items for cash on an Internet buy and sell page. We got hungry after we finished the arrests and paperwork." He spread his hands and sighed. "Hence my day off today in lieu of all the late nights I've spent pretending to purchase anything from jewellery to vehicles. I got up early, having planned to go to the gym, and then saw you speed off with trouble written all over your face. So, yes, I followed you." His jaw twisted to show through his cheek as a jutting line. "And just for the record, I didn't know what those boxes in the victim's garage contained. Draw your own conclusions. You usually do." Cold air blasted around Kit's legs as he popped open the door and slammed it behind him. Her door wrenched open with an agonising creak.

"What about last night, then?"

"What about it?"

"You followed Jerry's car home, and he saw you."

Jackson pursed his lips but offered no reply. Kit sighed and exited the vehicle, watching as he locked it. He lifted her hand and dropped the key into her palm. "What happens now?" Her voice held sadness and vulnerability.

Jackson glanced behind him at the concrete facade of the police station. His brow furrowed. "You speak to Lane. He shouts for a while. You drive home. He shouts a while longer but not at me because I'll grab a ride with one of the traffic guys to my car." His lips quirked into a smile. "He'll release your phone and belongings if you ask him."

Kit nodded. The icy pavement numbed her bare toes as she stared down at her feet. "How did Debbie die?"

"The killer throttled her with a length of strawberry netting her husband left in the garage. The nylon cut into her throat and stopped her breathing." He cocked his head and lowered his voice. "She died an hour earlier than initially suspected. Lane knows you didn't do it."

"Jen wanted her to ruin our group's hair. But like all cheap deals, word spread and the women in her own group started buying it. She just needed to tell Debbie she'd made a mistake, and she'd have stopped selling it." Her lips tightened. "I tripped over a funnel in Debbie's garage. It never occurred to me to mention it. She must have used it to pour the inferior products into the women's bottles while they waited outside for her."

"We found it." Jackson jerked his head towards the front doors. "Come on, let's get this over with so I can go to the gym."

"Okay." Kit followed him along the pavement, standing aside for uniformed officers to pass them. "But I don't know who killed her. Jen was in the house when I arrived. She thought I'd seen her, but those blue flip-flops are Vanessa's."

"Maybe." Jackson sounded uncertain. He held open the front door for her and she slid beneath his arm to find herself in the reception area. People sat on the ripped vinyl benches waiting to complain to the officer who listened from behind a layer of protective Perspex. Heads bowed as though in prayer as they engrossed themselves in the ready entertainment on their phone screens.

"Through here." Jackson indicated a security door to the right and turned his back on her to press numbers into a keypad.

Kit screamed as someone body-slammed her from the side. Quick feet and sensible soles pattered across the tiles without making a sound. The world tilted on its axis as she pitched over backwards and hit the floor with a thud. A terrible wailing filtered through her left ear drum, deafening her to all other noises.

Chapter Fifty-Four
Flippetty Flop

The pressure around Kit's neck lessened at the same time as the heavy object on her chest disappeared from view. Feet moved in her peripheral vision, and Jackson's face blocked out everything else. She pushed herself to a sitting position and accepted his outstretched hand. Once upright, she dipped forward to catch her breath and pressed a tentative hand to the bump at the back of her head. Frizz met her palm in a testament to her miserable day. A glance sideways showed the camera lenses of at least three phones as the bored occupants of the police station filmed the attack. One man commentated, complete with dramatic gasps and deliberate movement of the device as he tossed himself around to infer his heroic involvement in the incident.

"Come on." Jackson slipped his arm around her shoulders and ushered her through the security door. "Your makeshift lawyer is waiting." Another officer held it open until they passed and then sealed it against curious eyes. Wailing issued from along the corridor, echoing from inside the room occupied by Kit's assailant.

Jerry rose from his chair opposite Lane in an interview room nearer to the bathroom. His brows creased when he saw Kit. "What's all that noise?" he demanded. His eyes narrowed at Detective Lane, as though holding him responsible. "Why is she covered in blood? What happened to her face?"

"Mr Rashid is guilty of the noise. The blood is a longer story." Kit accepted his embrace and slumped into the adjacent chair. "He's incoherent."

An officer bearing a clipboard appeared in the doorway. "What should I do with that guy?" He paused for effect as hammering sounded on a door somewhere along the corridor. "He's confessing to everything from back taxes to embezzlement."

Lane wrinkled his nose. "Nothing to do with me." He turned to Kit with a shrug.

"I'll deal with him." Jackson raised clasped hands to the ceiling in a stretch before releasing an exaggerated sigh. "He's saying he's sorry, but it's perhaps not a word he uses often enough to realise violence isn't required."

"He hit you!" Jerry spun sideways in his seat.

"No." Kit shook her head. "Sort of bowled me over like an excited Labrador. I drove to the shop and told him I quit."

Jerry's features creased into a grimace. "You already told him that."

"But he didn't believe me. Now, he does." Kit rubbed the back of her head. "Please, may I have a drink of water?"

Jerry's knee bumped hers as he turned his attention to her cheek. "I want to know everything," he demanded. He produced a packet of tissues and pressed one over the wound. She winced as the pressure sent paper cuts of pain smarting from her cheek to her jaw. She swapped Jackson's stained handkerchief for Jerry's cleaner offering.

Kit skimmed through the retelling while Lane took notes and Jerry pulled a range of faces stretching from exasperation to horror. Lane scratched his head with a bony finger. "We didn't interview anyone named Jen." He dug through his notebook. "She isn't listed as an acquaintance, although we're still sifting through the list the victim's husband gave us."

Kit squeezed her eyes closed. "Jen was definitely at Debbie's house when I arrived because she admitted it. She figured I'd recognised her because I left the group meeting in a hurry. I was actually just tired and miserable."

After knocking on the door, Jackson re-entered, bearing a plastic cup of water. The wailing from along the corridor had stopped. "The duty doctor is here to check Miss Maguire," he said. Water slopped over his fingers as he set the cup in front of Kit. "I've threatened Rashid with obstruction of an ongoing investigation and lying to a police officer. He's quiet for now. What do you want to do with him?" He turned to address Lane.

"Let him stew for a while. Did he supply any of the fake alcohol?" His bushy eyebrows rose in a predatory salute.

"No." Kit answered for him and glared at Jackson. "Though I can imagine why it might be fun to make him believe he did. I always stock the alcohol shelves and I would have noticed any boxes with that same black line drawn across them." She stared at Jackson through narrowed eyelids, calling him out on his earlier untruth. "But it's probably why he's panicking, because he supplied counterfeit hair products." She exhaled. "I can testify he didn't know at the time. He's a speculative idiot but not a deliberate cheat."

Jackson's eyes glittered like diamonds, and he pursed his lips to avoid smirking. "Should I send the doctor in here?" He addressed Lane, but his gaze raked Kit's cheek.

"Yeah." Lane sighed and waved his hand. "Why not? Let's have a party."

The female doctor hailed from a local surgery, hauled away from a waiting room groaning beneath the weight of coughs, colds and more permanent ailments. Business-like and practical, she provided cleaning wipes for Kit's hands and a toe-curling antiseptic spray for her cut. Jerry rose so she could commandeer his chair and she huffed as her gloved fingers prised apart the edges of the wound. "It's deeper than it looks," she concluded. "I don't enjoy stitching faces if I can avoid it." Her blonde brows drew into a line as she surveyed the damage.

Jackson leaned against the wall, staring at his boots and chatting to Lane in a low voice. Jerry sat on the edge of the table with his phone lifted to his ear. His lips twitched as he filtered his voicemails, looking more like a lawyer than a vicar despite the dog collar.

Kit leaned closer to the doctor. "There's another one," she whispered. She turned away from the men and lifted her shirt to reveal the cut over her ribs. The doctor winced and raised the spray bottle.

"This is gonna hurt," she warned.

Ten minutes later, Kit sported two glued cuts and an array of fabric stitches butterflied over her cheek and ribs. The antiseptic spray had provided a degree of welcome numbness, and as the pain receded, she regained more of herself.

"I didn't know she stabbed you twice." Jackson's tone held an accusation. Kit pursed her lips, not wanting to point out they'd spoken more of kisses and betrayal than wounds.

"I'm fine now." She squared her seat in front of the table and regarded Detective Lane through narrowed eyes. "So, Jen went to Debbie's house, but I'll bet those blue flip-flops belong to Vanessa. They're in it together somehow."

Jerry gave a low whistle. "I don't mean to sound like a party pooper, but Vanessa is a pillar of the church. She runs all the community groups and is one of the sanest people I know. Do you believe she went with her sister-in-law to kill a woman selling fake conditioner?" He shook his head. "I worked as a defence barrister for a lot of years, and I've seen some terrible crimes. There's something not right about this."

Kit exhaled and her shoulders slumped. Her neat theory about the killing stumbled and tripped, leaving her back at the beginning. And exhausted in a bone aching tiredness which sapped the rest of her energy. She flapped her hand towards Lane and rose. "You work it out. I'm past caring." She sighed. "I've told you everything I know. Jen became violent when she realised I'd seen the blue flip-flops and recognised them from Debbie's house. There's something about their presence which acted as a trigger." She covered a yawn with her hand. "And whatever that is, the stakes are high enough for Jen to want to silence me."

Chapter Fifty-Five
Back Curl

Jerry paced the pavement outside the police station as Kit sat on a bench next to Mr Rashid. Jackson slumped on the low wall opposite. His hands dug into his jeans pockets as he stretched out his legs.

"Why would you do that to Kit?" Jerry demanded. He straightened his wonky dog collar and moderated his tone as though it had reminded him of his vocation. His gaze remained on the contrite shopkeeper.

Mr Rashid hung his head, defeat in the bowed set of his shoulders. "Panic," he admitted. "The woman died, and I feared any implication in her death. I made such a profit on the hair products, I paid up front for another consignment. It didn't occur to me it wasn't genuine. The purple lube sold well, apart from those few explosions." He picked at a hangnail and glanced sideways at Kit. "Thank you for vouching for me with the detective. And in a spirit of truth, the only reason I didn't supply the alcohol was because I didn't know about it." He released a shuddering breath, and his black brows drew together in a line. "I wonder why she didn't tell me."

Kit's jaw dropped, and she shook her head in disgust. "Always looking for a fast buck," she breathed. "And now you're offended she didn't drag you into the entirety of her lucrative counterfeit goods operation?"

"No, no." Mr Rashid turned to face her, straightening his left knee for balance. "Please don't quit. My wife will divorce me if you don't come back to work."

Kit exhaled. "I can't do it anymore. The early mornings are killing me, and I hate working the entire weekend. You need to find someone else."

"I'll pay you to Plop as often as you want." A beseeching tone entered Mr Rashid's sentence, and his eyes widened to form an expression of pleading. He edged nearer, his trousers scraping against the rough surface of the bench.

"What?" Jackson's lips drew back in disgust. "Plop! Is that even legal?"

Jerry slumped onto the wall next to him. He patted his curls with speculative fingers. "It's when you wrap your wet hair in a tee shirt and soak up the excess water. It helps with forming a cast."

Jackson jerked his body away from Jerry's. "Right." The single word contained dismissal. "If you say so." A light went on behind his eyes. "Does this Plopping involve lube?"

"Oh, yes!" Jerry squeezed his fringe in a shameless Scrunching Out the Crunch. "Nothing seems to get it quite so hard."

Jackson popped up in a fluid motion. "Plop. Lube. Hard. Those are words I don't want to hear in a single sentence from a vicar." He moved away from Jerry on a pretext of checking his phone.

Kit's fingers shook as she removed her phone and wallet from the transparent plastic bag Lane handed her after her interview. White dust covered them, and she wiped each item on the hem of her shirt before reinstating them in her pockets. "My phone is dead." She blinked up at Jerry. "I need to ask Piper what she meant by that look she gave me when I asked if she'd visited Debbie on the morning she died. I've gone off on the wrong track somewhere and instinct tells me that's where it happened."

Jackson exhaled. "Stop sleuthing, Kit. How many more injuries are you prepared to suffer to sort this out? Lane doesn't suspect you of anything. Leave it to him."

"Sorry, but I agree." Jerry winced and cocked his head. "You're off the hook. Get on with your life and let the cops sort out this mess."

Kit spread her hands out on either side of her. Blood stains still congealed between her fingers. "I don't want to remain disenfranchised from Women with Curls." Her tone held a faint whine. "I need their support and right now, I'm unwelcome in two different groups." She rose to emphasise her point.

"Start your own." Jackson whirled around to face her, towering over her as he closed the distance between them. "Do something different. Include men and other outliers who need help with their hair."

Kit's gaze strayed automatically to his head, and his eyes narrowed. "Not me." He fired the denial as his lips raised in one corner. "So, don't even go there."

She leaned her head back on her shoulders and stared up at the sky. Fluffy clouds scooted overhead like bubble cars in an eternal race. "I can't think about it," she admitted. "It's all too difficult."

"Good." Jerry's fingers closed around her elbow. "Go home and watch TV. You've already decimated the church's women's ministry and the parish council by taking out Vanessa. I can't risk you disrupting any more sub committees. Langdon will go nuts."

"Haha, funny." She allowed Jerry to lead her a few steps along the pavement towards the road. A traffic warden strolled along the street, checking parked vehicles with a mobile device. Kit tensed, not wanting to add a parking ticket to her woes.

"A pay rise." Mr Rashid bounced to his feet. He took a step along the path behind her. "No more early starts and no weekends."

"What?" Kit's head jerked back hard enough to give her whiplash. She narrowed her eyes. "I almost believed you."

"I'm serious." Angst knitted Mr Rashid's brows into a woolly black stripe across his forehead, and he wrung his hands in front of his chest. "Sunita loves having you work for us. You running the shop has spared me the horror of retirement. I'll find someone else to do the shifts you don't want and let you work part time."

Kit groaned as a dilemma opened up at her feet. She could run the dairy with her eyes closed, but it didn't challenge her. Yet, a part-time role would enable her to pay the mortgage and set up her Curly Cutting business. She exhaled and offered Mr Rashid a faint smile. "We'll talk some more," she promised. "I have some other human rights issues we'll need to discuss."

Jackson's jaw dropped, and he stared from her to her employer. "Yessss!" Mr Rashid bumped his own fists together when no one else shared his jubilation. He set off up the street at a run as the traffic warden stopped next to his car. A heated conversation ensued, and Kit turned her back on the scene.

"I'm going home," she announced.

Jerry wrinkled his nose and stared at Jackson. "Do you believe her?" he asked.

"Totally." He gave a definitive nod, and Jerry's shoulders relaxed.

"Okay." He pressed a kiss to Kit's forehead and drew back with a smile. "Stay out of trouble. I'm taking two funerals and a table mass this morning so I can't help you."

Kit rolled her eyes and pursed her lips to suppress the derisive comment bubbling free. On the street, Mr Rashid snatched a parking ticket from beneath his windscreen wiper and stamped like Rumpelstiltskin. Jerry's dog collar earned him a nod and a free pass from the traffic warden who made a bee line for Kit's Bug.

"I should go home." She held out her hand for her car keys, and Jackson's lips split into a wide grin.

"I told your vicar friend I believed you." He threw the keys up in the air and Kit dived for them. They landed in his other hand, and he looked down at her with mischief glittering in his hazel irises. She bounced off his chest like an insect. "I know you're going home because we're picking up my SUV and then I'm following you to your house." He laughed at the venom in Kit's scrunched features. "I have a day off and nothing better to do with it."

"We are not friends," she growled. "You're much too irritating."

"Ditto." Jackson threw the keys in the air again and glanced over his shoulder at her. His long strides took him across the pavement to the Bug.

"Morning, Officer." The traffic warden bobbed his head in acknowledgement, and Jackson nodded.

"Hi, Billy." His gaze tracked to the street as Jerry honked his horn and sailed past them. Having torn up the ticket, Mr Rashid played a game of individual hopscotch. His rubber-soled shoes thudded onto the scraps of paper as they skittered around his feet.

Jackson lifted his voice to a shout. "Littering is an offence."

Mr Rashid threw his arms in the air and released a wail of dismay. He bent to collect the pieces in a series of peculiar bunny hops.

"Get in the car, Miss Maguire." Jackson used the key on the passenger door and held it open for her. His stern expression invited obedience.

Kit slumped into the seat and glared at him through the window. She'd fastened her seatbelt and plugged her phone into the charging cable by the time Jackson settled in the driver's seat. Fifty-four missed calls showed on the screen as it charged, and she wrinkled her nose. "I don't know most of these numbers." She used her thumb to flick through them.

Jackson took two attempts to close the door before satisfied the Bug wouldn't propel him out sideways at the next roundabout. "Delete them," he advised.

"No. They might want Curl Consultations." Kit frowned. "Ah, Piper called me twelve times."

Jackson's coal eyelashes fluttered in an exaggerated blink. "And you're pleased about that because?" He started the ignition and waited for the Bug to finish its impromptu coughing fit.

Kit leaned back against the seat with a satisfied smile. "It means she's still my friend." She pressed a button to activate the call and the dashboard speaker amplified the telephonic ring like a klaxon.

A man sped past the car on running feet, his ponytail spiralling behind him. Misery creased his familiar face into a frown. Kit leaned sideways to watch his impatience as the front door of the police station creaked wide enough for him to enter, still at a jog.

"Hello?" Piper's voice filled the car as the call connected. Kit didn't answer.

Chapter Fifty-Six
Buzz Cut

Jackson nudged her thigh as Piper's voice betrayed her concern. "Kit? Is that you? Are you okay?"

She swallowed and blew out a breath through pursed lips. "Hey, I'm fine. Sorry. Poor connection."

"I've called you a few times." Her friend's voice held a plaintive element. "I don't want to lose our friendship over a stupid Expo."

Jackson fought the gear lever into drive but kept his foot pressed on the brake. Kit frowned as he jerked his head towards her seatbelt, showing he wouldn't join the traffic until she'd buckled herself in as the law dictated. She wrinkled her nose at him but complied. "I agree. I tried to pull out of the cutting competition, but the Huntly group already paid for my entry. It's non-refundable. I'll make it clear on the night that I'm independent and pay them back as soon as I can. Are you still interested in modelling for me? I'll understand if it's too difficult."

"I'd love to!" Piper's enthusiasm filled the car. Jackson smirked as he checked the mirrors before edging the Bug into the queue filing past the police station. Piper exhaled. "I used dish washing liquid on my hair and then rinsed with apple cider vinegar. The itching stopped straight away, but the curls aren't bouncing like they should."

"I'll look at it one evening. It might need a deep condition, maybe an Olaplex treatment." Kit glanced sideways at Jackson's expression of incredulity.

"Apple cider vinegar?" he whispered, and she slapped his arm.

"Are you driving?" Piper tutted as a child squawked in the background.

"Yes." Kit glared at Jackson and pressed a finger over her lips. "I just need to ask you a question. Remember when I visited your house and asked if you'd bought conditioner from Debbie on the morning of her death?"

"I didn't." Piper's quick reply held suspicion. "I bought some a few weeks ago and didn't need any more. That's the first time I did the refill option on the Naturals brand, but it obviously didn't agree with my hair."

Kit clamped her lips closed to keep in the comment about the inferior brand not agreeing with any Curly's hair. She exhaled. "I know you didn't visit Debbie's, but you implied you knew someone who did. I thought you meant Pam, but she had an alibi." She crossed her fingers and hoped Piper didn't ask about it. To her surprise, she snorted.

"Ah yes. The boobie appointment. If you want to ask her how she's doing, the code words are '*How are the boys?*' Her husband still hasn't realised. Their marriage grew a little stale over the last year and she wants to pep things up a bit.

Having nipples pointing in the same direction is an important start, I suppose. She's waiting for the bruising to go down and then she'll do the big reveal."

Jackson clapped a hand over his mouth and pressed. His eyes watered. Kit jabbed her knuckles into his thigh, and he swerved towards the curb. He clamped his hand over hers and kept her pinned there as she fumbled with the phone and almost dropped it. "Who visited Debbie's house?" She gasped as Jackson released her fingers.

"You did." Regret loaded Piper's tone. "You went to her house. I called into the shop to see you and that other chap said you'd gone to fetch supplies. Not the old man, the handsome one."

"Raj." Kit exhaled. "How did you know I'd gone to Debbie's?"

"He said you drove to pick up some hair products from Flagstaff. It's a residential area, so I guessed. Your shop stocked her lube, so I assumed. I waited for about twenty minutes, but you didn't come back." She lowered her voice. "I didn't mention it to anyone because of what happened before with Cindy. My anger didn't extend to disloyalty."

Jackson's head whipped around, and he narrowed his eyes at Kit. She read his expression as distaste. Lane had interviewed each of the WWC committee members as part of his investigation and Piper had withheld damming evidence. Kit pursed her lips and stared with fondness at the speaker unit. "Thanks, Piper. Pam phoned the house earlier this morning. Her son found my scissors down the back of their sofa. That means Debbie had someone else's in her neck."

Piper made a retching noise. "I can't think about it. I'm relieved your scissors are out of the picture, anyway. Do you think Cindy stuffed them there while we were in the bathroom?"

"She said she didn't, but I'll never know the truth. That's twice she's dropped me in the crap on purpose." Kit sighed. "I can stomach seeing her at group meetings but I don't want to re-join a committee where I have to interact with her."

"Do nothing hasty," Piper urged her. "Let's get the Expo out of the way first and see what happens after that."

Kit agreed and ended the call. Rural roads sped by as Jackson headed out of town. "Dish washing liquid and apple cider vinegar?" He repeated Piper's words with disgust. "It sounds like low level self-harm."

"Whatever!" Kit wrinkled her nose and smiled as he ran a hand through his hair as though self-conscious about his own curls. "Instead of hiding yours under a hat, you could release them into the wild."

"I'm not wearing a hat now." Jackson exhaled. "But I spend two-thirds of my life needing to wear one. Buzz cuts are the answer. You should try it."

Kit winced, and an image of Raki's butchered scalp drifted through her mind. "I'll pass but thanks." She sat up straighter. "Time for one more call. Mr Rashid should have made it back to his shop by now." She reached for her phone and found his number. The speaker amplified the ring tone as she waited for the call to connect, and Jackson grabbed her wrist.

"You can't do Lane's job for him," he warned. Before she could respond, Mr Rashid answered.

"Hi, it's Kit." She pressed on, not wanting him to direct the conversation to his offer of changed employment terms.

"You sent me to Debbie's house on Monday to pick up product you'd already paid for."

Mr Rashid grumbled into his phone, the subject a sore point in his memory. "Yes. Two thousand dollars' worth of women's haircare items and health products. Conditioner, shower gel, and other things. I paid cash for guaranteed pick up within two days."

Kit exhaled. "Yes, but who collected the money?" She tapped her lip in a gesture of impatience. "I saw Debbie thirty-six hours before she died and she asked if you'd be interested. I said no, not after the lube debacle. So, if you paid someone, it wasn't Debbie. And you took delivery of samples of conditioner at some point before she died. I realised that because Danni bought some."

"I didn't say I paid Debbie." Mr Rashid bristled, his voice acquiring the whine of injustice. "Her business partner made the deal. I didn't connect it with her until I got the address to pick up the product. I'd told her I wasn't interested after the exploding lube."

Kit swallowed. "Did you explain all this to Detective Lane?"

The bell over the shop door clanged, and Mr Rashid split his attention between the customer and Kit. "He didn't ask. Four dollars and fifty cents." The cash register pinged, and the shopkeeper swore as the drawer snapped at his fingers. "Can we talk about you coming back to work?" His wheedling tone set Kit's teeth grinding.

"Not yet. Tell me about Debbie's business partner. Is it a man or woman? What's their name?"

"I don't know her name!" Mr Rashid huffed like a bull, and a flash of inspiration revealed the root of his anxiety over the money he'd lost. "A woman approached me a week ago. She said she knew you. Her hair was all curly wurly like yours. She left the samples and said she would come for the money up front for future deliveries. The samples sold so fast, I figured it must be good stuff. So, I paid her when she returned. I didn't know it had anything to do with the exploding-lube-woman."

Kit groaned. He'd handed cash to a stranger on the strength of a dishonest claim of friendship and an empty promise.

"Describe the person who collected the money!" she snapped. Mr Rashid launched into a vague description of a curly haired woman who'd collected the cash and promised him more cheap products. She'd left an address for collection and a time. Kit closed her eyes and let the information percolate into her brain. She exhaled as her boss ground to a halt. "Okay," she conceded. "I'll come back to work. Find someone else to cover the early shifts and the weekends and I'll do it." She ended the call as Mr Rashid's whoop of joy deafened her.

As her phone dropped into her lap, Kit pressed her face into her hands. She exhaled and watched the clouds scud overhead. "I know who killed Debbie," she whispered. "And I think I understand why."

Chapter Fifty-Seven
The Missing Curl

Jackson pulled the Bug into a layby south of Gordonton. The tyres bit into the gravel as they slewed to a stop. "You can't be serious!" His half shout ricocheted off the walnut dashboard, amplifying his disbelief. "I refuse to drive you to visit a potential murderer."

"He isn't there." Kit spun in her seat to face him, and her spine complained. She contorted herself to rub the bruise caused by the fall downstairs. "I know where he is."

Jackson raised his hand in the universal halt sign, his fingers centimetres from her nose. "Let me make a phone call. We can't deal with this."

Kit flattened her lips. "I'm not talking about us dealing with anything. I need to go alone."

"Absolutely flamin' not!" He threw himself back in the seat and it gave a disturbing creak. Jackson folded his arms across his chest. "Not on my watch, Maguire."

"Then, don't look," she snapped. "Move over, and I'll drive you to fetch your SUV from outside Vanessa's house.

I'll go alone."

"Nope." Jackson lurched for the Bug keys at the same time as Kit. They bumped heads, and he jerked back, defeated, as her fingers closed around the wooden keyring and tugged. The letter 'K' flew from her hand in an aerial arc, taking the ignition key with it into the back seat. After a moment of stillness, Kit released her seatbelt and dived over after it.

Jackson fumbled with the driver's seatbelt as the Bug showed loyalty to its owner. Kit bent over the passenger seat, her bottom almost touching the ceiling as she searched for the key. Jackson's shoulder dug into her thigh when he turned and joined her in her scrabbling. The lack of a head rest on the older Bug model assisted them in their hasty access. Jackson's fingers closed around Kit's shoulder as he attempted to drag her back into the front. "Stop!" he demanded, but she ignored him. He knelt on the seat and used both hands to grab her waistband, and she shrieked as her jeans tugged over the crest of her hips to expose her underwear.

"Don't you dare pull my pants down!" she raged.

The backward pressure of Jackson's tugging ceased with such immediacy, Kit plunged head first into the foot well behind the passenger seat. She bumped her face on the ice scraper sticking out of its pocket on her way down, and her feet hit the ceiling. A glint of metal flashed from the opposite end of the vehicle and Kit lurched for the keys. The driver's door opened, and the seat tipped forward, allowing Jackson to reach in and snag them. He batted away her flailing hand. "Happy now?" he growled.

Kit grunted in reply, unable to do much more in her predicament. She placed her palms flat on the floor and tried to push herself back over the seat without success. Giving up, she hung like a discarded rag doll. Jackson's footsteps scrunched around the vehicle, and a whoosh of cold air signified the passenger door opening. "I am so tempted to drive you home like this with your ass in the air!" he bit. "You're the most frustrating woman I've ever met." He hauled on the back of her jacket and she made gagging noises as it restricted her airway. She slithered onto the seat on her knees and spun around, venom already spitting from her lips.

"I bet you don't find Officer Barbie frustrating!" She coughed and pulled her collar away from her throat.

Jackson muttered something incomprehensible and stamped back around the vehicle to throw himself into the driver's seat. "Finished now?" He jammed the key into the ignition and pressed hard on the gas pedal. The Bug spluttered in shock and stalled.

"He doesn't like you," Kit grumbled. "Let me drive."

Jackson snorted. His hand shook as he ran it across his chin. "I don't trust you." He leaned back to haul his phone from the front pocket of his jeans. "I'm calling Lane."

"No!" Kit reached across and squeezed his wrist. "Please, let me at least make a phone call before you unleash the nightmare. Let me get my facts straight."

"Fine!" Jackson stared through the side window as Kit dialled the number from her list of contacts. "Leave it on speaker."

She gnawed her lower lip as she waited, the ring tone jolly and irritating as the heavy emotional distance stretched between them. They both tensed as a click preceded a tentative female voice.

"Hi, Kit."

"How are your boobies?" She paused to let Pam answer.

"Brian wants a divorce."

"Wait, what?" Kit exhaled, knocked off balance by the revelation. "That sounds drastic. He must have liked the old boobies more than you realised." Jackson stared at her, lifting his hand in a circular motion to encourage her to get on with it.

"It's not that." Pam sniffed, and her chest hitched. "I spent money from the savings account. I checked a few weeks ago and didn't realise we'd built up such an enormous amount. A couple of thousand made little difference. He still has enough to clear the mortgage."

"Oh." Kit swallowed. "Where is Brian now?"

"I have no idea." Pam blew her nose. "He told me he got that promotion, but Debbie's husband called round earlier and said they both missed out on the new job. I don't understand what's happening. Where did all that money come from?" Her voice rose to a wail. "My boobs hurt, and I think they're infected."

"It's okay." Kit swallowed and released a ragged exhale. "Is anyone else at home with you?"

"No." Pam's sobs tugged at her empathy.

"Give me ten minutes," she conceded. "I'll see you soon."

Jackson slapped the steering wheel as soon as the call ended. "What the hell?" he demanded. "You're not going round there!"

"Yes, I am!" She raised her voice to a shout. "You have no legal reason to stop me."

"I'm calling Lane." Jackson lifted his phone and jabbed at the screen.

Kit gritted her teeth. "To tell him what? The second you mention it's my theory, he'll laugh himself sick."

Jackson dropped his phone into his lap. "You're right." Defeat slumped his shoulders, and he shook his head. "What do you suggest?"

Kit sat sideways in her seat and lowered her voice. "Jen lives with Vanessa. The blue flip-flops were at Debbie's house when I arrived and then gone when I left. Vanessa has enormous feet, so I thought they were hers and that she and Jen visited Debbie. Apparently, all the Huntly committee attended the trial cutting course run by Vanessa's sister. Any of them could have owned the matte black precision scissors stuck in Debbie's neck." She reached out and clasped Jackson's writhing fingers. "I think either Jen or Vanessa is having an affair with Pam's husband. The flip-flops belong to him. I saw Brian arrive at the police station as we left, and both Jen and Vanessa are there. One of them must have called him for help."

Jackson slipped his hand free, and she swallowed as unexpected disappointment coursed through her. He stared at it for a moment before pressing his palm against hers and linking their fingers in a jointed steeple. "What do you think we should do?"

Kit gave a long exhale and shrugged. "Pam's unwell, so I should see if she needs a doctor. She's also my friend and I'm aware it colours my judgement. You could come with me and wait in the car?"

"Okay." Jackson's concession came with conditions. "But we're dumping this rust bucket and going in mine. Agreed?"

Chapter Fifty-Eight

Boobalicious

"We can go in your rust bucket for sure." Kit fixed a sweet smile onto her lips. Jackson's grammatical error provided small comfort as he ground the gear lever into drive and bunny hopped the Bug from the layby. He drove first to Vanessa's house to retrieve his SUV, stopping to converse with the lone officer charged with photographing the site of Jen's assault on Kit and bagging any evidence. Kit set off home to drop off the Bug, although she fought the temptation to drive straight to Pam's and cut Jackson from the equation.

She pulled onto the verge a kilometre before her house and got out of the car. "What are you doing?" she demanded.

"Walking the horse." Raki held the lead rope in his left hand, using his right thumb to scroll his phone screen. Bouffant's enormous hooves clumped in lazy arcs as his eager lips snatched at the long grass. His curly tail swished against his hocks in a regular rhythm which deterred imaginary flies.

Kit placed her hands over her hips. "Does Langdon know you're doing this?" Her voice rose at the end of the sentence. The vicar had bitten off much more than a bite size when he gave the enormous animal a home. His Saturday riding lessons had become weekly entertainment and the girl who drove out to the paddock to school him had visibly aged.

"Yeah." Raki pulled his gaze away from his phone. He lifted the peak of his baseball cap to reveal the shadow of dark regrowth on his head. "Is it ready yet? I've picked some symbols I'd like on my head."

Kit frowned. "Not quite. Hair grows around one and a half millimetres every month. I'll look at it again next weekend."

"Okay." Raki nodded. "Sounds great." He tugged the lead rope to discourage Bouffant from reaching so far into the ditch after the greenest shoots of grass. The promise of spring sent a newness into the air. "What happened to your face?" He squinted at her cheek.

"A silly accident. Why are you walking the horse?" Kit turned back to the car to avoid his scrutiny.

"Langdon wants him to have a varied diet and a change of scenery." He shrugged. "I don't mind. It's thinking time for me. Did you know the element Tennessine decays in less than a second?" Bouffant lifted his head in reply and blew out a warm breath, which ruffled Raki's jacket. A sense of peace surrounded them, and Kit envied it.

"You're a good friend." She sighed. "We'd all be lost without you."

"Thanks." Raki's body tipped as Bouffant tugged on the lead rope attached to his head collar. They continued their rambling gait as Kit drove past them with care. She glanced in the rear-view mirror to see Jackson's SUV slow behind them and use the other side of the carriageway to overtake. His consideration reminded her that he'd been a good friend, too.

She bounced the car onto the driveway and sat for a moment beneath a stray shaft of sunlight. The side gate to Bouffant's paddock stood open, and a wild turkey pecked around in the horse's giant footprints. Fuzzy thoughts of Raki and Jackson coupled with the sight of the dents from Bouffant's feet merged into a conclusion in Kit's mind. She held her breath and let it percolate.

A knock on her window made her jump, and the door popped open to reveal Jackson's impatient glare. "Come on, Maguire. Are we doing this or not?" He wagged a finger at her. "Don't expect me to look at infected boobs!"

Kit dived from the Bug and examined her phone screen. "Fifteen percent battery." She shrugged. "It'll have to be enough for now." She pushed it into her jeans pocket. "I've got some facts wrong." As she shoved a curl behind her ear, a camellia leaf came away in her fingers.

"What's new?" Jackson turned his back on her and strode away, but he waited for her next to the passenger door.

Kit paused and glanced down at her muddy feet. "I've run out of shoes and I'm still filthy."

His fingers closed around her chin. "Yeah." He tilted her face and his lips grazed the end of her nose. "Filthy but compelling." He held the door as she clambered onto the runner board before slamming it behind her.

"What did you get wrong?" He started the diesel engine and the vehicle chugged away from the curb.

Kit blew out a breath through her nose. "This isn't about counterfeit hair conditioner or embezzlement. It all comes down to big feet and a specific kind of friendship."

"What other sorts of friendship are there?" Jackson leaned forward to check the intersection before driving the vehicle onto the main road. His strong knuckles bent and flexed as his fingers curled around the steering wheel. Kit settled back in her seat, the belt hugging her stomach and dividing her breasts like a boundary fence. She lifted her fingers to list them.

"According to studies, there are four types; acquaintance, friend, close friend and best friend."

"What are we?" Jackson glanced sideways at her, a smirk lifting a corner of his lip.

Kit blinked, clinging to her train of thought. "Ask me again after today." She pursed her lips and loosened the grip of the seatbelt. "This is about a special kind of friendship, one which calls for something extra. That's what I missed." She clicked her fingers with a grin of satisfaction. "Stay in the car. I'll call you and leave the connection open between us. You'll hear everything."

Jackson huffed out his exasperation and made the turn into the Flagstaff suburb. "It's not admissible unless your friend knows I'm listening."

"Come in with me then." Her irises sparkled like gems. "But don't blame me if she wants to show off her new boobies."

He tutted. "I live on the same street, remember? I've seen her putting the rubbish out in her dressing gown."

Kit sighed. "That's a relief. I'd hate to think of you relying on Officer Barbie for your thrills."

"Jealousy looks good on you, Maguire." Jackson stopped by the curb outside Pam's house, lining the vehicle up with her front lawn. He pulled his phone free and dialled a number.

"Hello?" Kit answered the call and held the phone to her ear.

"It's me, you idiot!" Jackson snarled. "And I intend to record this conversation so keep it clean."

"Right." Kit stared at the device. "Where do you suggest I put it, so I don't disconnect the call by accident?"

"I don't know! In your jeans pocket?"

"Not a good idea. I bent over once and called the fire brigade."

Jackson bowed his forehead to touch the steering wheel, and the horn tooted. A dog walker across the street jumped and clutched at her heart. "Just get in there and look at her boobs," he groaned. "I still don't understand why I need to listen. Are you afraid of medical misadventure litigation?"

"Not quite." Kit pulled her shirt away from her chest and slipped the phone into her bra. "Just shut your eyes a second," she commanded. Her fingers paused as she waited for Jackson to clamp his palm over his face. "I need to turn it round, so the microphone faces outward, or you'll hear me breathing." She peered into her bra and released a nervous giggle. "Good job it's not a video call, or you'd have to arrest yourself."

"I'm considering it."

"You can put your hand down now." Kit jiggled in the seat to adjust her shirt. She nudged Jackson's elbow when he kept his face covered. "I'm decent. You can come out now."

"Leave me alone. I'm practising yoga breathing."

"Oh." Kit paused with her hand against the door. "The boys do yoga. They like to get hot. I'll tell them you do it too. Perhaps you could make a threesome."

"Get out of the car." Jackson's flat tone held a warning.

"I'm trying." Kit pushed the door open and dangled her feet over the runner board. "It's quite high up, isn't it?" He didn't respond, not even when her bare feet slipped on the board and she sat in the foot well with a bump. The impact jolted her already painful tail bone. She glanced back at him, but he kept his eyes covered. His lips moved as though in prayer.

Kit slammed the door behind her and ran across the damp lawn. The disappearing frost left the grass crunchy underfoot, and she wrinkled her toes against the icy sensations. After a moment spent straightening the phone in her bra and fastening another button to disguise its presence, she lifted her knuckles and hammered on Pam's front door.

Chapter Fifty-Nine
Bad Feet

Pam pulled open the front door by degrees. She bent double and shuffled with a stoop. Her shoulders shuddered with the force of her pitiful sniffs. "What happened to your face?"

"Silly accident. What can I do to help you?" Kit glanced back at Jackson before stepping over the threshold and following Pam along the hallway. She left the door ajar, in case she needed his assistance.

"Nothing." Pam slumped into a dining chair with a groan. "Instead of fixing my marriage, I've messed up everything."

Kit settled in the seat next to her, stroking Pam's shoulder in an ineffectual patting motion. When Pam winced in pain, she removed her hand. "Let's deal with the first issue," she suggested. "You mentioned an infection. Can I run you to a doctor?"

Pam whipped aside her dressing gown to reveal brown tape overlaid by a soft white bra. Perky breasts poked from beneath their covering, mismatched against the stretch marks crisscrossing her flabby stomach. Kit forced her expression into a fake smile. "Lovely." She wagged her fingers to encourage Pam to put her boys away again.

"No! Look!" She widened the aperture in her dressing gown and Kit leaned closer.

"What's that?" She pointed at the lower section of the left boob and recoiled. "Oh, dear. You're leaking yellow stuff."

"I know!" Pam rose, bumping her hip against the dining table as she stumped across the kitchen. "I noticed it this morning after my shower. The antibiotics aren't working." She snatched a container from the counter and shook it. Pills rattled inside and she peered at the label as though it might provide answers.

"Why don't you call the surgeon who did your operation?" Kit employed her most soothing tone. "I could drive you there."

"Did you ever notice Debbie's boobs?"

Kit held her breath. "Before or after she died?" she whispered. She closed her eyes as embarrassment flushed her cheeks. The conversation veered away from its imagined direction, and she pictured the disgust on Jackson's face as he listened from the SUV.

"Before!" Pam's voice rose to a shout. She dropped the pill bottle on the counter and it rolled until it butted up against the sink. The tiny tablets shuffled around inside like marbles. Kit's eyes widened as Pam lifted both hands and mimed a cupping motion. "Two perfect melons!" she spat.

Kit floundered. Her mind's eye conjured an image of Jackson rolling around in the SUV, covering his laughter with his hand as she made a fool of herself in a bid for truth.

She rallied. "I noticed. Remember the official group photo last Christmas? The committee sat on chairs in the front row and Debbie stood behind in a temper because we didn't arrange enough seats. She posed between Sharon and Piper and it looked as though she balanced her breasts on their shoulders."

Pam snorted. She jabbed her sternum with her index finger and hissed in pain. "I didn't arrange enough seats on purpose. I told her to stand behind us because I didn't want her on the committee." She waved her right arm in a wooden arc. "You idiots voted her back in power year after year. I tried to resign and you wouldn't let me." Her voice held a hint of hysteria.

"I'm sorry." Kit's shoulders sagged. "I didn't realise you felt so challenged by her." She paused for a moment and thought through the last six months of committee meetings, finding she'd attended in body only. Her mind had been on her duties at the shop or the next assignment for her course. "I'm a rotten friend. Sorry. You tried to resign, and I resisted because it made life easier for me." Kit rose and took a step towards her. "Resign now and I'll accept it on behalf of the other girls."

"You're not on the committee anymore." Pam's shoulders shuddered as tears fell from her cheeks onto the dressing gown. They zig zagged along the fluff, driven by gravity and a desire for escape.

"True." Kit frowned. "Let's call Piper. She can accept it." She lifted her fingers to touch her phone through her shirt and winced, wondering if Jackson would understand why she killed the call. He might show gratitude if still recovering from Pam's obsession with a dead woman's breasts.

"This is all your fault."

Pam's eyes flashed with a dangerous light, and Kit froze. "How?"

She edged backwards as Pam's venom found an outlet. The woman's hands balled by her sides, flexing and opening like pincers until she raised a finger and jabbed it in her direction. "You started it with all that lube you ordered by mistake. It gave her a taste for selling from her garage, working for herself and answering to no one. You let her push you out of the committee without putting up a fight. Debbie wanted you gone, and you just walked away from us like we meant nothing to you."

Anger flared in Kit's chest. She gritted her teeth and defended herself. "Not one of you spoke up for me that night. You all sat there watching as she pushed me around and made it impossible for me to stay. I arrived with such excitement, desperate to show you my new scissors and Cindy ruined that too." She frowned. "Where are they? I want them." Kit stuck her chin in the air. "I'm accepting no responsibility for this fiasco. Give me my scissors and I'll leave you alone." She spun on the spot, checking the counters and the table for the familiar velvet case. "Did the detective take them already?"

Pam squeezed the bridge of her nose and sniffed. "Brian's gone to the police station, and he took your scissors with him."

Kit froze, wondering how much Pam knew of her husband's extra-curricular activities. "Okay. I'm sorry he wants a divorce." She softened her tone to suit the moment, but her body exacted its revenge. A loud hiccup emerged at the end of the sentence. Pam glared at her.

"Nerves. Sorry." Kit hiccupped again and clutched her chest. "It's embarrassing. Sorry." *Hiccup*. She wished with all her heart Jackson couldn't hear the unfolding disaster. "Does he know anyone called Jen or Vanessa? It's what I wanted to speak to you about. Money, lust and jealousy are the only things that make sense in Debbie's death. All murder starts with a particular relationship between two people."

Pam's lower lip trembled and fresh tears plummeted onto her dressing gown. "Who?" Her face creased in confusion. "I don't know them." Alarm back lit her irises. "What are you suggesting?" Hysteria rose in her voice. "What are you saying?"

"Forget I mentioned it." Kit backed towards the kitchen door. She hiccupped as her spine hit the frame. "I don't suppose Brian owns a pair of blue flip-flops?" She exhaled. "Of course, he doesn't. My mistake."

Pam snivelled into the cuff of her dressing gown and shook her head. "He hates anyone seeing his feet!" she wailed. "And I hate him."

Chapter Sixty

Tarts and Vicars

Kit closed the front door and screamed as she ran into Jackson's chest. She buried her face in her hands to avoid hurting her cheek. Another hiccup rocked her torso, and she jumped as his fingers closed around her wrist.

"Why did you turn your phone off?" he demanded. "What did she say?"

"I didn't!" Kit hauled the device from her bra and stared at the blank screen. She hiccupped again and pressed the power button. Nothing happened. "It's dead again." She narrowed her eyes at him. "It died in Lane's custody!"

Jackson blinked and dropped his chin. "It died in yours. Why didn't you check the battery before you went in there?"

Kit hiccupped again, midway through a deep sigh. "You saw me charge it. I thought fifteen percent would be enough! How much did you hear?"

He ran a hand across his head and shrugged. "A naked photo shoot with women putting boobs on each other's shoulders. The connection disappeared, and I got concerned. I pushed the front door open and heard you both talking about a committee. I waited out here in case things turned ugly."

"She's got antibiotics." Kit shifted from the gritty path to the lawn to avoid hurting her feet. "My scissors are at the police station with her husband." She glanced back at Jackson. "I thought he was having an affair with Jen or Vanessa." Kit shook her head. "She holds me responsible for everything. What a bloody laugh!"

"Where to next?" Jackson gave her a shove into the passenger seat. "Do you want to talk to Lane?"

Kit sagged against the leather. "No. He doesn't believe me. I'm sure Jen and Vanessa killed Debbie. Jen told me she saw me at Debbie's house. Mr Rashid's description of a curly haired woman could fit her." She whirled to face him. "You could ask to look at the security footage from the shop. Then, you'd know for sure."

"True." Jackson started the engine. He shook his head as she opened her mouth. "But we're not going back there today. You're staying out of this and it's my day off."

Kit tapped her chin and continued with the washing machine of facts swilling around in her brain. "I heard someone pulling boxes across the concrete floor when I arrived at Debbie's and if Jen's having an affair with Brian, he might also be a partner in the conditioner scam. That's where the extra money in Pam's bank account came from. Only, she spent it on a new pair of infected boobs."

"Oh, dear." Jackson tutted and straightened his lips into a solemn line. "Then, her new boobs are an asset purchased using the proceeds of crime. She'll have to give them back to the state."

"What?" Kit inhaled in a shock substantial enough to dispel the hiccups. "You can't do that!" Jackson's snort of laughter induced a writhing sensation in her gut. She shook her head. "I give up for today. My hair needs washing and I'm hungry." Her jaw ached from clenching her teeth. "I want my scissors back and for life to return to normal."

Jackson laughed. "Whatever normal looks like for you."

He drove Kit home, but seemed reluctant to leave her there. She left him making toast in the kitchen while she took a shower and used Sugar Scrub on her hair. The hot water soothed her bruises, although the water soaked the gauze over her ribs and cheek. "You're a useless sleuth," she whispered to her reflection.

She clattered down the stairs at the sound of the doorbell. Jackson emerged from the lounge with a plate of toast in his hand. "What's that noise? he demanded.

"Doorbell." Kit's fingers closed around the handle. "It sounds more like a fart because the batteries leaked and Raki did one of his special fixes."

"Right." Jackson leaned against the wall and watched as she hauled open the front door.

A petite blonde stood on the porch, red manicured nails clutching a fake Louboutin handbag. A heavy coat shrouded her slender frame in a layer of faux fur, and her scarlet stiletto heels scraped against the wood. She spoke from behind a collar turned up to cover her chin. "Do I have the right address for the Reverends, Langdon and Jerry?" Her clipped tone rubbed Kit up the wrong way.

"Not another one!" She rolled her eyes. "At least you're older than the last girl."

"Sorry?" The woman cocked her head to one side and stepped closer. "What last girl?"

"It's kind of you, but we don't need anyone. I'm capable of taking care of the boys myself." Her gaze flicked to the woman's straightened hair and her fingers itched to fix the repressed curls screaming beneath a layer of hair spray. The damp air attacked it so that a layer of frizz rose in rebellion like a haze.

"Taking care of the boys?" The woman frowned. She pulled her chin from her collar to reveal matching red lipstick. Her blue irises sparkled like gems. "I'm passing through and thought I might catch one of the reverends."

"But they don't want to get caught." Kit rolled her eyes. Her chest gave a minor hitch as a remnant of the hiccups returned. "They're more capable than everyone thinks. They can pick up their own underpants!"

She closed the door in the woman's face and met Jackson's confused expression. Butter dripped from the toast suspended in his hand to create a yellow pool on the plate. Kit sighed. "At least you look house trained," she commented. She moved to the lounge window and watched the woman clatter back to the road with spiky footsteps.

"Why did you send her away?" Jackson followed her and joined her nosey vigil.

"The mothers in the church congregation send their daughters to clean the house. It's their way of pimping them to the boys in the hope they'll fall in love at the sight of them wearing yellow rubber gloves and want to marry them. It's the Christian version of an aptitude test. If you can cope with Jerry's famous melting socks and Langdon's colour coded shirts, you can progress to the next stage. An unfortunate side job is dealing with Raki's days-of-the-week underpants which he wears out of sync, but I figure any prospective wife will plan to evict him. He's not marriage material. I chased off one girl last Saturday but Raki said she wasn't the first."

Jackson twisted his lips. "Didn't she look too old for that? And she wore a wedding ring."

"What?" Kit rounded on him, pressing her fingers over her lips. "Why didn't you say something?"

He shrugged and pushed a crust into his mouth. "Looked like you had it sorted, Maguire. Like the Debbie thing. Clueless, but as fascinating to watch as a traffic accident you're powerless to stop."

Kit swore and ran to the front door. She hauled it open, but the woman's car slid away from the house and moved out of sight beyond next door's hedge. "Give me your phone." She returned to pat his clothes, finding the device in the back pocket of his jeans. "Mine is still charging." His big toe poking through a hole showed he suffered the same sock issues as Jerry. "Code!" she demanded, turning the screen towards him.

Jackson obeyed, leaving a buttery streak on the surface. Grease stuck to Kit's fingers as she called up a web browser and performed a search. Her shoulders slumped and her head drooped forward as she spun the screen around to show him the result. He winced at the image of the visitor wearing a purple shirt and white dog collar at her inauguration two years earlier. "You just shut the door on a bishop after calling her a tart," he said with a grin. "Stick to hairdressing."

He ambled back to the kitchen and jammed two more pieces of bread into the toaster. Kit sank onto the sofa and stuck her head between her knees.

Chapter Sixty-One
The Wrong Curls

Jackson took a call as he finished working his way through the loaf of bread. Kit confiscated the toaster as he turned to answer the jaunty ring tone. "Delaney. What have you got?" She raised an eyebrow at his curt salutation, wondering if she'd get away with responding to her callers with such a crisp reply. As he stepped into the lounge and out of earshot, she loaded the dishwasher with his plate to halt the feeding frenzy laying waste to her shelf of the fridge.

Her phone buzzed on the counter and she washed her hands and lifted it to her ear. "Maguire. What have you got?" The charger cord stretched taut.

"Nothing!" Marian's voice rose to an instant squeak. "I've got nothing."

Kit realised her new technique wouldn't wash with her mother and moderated her tone. "I'm not suggesting you're infectious," she soothed. "It's a new way of asking what you want."

"I don't want anything! Why do you assume I want something from you? Can't I phone my daughter to see how she is?"

Kit blew out a breath which disturbed her damp fringe. She tested the coil with tentative fingers, estimating the drying time until she could Scrunch Out the Crunch again. She'd foregone the Plopping process with Jackson still in the house. He'd seen her wearing Mrs Rashid's green hijab before and didn't need a repeat.

"Why have you ignored my calls?" Marian's voice wobbled. "Have I offended you?"

"No." Kit leaned against the counter and contemplated a noodle encrusted bowl abandoned in the sink by Raki. The charger cord stretched to its limit and she sank onto a stool. "Sorry. I lost my phone for a few days."

"Oh." Her mother sounded mollified enough to continue. "I wondered if you'd trim Stephanie's hair. She's trying so hard to do this Curly thing but it's looking like a haystack at the back. I haven't mentioned it to her because I don't want to ruin her confidence. She's working on the fringe at the moment."

Kit exhaled into the phone. "It doesn't work like that. You can't do the process one hair at a time. I know for a fact she's dyed it purple at the back, Mum. That's why it's a mess. It's like shaving your legs but only doing your shins because that's the bit you can see. Meanwhile your calves look like they belong to a horse."

"There's no need for rudeness." Marian's tight tone acted as a hazard warning and Kit tensed, waiting for the familiar mantra. "I know you don't like Steph, but she has extensive emotional needs. You of all people should extend Christian kindness to her."

"Because I live with two vicars?" Kit wedged her tongue into her cheek to stop it wagging her into any more trouble. She'd lost the battle before it began. "Fine," she conceded. "I'll make time to trim her hair next week. But you need to stay in the room because otherwise she'll blame me for everything that goes wrong in her life from that moment. I need witnesses to prove I didn't make her face spottier or put extra weight on her hips."

"Okay dear. We'll pencil it in for Monday of next week. I'll provide dinner."

"And the antidepressants."

"What? I didn't catch that last thing." Marian feigned ignorance and ended the call after blowing a wet kiss through the speaker.

Kit tilted her head back to stare at the ceiling. Fly poop collected around the overhead spotlight and she grimaced while contemplating standing on a bar stool and attacking it with a baby wipe. Raki detested flies and often performed an effective contemporary dance using chopsticks to catch them. It worked better than the vile concoction which passed as his homemade fly spray and made everyone cough up a lung.

"What are we looking at?" Jackson appeared next to her, his footsteps approaching with worrying stealth.

Kit sighed and set her phone back on the counter. "Do you think it's unreasonable to ask a free cleaner to wash the ceiling?"

He blinked. "How can I get one of these free cleaners?"

"Wear a long black robe and pretend you're nice." Kit sniffed. "It wouldn't work. She'd need to take off her stilettos and her skirt is too short for aerobatics."

"Wow. Does she take bookings?" Jackson sank onto the stool next to her. "Did you get hold of your flat mate?"

She shook her head and cringed. "I left a message. Perhaps I should move in with you until they cancel the hit on me."

"That's a little forward of you." Jackson grinned, revealing the dimple in his right cheek. "I'm sure the bishop's taken worse insults than 'skanky cleaner' in her chosen career."

Kit groaned and rested her forearms on the counter. "They're both terrified of her. I probably just cost them their parish. Why didn't you stop me?"

Jackson jerked backwards on his stool. "Again, I'm not your keeper, Maguire." His gaze flicked to her lips and his sparkling irises lost their humour. He cleared his throat. "Lane called me. His murder case is unravelling by the hour. The victim had a lover. Lane's interviewing her husband to see if he knew. If he did, that's a motive."

Kit's jaw dropped open in an unladylike gape. "Debbie? Are you sure?"

Jackson shrugged. "Lane released the woman who attacked you. He thinks an assault charge would be too sketchy as she was technically carrying a knife on private property and claims you attacked her. He said the other one didn't have anything useful to add about your assault, so he let her go as well."

Kit edged off the stool as confusion descended over her like a cloak. She shook her head and stared at Jackson. "Jen was in Debbie's house when I arrived." Her voice rose. "She admitted it before she attacked me. I told you that!"

"Hey." Jackson rose and caught her flailing hands. "He's under pressure but he'll put the pieces together. He always does. Maybe there's stuff going on that he isn't sharing with me because you called me first, remember?"

Kit's breath caught in her chest as his fingers smoothed along her arms and wrapped around her shoulders. Dismay consumed her in the same way it did in Debbie's garage. "I'm sorry you're still suffering but he's got it wrong," she whispered. "He's got it all wrong!"

Jackson inhaled and folded her against his chest, resting his chin on the top of her damp curls. "Then he'll find that out, won't he? He's not interested in my contribution, not since you phoned me instead of the emergency services. He's banned me from getting involved."

Kit's phone rang again and she groaned. Jackson released her from his embrace as she lifted it from the counter. "Damn!" she hissed as she peered at the screen. "I just agreed to cut my stepsister's hair on Monday and that's the night of the Huntly Curly meeting." Jackson took a step back while she answered the call. Her tone changed when she heard the other person speak. "Hi. What do you want?"

"To talk." A sniff punctuated Vanessa's tearful voice. "You don't have to come to the house. We can meet at a coffee shop if you'd rather. I know your last visit to mine didn't go so well."

Kit snorted. "You think?" She ogled Jackson's physique as he strode across the tiles and rifled through the cupboards for a clean glass. His biceps flexed as he ran the tap and scarfed an entire half pint. She toyed with the idea of inviting him to tag along to meet Vanessa and then discarded it. He'd baulked at her joke about moving in with him to avoid the forthcoming clerical showdown with her house mates. She needed to file their relationship back in its correct slot of cop and regular victim. "Fine!" she snapped. "Two o'clock at that cafe near the Flagstaff roundabout."

She ended the call and bumped her phone against her lower lip in thought.

"I'll head off if you've got a date." Jackson opened the dishwasher and placed the glass on the top rung.

Kit opened her mouth to reply and her phone trilled again in her hand. She recognised the jaunty jazz ring tone and almost dropped it. "It's Langdon." She swallowed and her complexion paled. The white fabric stitches on her cheek blended with her waxy hue. Her fingers shook as she pressed the button to connect the call and lifted the device to her ear. She thought for a moment she'd put it on speaker by accident as the volume of Langdon's shout filled the room. It bounced off the cupboard doors and the ceiling before hitting Kit in the face.

"What the hell did you say?" he yelled, hysteria nipping at the fringes of his wail.

Chapter Sixty-Two
Curly Con Merchants

"I'm so sorry, is that what Jen did to you?" Vanessa rose as Kit stalked across the cafe. She stared at her cheek, reaching her arms out as though to hug her before stalling. The look of derision fixed over Kit's slender features created a barrier. She yanked her purse from a patent handbag and jerked her chin at the counter. "What would you like? My treat."

Kit sank into the seat opposite and sighed. Having recovered her belongings from Detective Lane, she'd discovered her best plimsolls in a terrible state. White fingerprint powder coated the uppers and laces while a sticky substance caused the soles to stick to everything they touched. It smelled like floral alcohol, and the blatant disregard for her property rankled. She'd intended to continue the facade of disgust throughout the meeting with Vanessa, but found it too exhausting. "Chai latte, please," she conceded. Vanessa nodded and trotted towards the barista, already jabbing her index finger at the muffins nestled behind display glass. Kit frowned at Vanessa's enormous feet snuggled in her blue sandals. Her ankles tipped inward, compressing the soles on the inside edge.

Vanessa returned smiling and waving a stick with a table number attached. "I've ordered a selection of muffins and a large chai latte for you." She swallowed. "It's the least I can do after what happened."

Kit leaned back in her chair and said nothing. She studied Vanessa's discomfort from the perspective of a passive observer. Guilt and anxiety stripped away the woman's usual confidence and left her a shambles. "So, you lied to the police." Kit sat forward and leaned her forearms on the table between them. "Jen admitted she saw me at Debbie's house and I noticed your flip-flops outside the door. Either you tell me what happened now, or I'll draw my own conclusions and make a statement to Detective Lane."

Vanessa's lips twisted into a reluctant smile. "He wouldn't believe you. It's so fantastic, he'd think you fabricated the whole thing."

Kit jerked back in her seat, her brow furrowing. "Are you threatening me?"

Vanessa shrugged. "No. Just letting you know what you're up against."

The barista arrived bearing a tray of food, a berry smoothie and Kit's chai latte. She placed the items on the table and snatched the number before returning to her post behind the coffee machine. Kit eyed the feast, performing a mental tally of the carbohydrates lurking within the sugary pastry, and prepared to pass on the proffered late lunch. She snagged the handle of her mug and dragged it towards her. Vanessa plucked a donut from the platter between finger and thumb, sprinkling sugar over her smoothie as she took delicate bites. "I'm starving," she complained through the dough rolling around her mouth. "I got a ride home, so I could fetch my car after the police officer took my statement. It's taken me all morning to catch up on appointments." She exhaled and sugar dusting sprayed onto the table.

"Yet here we are." Kit stared around the cafe at the other customers. Some waited for their drinks to arrive in cardboard cups and others settled into seats. Her gaze pinned Vanessa in place, demanding explanations. "Do you know a man called Brian?"

Vanessa's face creased into lines, and she shook her hair. Ringlets bounced against her shoulders before settling. "Probably. I know lots of people through the church."

Kit exhaled. She needed to let her theory die a quiet death. "Never mind. What do you want to talk about?"

"Where do I start?" Vanessa dabbed her lips with a napkin and eyed up a chocolate chip muffin spilling over the side of its case. Irritated, Kit glanced at her watch and then folded her arms. Vanessa dropped the muffin onto the plate and sighed. "I didn't kill that woman." She steepled her fingers in front of her. A blob of blue icing coated her thumbnail.

"Why were you at her house on Monday morning?"

Vanessa blinked at the force of Kit's question. A customer waiting for his coffee glanced their way and slid his phone into his pocket. "Keep your voice down!" Vanessa flapped her hands and her ringlets swished as she turned her head to survey their audience. She lowered her voice to a whisper. "My office received a call from a potential new client. They'd set up a sole trader distribution centre at home and needed help with the accounting. There are discounts available from the tax office for people who use part of their dwelling as a business, so it's better for me to visit and work out the percentages on site. The woman said she didn't want a home visit, as she intended to move premises. The receptionist persuaded her to set her accounting up properly from the start as it's easier to tweak than reinvent after the fact. She agreed and left her name and address. The receptionist printed off her details and gave them to me last Friday. I often work from home, so I drove straight to the address for our nine thirty appointment on Monday."

Her lips closed over the straw protruding from her smoothie, and she sucked up a mouthful of the fruity pink liquid. "I figured she left the front door open for me, so I called to her and walked inside the house. No one replied, and I checked the downstairs rooms before finding her in the garage."

She gulped and wrinkled her nose at the memory. Her glance at the muffin suggested she regretted gorging while retelling her story. "She sat on a low stool with her back to me, bending forwards over a gigantic box. The way she'd bent trapped the side of the box under her chin. I shook her shoulder when she didn't respond and when I bobbed down, I saw her staring eyes." Vanessa flapped a hand at her mouth. "Her lips were blue, and I could see she'd already gone. She tipped sideways, and I panicked. I hauled her upright and pushed her hands into the box to keep her body in place."

Kit reached for her drink and took a fortifying sip. She cleared her throat. "They'll have your fingerprints and DNA on everything. Why didn't you call an ambulance or the cops?" Hypocrisy bloomed as a pink hue over her cheeks as she recalled phoning Jackson instead of the emergency number. It proved a mistake for which he'd taken an unwarranted punishment.

Vanessa groaned and leaned back in her seat. "I've wondered why I didn't call the cops a million times. Panic, perhaps? I called Jen, and that's where it gets messy."

Kit nodded. "Because Jen knew Debbie. She'd convinced her to buy the cheap conditioner and pass it off as Naturals products. But Debbie spread it through the community and the Huntly Curlies got hold of it."

Vanessa nodded. "Jen's a compliance officer for the council. She'd just finished surveying a house around the corner and arrived before I disconnected the call."

"She stuck the scissors in Debbie's neck?" Kit continued at Vanessa's shallow nod. "Why?"

"Temper." Vanessa swallowed. "Jen has always struggled to control her anger. She stabbed them into the poor woman and ranted. I'm rather afraid of her when she gets like that."

Kit ran a shaking hand over her face. Her palm caught the stitches holding her cheek together, as though to remind her of Jen's fury. She nodded. "Who locked the front door?"

"Jen. She didn't want someone stumbling across the body by accident."

"I heard boxes moving. Why?"

Vanessa exhaled. "You arrived as I got ready to leave, and I tripped over a box near the door. We'd packed up all the empty Naturals bottles, and the funnels used to fill them. Jen said the woman took orders from people and provided a refill service on a Monday, so we had to hurry. Jen ran the stuff out to her car in a box. I left my vehicle on the road, but she'd parked on the driveway and needed to leave. The city council logo makes her vehicle more memorable than mine. I wiped our fingerprints off the things we'd touched." She gave an involuntary shudder. "I almost threw up wiping the handles of the scissors. The blades were stuck in deep." Her eyes glazed as her mind transported her back to the garage and the scene of a woman's death.

"So, Jen used a box from Debbie's house to transport the bottles?"

Vanessa nodded, still distracted by the memory of Debbie's staring eyes. Strangulation created a horrific visage and Kit felt no sympathy for the nightmares waiting to pay the woman regular visits. She turned misted irises on Kit. "You recognised the box at my house, didn't you? My husband grabbed it for recycling some wine bottles. I couldn't think of a valid reason for stopping him without explaining." She blinked and swallowed. Her fingers trembled as she reached for the muffin, unable to reject its siren call.

"What did you do with the Naturals conditioner bottles and funnels?" Kit cocked her head.

Crumbs fell from Vanessa's lips as she spoke. "We needed to burn some household waste before the fire bans start. Jen got rid of everything before the WWC meeting while I cooked dinner. But my husband snagged the box off the deck and put it behind the chair."

Kit nodded. She recalled the smoky scent as she arrived at the first Huntly WWC meeting. The floral aroma of the conditioner had implanted a subconscious reminder of her mother's washing powder. They'd destroyed the evidence. "And why not take all the conditioners? Why only that one?"

"Jen rifled through the bottles on one side of the box. She told me the woman had been selling fake Naturals products to our Curlies. She told me to grab all that brand and I did what she said. I didn't notice her touch any of the others, so we left them. But as I emptied the box, they all started falling over sideways." She squeezed her eyes closed. "I admitted to the detective that I looked for my client but denied going as far as the garage. That takes care of my DNA. A draught can spread hair or skin through an area. And Jen knows Debbie through the council, so she's visited her house." She pursed her lips. "She can make her own excuses, anyway."

"I entered through the garden, but how did you leave through the front door? It takes ages for the spring to close."

Vanessa shrugged. "I found it hard to open, but I ran as soon as I got onto the driveway and saw a delivery van."

"So, you've lied to Detective Lane?" Kit spoke through gritted teeth. "Did you know he held me for questioning and suspected I'd killed her?"

Vanessa winced. "I can't go to prison." She flapped her hand and cake crumbs cascaded from her fingers. "What would the church think?" Her eyes narrowed in warning. "The detective won't believe you if you tell him, anyway. My husband golfs with his superiors."

Kit rose, startling Vanessa as she pushed her chair into position beneath the table. "Thanks for the chai latte," she said. A sense of defeat shrouded her, tugging at her need for fairness and consistency. Another visit to Lane would achieve nothing. He didn't want to hear the truth.

Vanessa frowned, her lips parted in surprise and her mouth swilling the remains of the muffin. "Don't you want something to eat?" She indicated the plate's remaining contents of a square of caramel slice and a second donut.

"Thanks." Kit peeled a napkin from a pile and wrapped the caramel slice into it. "One more question. Was your WWC group involved in Debbie's supply venture? You mentioned a fund awarded by the committee as grants and loans for new businesses which promised to benefit Curlies. But I can't imagine you giving a loan to a member of another group."

Vanessa's shoulders stiffened. She used her damp index finger to collect crumbs from around the plate. Her forgotten smoothie oozed condensation, which created a pool on the table. "I didn't know Jen gave her money." Her chest rose as she inhaled. "This is the last year for winning the Expo competition. She figured sabotaging the Hamilton group might give us a better chance. A new girl came to the meetings for a while and Jen became friends with her. They met for coffee a few times." She cocked her head. "You know her. Something happened between the two of you and she felt she needed to leave your group."

Kit clamped her teeth together hard enough to trap her tongue. "Cindy," she growled, without moving her lips.

Vanessa nodded. "That's her, yes. Jen gave the money to her. She's Debbie's business partner."

Kit stumbled from the cafe without recalling the details of her exit. She didn't notice the chair she sent skittering across the floor or the customer who held the door open for her. The passenger door of the car opened to her touch, and she clambered inside the vehicle, her chest thudding and her eyes filling with angry tears. "Did you get it this time?" she snarled. She dropped the caramel slice into his lap as an afternoon snack before the fun started.

Jackson grinned and waggled his phone. "Sure did, Maguire," he said. And smiled.

Chapter Sixty-Three
Exposed Curls

"She said Lane won't believe me." Kit's nails caught the fabric stitches as she scrubbed at her face. "He let them go because they told him a pack of lies and half-truths."

"He's not an idiot." Jackson peeled napkin fluff from the caramel slice and wrinkled his nose. "Do you mind if I don't eat this? I'm not a fan of carbs."

Kit leaned her uninjured cheek against the head rest and sighed. "If you weren't a cop, you'd be my perfect man."

Jackson narrowed his eyes and leaned closer. "What if I was a vicar? Or a lawyer? Both, maybe."

She dodged the question with a shake of her head. "You keep saying Lane's not an idiot, but I don't believe you."

"He has a suspect, Kit."

"Yes, me!" She slapped her thigh and winced. "Even my legs hurt. So far this week I've walked in on a murder, run away from rabid Curly women, fallen down the stairs and got into a fight with a ninja."

Jackson raised a finger. "You forgot about sitting in a police station naked, tipping coffee over Senior Constable White, making a scene at a dairy, quitting your job and then getting it back again."

"I wasn't naked, smart ass!"

A dimple appeared in Jackson's rugged cheek. "Those paper jumpsuits are a human rights issue."

Kit grabbed her throat, her voice a strangled croak. "You saw things through the suit?"

"I'm shutting up now." Jackson placed the sticky slice and its disintegrating wrapper into the cup holder between them. "Buckle up, Maguire. I'm taking you home. Then, I need to return Lane's call. I couldn't answer it and record your conversation with that woman."

Kit fumbled with her seatbelt. "If you don't eat carbs, why did I see you in a fast-food restaurant late at night?"

"Why did I see you there?" Jackson shot her a sideways glance as he gunned the gas pedal and slipped the SUV into the traffic.

Kit shrugged and studied the logo on a truck in front of them, in the queue for the traffic lights. "I wanted to stuff myself silly with awful food after the Huntly Curly meeting. Jerry seemed complicit, but then Langdon acted as our combined conscience. I arrived home hungry but victorious. The sugar free hot chocolate tasted fine, and I abstained from the cookie fest." She chewed on her lower lip. "You looked cozy with Officer Ponytail."

Jackson clicked his tongue, and a smile spread across his lips. "Very cozy," he agreed. "My wife of choice for the night, in fact. And the only way to get me in any kind of marriage again."

"Again?" Kit seized on the morsel of personal information as though starving and her eagerness embarrassed her.

He snorted. "That's all you got from that sentence, Maguire?"

"No." She sat up straighter to defend herself. "You said before that you staked out fake sellers. Will you be doing it again?"

Jackson wrinkled his nose. "I told you that, didn't I? Well, we also watched another clandestine operation. My colleagues made the relevant arrest half an hour ago."

"I haven't watched the news since I saw Debbie's death announced at Vanessa's." Kit sighed. "What have I missed?"

"We caught the guys making illegal alcohol."

"Wow! Well done. One of the Huntly Curlies lost her son because he drank that stuff."

He exhaled. "I know. Complete waste of a life for the sake of a sneaky drink."

"Debbie was supplying it, wasn't she? All those boxes with a line through the brand name."

"Yeah. Officer White and I spent a night outside the manufacturing plant, which is in a warehouse in Claudelands. The chief said it was the most unhygienic still he'd ever seen. The two kids making it didn't understand what they were doing and created the equivalent of pure isopropanol."

"Kids?" Kit frowned. "I wonder why they started doing that. It's not your usual teenage misdemeanour. Debbie had a heap of boxes, so they produced it at a tremendous rate. I thought making liquor took a long time."

Jackson raised his eyebrows and tipped his head from side to side. "It depends on what you're making. You could turn out a reasonable spirit in under ten days. And they had financial backing and adult help. The guy sitting at the table next to you in the fast-food restaurant is connected, but I only learned that today. Lane asked us to follow him that night and I assumed he was one of the bogus sellers from the other job."

Kit hung her head and fixed her gaze on the handle of the glove box. Her vision blurred as she remembered the interaction between Jerry and the man in the next booth. "Vanessa's husband," she whispered. She clicked her fingers. "That's where I knew him. I thought he looked familiar."

"Pardon?" Jackson blinked and waited for her to repeat the sentence. Kit figured he'd find out soon enough and considered the irony of Vanessa getting a different punishment than the one she'd avoided. The voice recording would give Lane enough to question her again, but it seemed her family's crimes reached beyond perverting the course of justice.

"Nothing," she said with a sigh. "Just rambling."

They travelled in silence until the SUV crunched across the gravel and onto Kit's drive. Jackson activated the hand brake and turned to face her. "Will you be okay?" His question stretched beyond the moment to encompass the rest of her life, and she nodded.

"I hope so."

"Nice working with ya, Maguire." His long black lashes grazed his cheek as he smiled. He took her chin in his fingers and tilted her head to examine the cut to her cheek. "Take care of yourself. I'll see you around."

"Not if I see you first." Kit clambered from the SUV and turned to close the door. "Good luck with finding out who killed Debbie. I know the voice recording isn't admissible in court, but I hope it helps you find what you need." She forced her lips into a smile and gave a feckless wave as Jackson's diesel engine roared and he reversed onto the road.

The front door whipped open as she crested the steps onto the porch. Raki flew past her, his coat flapping in his hand. He hopped on one leg as he pushed his raised foot into a shoe. "I left something cooking!" he shouted over his shoulder.

Kit stared through the open front door. Her fingers fluttered over her cheek. "Do you want me to turn it off for you?" she called after him.

He hauled open his creaky car door and threw his jacket across the seat. "No thanks. I left it cooking at the university. The professor just phoned." His eyes bugged like a frog's. "On the plus side, I've created a patentable product. On the downside, I'm in trouble." His suspension groaned as he drove over a flowerbed, swerved to avoid the post box, and bounced onto the road.

Kit rushed inside and checked the stove to ensure he hadn't left something else wreaking havoc. Finding nothing, she boiled the kettle and added a herbal tea bag to her favourite mug.

"Can I come in? A knock sounded on the open front door and Pam stepped into the hallway. She'd shucked the dressing gown in favour of sweatpants and a loose-fitting shirt. A waxy hue coloured her features, beads of sweat dotting her forehead.

"Yes, sure." Kit studied her movements as she bent to remove her trainers. "Don't worry." She held up her hand. "Bending down looks too painful."

Pam grunted in reply, and stiff movements carried her across the lounge. "I owe you an apology." She swallowed, and tears sprang into her eyes.

Kit gave an emphatic shake of her head. "You don't," she insisted. "Neither of us are to blame for what's happened. How's the infection?" She turned back to the kettle and flicked the switch. Already heated, it clicked in protest, and the light remained red. "Tea?" Kit reached across for the box of berry tea bags, her mind registering the sound of a movement close behind her.

"I'm sorry for this." Pam's voice wavered, anxiety and pain creating a heady mixture. Her hand touched Kit's shoulder.

"For what?" Kit dropped the tea bag into a mug and started to turn, missing the length of green wire which passed in front of her face and slipped beneath her chin. It happened so fast, she lost the opportunity to stop it tightening around her throat. Instinct sent her fingers to grapple with the ligature, blood soaking her nails as Pam pulled it tighter and twisted so it bit into her skin. Her brain focused on the immediate need to take oxygen as the wire cut off her airway and constricted the arteries in her neck. A rapid pulse occupied her eardrums, blood pooling in her forehead and rendering her vision hazy. The alerts screaming in her mind displaced any sense of logic or forethought. A decent punch backwards with her fist could have caught Pam's already painful torso and incapacitated her. Instead, Kit scrabbled at the wire and tried to pull away as Pam twisted the makeshift garotte once more before dropping her hands and standing back to watch.

Chapter Sixty-Four
Twisted Curls

Through unfocused eyes, Kit registered shadows moving around her. Her elbows slammed against the counter as she hauled at the wire without success.

"Stand still!" a voice commanded. The tension in her throat increased before air filled her lungs and she dipped forward, coughing. Ooze covered her fingers and she couldn't speak the words gagging against the back of her tongue. She sank to her knees and pressed her forehead against the tiles, closing her eyes and waiting for the spectre of death to slide back into the abyss.

"Call an ambulance." A woman's voice added a soothing lilt over the clamour in Kit's head.

"And the police." She recognised Langdon's urgency. "Is she okay?"

Her lungs ached from the greedy gulps of air she took. They locked up her chest and increased the panic raised by an excess of adrenaline. She lifted her forehead from the floor and uncurled her body, noticing the toes of Pam's trainers digging into the lounge rug. Her heels pointed at the ceiling.

It hurt to swallow, and Kit cleared her throat before rasping her question. Jerry's concerned face appeared in her peripheral vision. "Is she dead?"

He blinked and shook his head. "No." A length of rubber-coated green garden wire dangled from his fingers.

"You're hurting me!" Pam's wail cut through the silence. "Get off me. I have an infection. You can't make me lay on my boobs!"

"You have bigger problems than that."

Curiosity prickled Kit's consciousness as she recognised the inflection in the woman's voice. Jerry squatted in front of her, his forearm resting on his bent knee. "Help is coming," he promised. His eyes appeared wider, his brown irises pale against the frightened bloom of his pupils. A shaking palm rubbed up and down her spine, the fingers trembling against her muscles. Langdon's shiny shoes appeared in her view as she stared at the floor. He bent to speak to her, a wet cloth leaking in his fingers.

"I got this from the airing cupboard," he said. His knees clicked as he squatted to look into her face. "I ran it under the cold tap. It'll take down the swelling."

Kit peered at the dripping black flannel, but her fingers still gripped her knees. It looked familiar. She glanced sideways at Jerry, and he shrugged. "It might help," he urged. He took the cloth from Langdon and folded it into a long rectangle.

The initial cold sensation sent shock waves through her body, but as Jerry held it against the wound, the chill brought a welcome numbness. "Bloody hurts," she managed.

"I know." Jerry dropped the wire onto the tiles. "The paramedics will have something useful in their box of tricks to take the sting away."

"What happened to Pam?" She dragged at Jerry's sleeve and forced him to help her stand. He guided her around the counter to the scene in the dining room. His audible gulp stole any pertinent comment he might have made.

Langdon cleared his throat, and Kit spotted the nervous glance he shot in Jerry's direction. Jerry's eyes bulged, and he shook his head, his curls bouncing like bed springs. He took a step backwards, dragging her with him and leaving Langdon to deal with the situation alone. His arm slid around Kit's shoulders as though seeking immunity. Langdon screwed his head around to glare at him before clearing his throat again. "Er, Your Excellency, the police are on their way. Would you like me to swap places with you?"

"I'm fine, thank you, Reverend." The bishop sat on Pam's back, her painted fingernails clamped around the other woman's wrists. Her long coat spread on either side of her, creating a puddle of expensive fabric from beneath which delicate stiletto heels poked. The Louboutin bag spewed a matching purse and other paraphernalia from its innards, the unmistakable stamp of a genuine product decorating its side.

Pam rocked like a turtle, her painful breasts taking the brunt of her weight. Kit winced in sympathy until her throat treated her to a spasm like an electric shock.

"My throat hurts." Her voice croaked, and Jerry's arm tightened around her shoulders. The force of his grip crushed her to his ribs. He and Langdon seemed transfixed by their kick ass bishop sitting on the murderer. Pam's complaints grew in volume and Her Excellency ignored her.

The front door hit the wall behind it with a deafening clang, the glass window reverberating the sound. Jackson barrelled into the hallway and kept coming, his eyes wide and his hands balled into fists. He froze in the lounge doorway at the sight of the bishop riding Pam, and his frantic gaze crossed the room to find Kit. Then he swore with enough ferocity to curl everyone's hair, including his own. "She's the bloody killer!" Pants interspersed his words. "Her husband and the victim were partners in more than just business."

Kit gave a grunt of acknowledgement and pressed the flannel to her throat. The heat in her wound had warmed the rough fabric, and a funky smell rose from its folds. She pulled it away and examined it. Jerry jerked to life and plucked it from her fingers. "I'll wet it again." He jogged to the kitchen sink and a jet of water splurged from the tap.

"I'm so sorry." Jackson filled Jerry's vacancy, and his first words weren't what Kit expected. He rarely led with an apology. His hand cradled the back of her head, and he pulled her against his chest, enfolding her into a wall of muscle. "I called Lane on my way back to town and told him about the recording. Then, he informed me of what he got from Brian Porter. He wasn't there to bail out either of those crazy women. He and the victim got into an affair last summer and started building a nest egg to use when they left their respective partners. Lane said he confessed everything. They sourced the alcohol from the illegal still and distributed it around bottle shops in the city. His wife found the money last weekend, hidden in a joint bank account. She spent a chunk before he could stop her." He kissed the top of Kit's head and then pressed her away from him, so he could peer at her throat. "That's gonna scar on you." He pursed his lips and apologised again.

"Not if we calm the inflammation." Jerry's hand appeared between them and he held up the wet flannel as though presenting a gilded cushion. "I wrapped ice inside so don't jiggle it about," he advised. His tone lowered to address Jackson, the words backed by veiled aggression. "Shouldn't you handcuff the suspect, officer? I'm sure Her Excellency doesn't want to spend all afternoon on her knees."

Jackson blinked, and he jammed his teeth over his lower lip. He caught Jerry's Freudian slip and struggled with the internal laughter building in his chest. His usual blank mask crashed down over his humour, but not before Kit recognised the schoolboy bursting to escape. Oblivious, Jerry shouldered him aside and resumed his protectorate duties. His warm embrace body-checked Jackson.

Sirens filled the air outside, signalling alarm to the rural neighbourhood. Police vehicles stripped the turf from the front garden as they slid to a halt on the damp lawn, accompanied by a single ambulance. Kit sank onto a dining chair, keeping her chin lowered to stop the air from getting to the cut and making it sting. The dark flannel absorbed the blood, but the wound oozed soreness rather than terminal damage. She distracted herself from the bustle of first responders filling her house and focussed on the bishop's stunning red shoes. The woman had class.

A paramedic wearing latex gloves pulled the flannel away from Kit's throat to examine the wound. A whiff of something funky drifted into her nostrils again, and the paramedic frowned. Kit jerked her head backwards and pain blossomed from her Adam's apple. She pressed a hand over her mouth and retched. "Where did you find that cloth?" she rasped.

Jerry repeated the question to Langdon. Distraction filled his reply, his gaze studying the bishop as Jackson helped her off Pam's back. The cleric bounced up with the grace of a ballerina and Langdon's bottom lip hung low. "Upstairs bathroom," he murmured. A stupid smile fixed over his lips. "Isn't she wonderful?" he sighed.

"Upstairs bathroom." Jerry relayed the message with a frown.

Kit retched again, all her worst fears confirmed. "I need antibiotics!" she croaked at the paramedic. "Quick."

They'd found Raki's infamous missing bum flannel.

Chapter Sixty-Five
Done Up

"That plaster spray at the hospital hurt more than the actual cut." Kit sipped water through a straw and tried to keep her neck still. The action of swallowing induced a tingling ache across the raised skin, and her bruised windpipe gave a stab of complaint. She hardly recognised her croaky voice.

"It smelled weird." Jerry sat next to her at the counter, his arm brushing hers. He shook frozen peas into a smaller bag to create a neat compress. "This should help."

Langdon bustled around the kitchen, his blond head bowed in concentration as he put the remaining peas back into the freezer and fetched a clean tea towel from the drawer. He handed it to Jerry without speaking. Kit watched Jerry's deft fingers wrap the tea towel around the bag of peas. He folded the edges as though preparing a Christmas gift before giving the parcel an approving pat.

Kit lifted a hand to her throat. "No," she rasped. "It's too painful."

"Do as you're told." Jerry cocked his head and raised his eyebrow. "Or I won't explain why we all arrived home when we did."

Kit's shoulders slumped as her curiosity protested at the prospect of missing out on a vital piece in the crazy puzzle. She plucked the makeshift icepack from his fingers and held it against her injury with reluctance. The first contact ramped up the fire in her throat, but as the chill from the ice percolated through the cloth, a glorious numbing started at her Adam's apple and spread across the inflamed skin. Jerry grinned at the hint of relief in her expression.

Langdon leaned his right hip against the counter and folded his arms. He'd loosened the top buttons on his black shirt and abandoned his dog collar. "The bishop arrived at the church ready to reprimand us." His tone contained an accusation. "She called at the house on her way to a meeting in Auckland. But after her unfortunate conversation with you, she cancelled it and doubled back to visit the church." He exhaled. "What were you thinking? She imagined us abusing our position with the congregation. It took ages to smooth things out enough for her to agree to meet you again."

Jerry's shoulder bumped Kit's, and he lowered his voice. "Did you really think she'd come to clean the house?"

Kit exhaled. She lacked the energy to confirm or deny her unfortunate error. Jerry pursed his lips and slid his gaze sideways to meet hers. Langdon inhaled and ran a hand through his curls. "Stop doing that," she croaked. "Leave them alone or they'll turn to frizz." A cough punctuated the end of her sentence.

Langdon dropped his hand to his side. "Well, the bishop stayed for two weddings and a baptism. We'd just walked into the church car park when the police arrived. Apparently, they've arrested our head deacon. They wanted to search the premises for evidence of alcohol production or storage. It seems he spent more time covering up the mysterious disappearance of our communion wine bottles, than trying to solve it. I'm kicking myself for trusting him. Anyway, we waited while they searched the building and then set off home. We arrived here to discover a woman with leaky breasts garrotting you." Langdon frowned at a sentence containing verbs and adjectives he'd likely never pair together again. He crossed his feet at the ankles. "And then the bishop waded in and rescued you."

Jerry gave a low whistle through his teeth. "Did you know she used to be a cop, Langdon? I had no idea. She flew across the room and hauled that woman off Kit before either of us moved. And in those heels, too!"

Langdon gave a loud swallow and covered the lower half of his face with his palm. "Her Excellency pinned her face down on the ground before we realised what was happening." His brows furrowed, and he shook his head. When he looked up, his cobalt irises flickered. "That woman could have killed you."

Jerry tutted. "That's what she intended. How could she imagine she'd get away with it?"

Kit exhaled. "Easy," she whispered. "Make up lies about me after the fact. She could pin Debbie's death on me. If she had time to move my body, she could throw me in the river or bury me somewhere rural. She thought I'd lost my job and my friendship group, so she could claim I felt depressed."

Langdon frowned and shook his head so that his blond curls bounced. "But you thought you were friends."

Kit swallowed and adjusted the tea towel and frozen peas over her throat. "After this week, it's become harder to tell who my real friends are anymore." She blinked against the mental image of Jackson leading a hysterical Pam out to a waiting police car. To their credit, the boys didn't shower her with immediate platitudes regarding their loyalty. Gratitude blossomed in her heart and warmed her despite the ice pack.

"All murder begins in the heart." Jerry wrinkled his nose. "It starts with a thought and blooms into an action. I say that as a former lawyer and a cleric. Cain became jealous of Abel's right standing with God, not acknowledging that Abel sacrificed the best of what he had to achieve that relationship. It resulted in Adam and Eve losing two sons. Your friend's husband found love outside of his marriage and now he has neither his lover nor his wife."

Langdon sighed. "That's a horribly damning verdict on humanity." He shook his head and his curls bounced. "I wonder if I'm in the right job."

Jerry pursed his lips and winced at Kit. "I'm embarrassed they accused a parishioner of running an illegal still and supplying inferior alcohol to the community. Neither of us saw that one coming."

She groaned. "I recognised him when I arrived at Vanessa's this morning but I couldn't place him. He's the man from our late-night carb craving and Jen's brother. Vanessa thought he'd just appropriated the box from Debbie's garage by mistake, but he'd hidden it because he needed to reuse it. The Huntly chapter wanted to win that Expo so much and now they've lost everything." A thought flashed into her mind like a star burst. "Jerry, please, can you drive me somewhere?"

Chapter Sixty-Six
Finishing Touches

As Jerry guided his Mustang through the bends on the main road, Jackson phoned Kit with news. "Lane added Vanessa and Jen to his extensive list of arrests after listening to that recording. It's inadmissible for court purposes, but it can direct his questioning under caution. He's also confirmed Cindy's involvement in the victim's business dealings, and he's looking for her now. Stay out of it, please," he urged, his voice echoing from her phone speaker. Kit kept the melting packet of peas pressed against her throat and closed her eyes. "Kit?" She severed the end of his sentence by killing the call and shoving her phone into Jerry's glove box.

"He's trying to keep you safe." Jerry turned onto Thomas Road and shot her a glance through narrowed eyes. "If you're rebuilding your list of friends, you should add him."

Kit twisted her lips and stared through her window at the houses stacked together in neat rows. "I'll leave him off for now."

"Do you think Langdon will change his mind about the cleaning issue?" He raised an eyebrow, and his lips quirked upwards into a mischievous grin.

Kit snorted. "No. We left him praying for his remaining congregation members. And he wants a house meeting regarding rules for prospective cleaners. I'm happy to go back to our original rota. Nobody cleans like Raki."

"Nobody makes a mess like Raki either." Jerry laughed.

Raki had arrived home oblivious of the disaster which earlier befell his home, a massive saucepan cradled in his arms. "I made the most fantastic glue with the undergrads," he announced. A metal spoon stuck upright from the mixture like a flag pole. "I just need to work out how to get it out of the pan." His gaze fell on the discarded flannel, and he gave a whoop of joy. "And you found my bum flannel. What an awesome day."

Jerry eased the car into a familiar Flagstaff side street. "You realise this goes against everything Jackson just said to you." A heavy line bisected his dark brows. "I shouldn't aid and abet you in this."

"I need to do it," Kit pleaded. "Nobody will know."

"But that woman lied to your face about hiding the scissors. And she contributed to Debbie's scam, so she must also have known about the affair with Pam's husband."

Kit sighed. "Yeah but hating her gave me energy. What will I do now? She's going to prison."

Jerry eased the vehicle's chrome alloys next to the curb. He engaged the handbrake and leaned his elbow on the sill of the open window, gripping his chin in his hand. His fingers scratched across the bristles. "It didn't give you good energy, sweetheart. And newsflash, the prisons are full already. If she knew nothing about the alcohol and gets an excellent lawyer to defend her against involvement in the murder or the accidental death, she might serve her sentence as home detention."

Kit made a disparaging noise with her lips. "I'm not here for her."

Jerry studied her before releasing his seatbelt. "Want me to come with you?"

"No thanks." She hauled herself from the passenger seat and handed him the wilted bag of melting peas. "I won't go inside, so you'll see me the whole time." She flapped her hand around the car's vintage interior. "Can you do that thing for me that you do for other people?"

"Can I what?" He squinted at her, his black brows knitting into a line. As she reached the front door, she glanced back to see the realisation break out across his features. He closed his eyes and bowed his head. Sunshine created shadows across his glossy curls as he batted for her in the corridors of Heaven.

"Kit?" Alec hauled the front door open and smiled. "Good to see you again." His gaze drank her in from top to toe, and she sensed the moment he noticed the red line snaking across her throat and the cloth stitches on her cheek. He frowned and lifted his hand towards her. She experienced a flashback of the electricity that once drew them together and then blew them apart. Her feet moved backwards as though by their own volition, and she cleared her throat before rasping out her warning.

"Cindy's in trouble. You need to call the Hamilton police headquarters and ask for Detective Lane. If you lent her money or let her store anything on your property, you need to tell him and do it fast. Don't hide anything. Make the call now, Alec."

His fringe flopped over his left eye, giving him the bashful appearance Kit once adored. "What?" He stepped from his castle and met her on the doormat. "What are you talking about?"

"Two people are dead, Alec." Kit tried to raise her voice and failed, his name emerging as a squeak. "Call Detective Lane right now." She spun away from him and focussed on Jerry's bowed head. He'd left the engine running, still praying, but uncomfortable with their mission.

"I don't understand!" Alec called to her retreating back as she cut across the manicured front lawn to the street. "Is this about the boxes in the garage? What's inside them, Kit?" A phone trilled from his pocket and he reached for it, peering at the screen in confusion.

Kit paused with her fingers clasping the handle of Jerry's Mustang. "Don't answer it!" she squeaked.

Alec ran a hand through his wavy hair and lines appeared across his forehead. He lifted the phone to his ear and his eyes widened in horror at the series of wails which reached Kit's hearing. She shook her head in disbelief and threw herself into the passenger seat.

"Waste of time?" Jerry's lips flattened in consolation.

Kit shrugged and fastened her seatbelt. "Had to try. Let's go." She re-wrapped the packet of peas in the damp tea towel and placed it over the welt on her throat. It seemed more painful because a friend inflicted it on her. Jerry made the turn onto the main road as a police car careened in the other direction. Kit watched in the side mirror as its wheels squealed to a stop on Alec's drive.

"I wonder who the scissors belonged to," Jerry mused as they headed for home.

"Vanessa." Kit leaned her head against the seat and closed her eyes. "The girls said she kept them in her handbag. I needed to borrow them on the night of the meeting and she avoided lending them to me. She couldn't because she didn't have them. The excuse she gave involved disturbing her husband, but he wasn't at home. He sat in the booth next to ours at the restaurant." She imagined the Queen of Curl's dismay at discovering her sister's involvement with using a pair of the prized matte black precision scissors to defile a dead body.

"Wow." Jerry exhaled. "Do you think Langdon would notice if we sneaked through the drive through and stuffed our faces with ice cream sundaes?"

Kit nodded, and the action hurt. "He knows when I'm lying. We shouldn't risk it."

As if by divine intervention, Jerry's car speaker clicked to signal an incoming call. A disembodied voice created an amusing ring tone as he took it off mute. Langdon's name flashed on the screen at the same time as Yoda declared, "The master, it is."

Kit gaped and sat up in her seat, wondering if he knew about Jerry's ringtone. She guessed not. He wouldn't approve.

"Is Kit with you?" Langdon's baritone filled the car.

"Yes." Jerry clamped his bottom lip in his teeth and Kit smirked. She imagined he usually said the *'Master'* part under his breath. "We're heading home now."

Langdon grunted. "This journalist just called the house phone. Something about a hair cutting competition.

Anyway, she wants to interview Kit for the local newspaper. A spokesperson from Women with Curls has tipped her to win, so they want an exclusive."

Kit groaned, the sound vibrating through the ice pack and into her fingers. She squeezed her eyes closed against the next unfolding disaster. "Oh," Langdon added, "someone else called to speak to you about hair conditioner. They phoned from Australia and promised to try again later. He sounded quite upset and said it was urgent."

"Of course, he did," Kit whispered. "Of course, he did."

BOOK FOUR

Kit lifted her scissors into the air like a maestro waiting for the orchestra to ready itself. The fluffy head beneath her wobbled on a stringy neck supported by thin shoulders.

"Don't you need to wet it before you start cutting?" Her irritating stepsister sat at the kitchen table with a stack of toast piled up in front of her. She ladled treacle onto the uppermost level and licked the spoon as it dripped down the side of her bread building.

"Yes, don't you need to wet it?" Marian clattered cups and saucers onto a tray while her husband wandered around behind her, scratching his protruding hairy belly. "Put a shirt on, Kenny darling. Martha doesn't want to see your nipples."

"Could you do mine afterwards?" Kenny shoved his spiky head in front of Kit's face, his breath smelling of garlic and axle grease.

Kit ground her teeth in her jaw until it sent an ache blossoming through her cheek and into her forehead. She lowered her scissors, careful not to jab the bony shoulder of her client. "I can't do this here," she declared. "You're welcome to come back to my house, Martha. Or we can schedule another appointment and I'll do it at yours?"

The seventy-year-old self-confessed serial straightener turned huge blue eyes up to meet her gaze. "But I got so excited." Her chin wobbled, and she lifted a gnarled hand to caress the frizzled bird's nest at her crown. "Marian said you could fix it for me."

Kit swallowed, the action snatching at her painful throat. Her fingers rose to connect with the welt across her milky skin. "It's not an instant fix," she replied, her voice containing a croak. "Straightening it since 1987 means it's suffered lots of heat damage. You'll need to follow the Curly Routine I explained to you."

"She doesn't want me here." Steph's toast tower teetered as she rose and snatched up her plate. "I told you she wouldn't cut my hair. She hates me."

"No, Steph." Marian blew her cheeks out and defeat bowed her shoulders. "That's not true. Kit doesn't hate you, do you darling?" She turned her vibrant gaze on her daughter, channelling angst through the widening of her eyes. "Tell her, Kit. Tell her you don't hate her."

"I don't hate you." She spoke through gritted teeth, the admission for her mother's benefit and not because she liked anything about the selfish teenager. "But I need you all to leave, or I'm packing my gear and going home."

"Me too?" Martha spun her legs around to swivel her body around to face Kit. The revolving kitchen stool kept moving, and she gasped through several complete circles before Kit grabbed her shoulder.

"I'm not cutting with an audience." She pushed Martha back to her original position and drew in a controlled yoga breath.

"That means me!" Steph huffed to a standing position. She bounced from the room with a toss of her purple hair. "Told ya!"

Kenny ran his index finger through a blob of treacle left on the table. He sucked it with thought before following his daughter. Marian exhaled and pressed her palms over her cheeks, squashing her features together like wet clay. "I thought you'd enjoy the chance to practice in front of a live audience." Her voice held the traces of a suppressed wail.

Glossary of Terms

WWC - Women with Curls.

Curly/Curlies - individuals or a group with curly hair.

SOTC Scrunch Out the Crunch - cracking the cast on dry curls.

Plop/Plopping - wrapping a tee shirt or scarf around hair to absorb water.

Transition Stage - the in between bit when no longer using products containing silicone and sulfates.

Blip - when it all goes wrong and a Curly needs to go back to basics.

Flaxseed gel - homemade hair gel used to create defined curls.

Curly Approved - assessed by Curl experts as free from harmful chemicals.

Praying Hands - a method of applying conditioner to hair.

Finger Curling - using conditioner and fingers to create ringlets.

Curly Cutting - a curl by curl cut administered to dry hair.
Unicorn Cut - a way a Curly can cut layers in their own hair but watch lots of videos before attempting it.

Dear Reader

I hope you've enjoyed *Side Parting*. I would be grateful if you would take the time to leave a review at your usual retailer. I often feature snappy review comments on my covers. My work is also ranked on reviews and your comments will allow me to reach a wider audience.

It doesn't have to be an essay - I will be grateful for a few words.

Thank you for doing this for me.

About the Author

K T Bowes is a bestselling teen and women's author.

Her novel, *A Trail of Lies*, was the winner of the genre award for Author's Cave in 2014.

Phoenix Du Rose was considered for the prestigious Ngaio Marsh awards for 2021.

K T Bowes is an Englishwoman in exile in New Zealand, swapping rugged cosmopolitan for mountain ranges and terrifying rivers. She loves Māori culture and has learned to weave flax using traditional methods. Her other passion is Rongoa Māori, which involves creating medicines from native plants. She is a student of Te Reo Māori.

You can find her hanging out on social media in the following places.

Check in and say hello. Maybe suggest she gets back to writing and stops watching cat videos.

FACEBOOK
https://www.facebook.com/NZauthorKTBowes/
TWITTER

https://twitter.com/ktboweswrites
INSTAGRAM
https://www.instagram.com/k_t_bowes
PINTEREST
https://www.pinterest.nz/hanadurose/
LINKEDIN
https://www.linkedin.com/in/ktbowes/

Other books by this author:

The Hana Du Rose Mysteries in order:
Logan Du Rose
About Hana
Du Rose Legacy
The New Du Rose Matriarch
One Heartbeat
The Du Rose Prophecy
Du Rose Sons
Du Rose Family Ties
Du Rose Vendetta
Phoenix Du Rose
The Calculated Risk Series:
The Actuary
The Actuary's Wife
The Actuary in Trouble
The Heart of The Actuary
Troubled series for teens/young adults in order:
Free from the Tracks

Sophia's Dilemma
A Trail of Lies
Gone Phishing
New Zealand Soccer Referee Series:
All Saints
Escaping the Back Country NZ Series:
Pirongia's Secret
Deleilah
A Keeper's War Fantasy Trilogy:
Perpetual Winter
The Bee Queen
Hive
UK based mystery/romances:
Artifact
Demons on Her Shoulder
The Curly Fan Club
Dead Straight
Bad Hair Day
Side Parting
Take a look at all K T Bowes' novels at ktbowes.com

www.ingramcontent.com/pod-product-compliance
Lightning Source LLC
Chambersburg PA
CBHW011405070526
44577CB00004B/402